Through The Years With Prince Charming:

The Collected Music Criticism of Paul du Quenoy, 2010-2020

Paul du Quenoy

Through The Years With Prince Charming:
The Collected Music Criticism of Paul du Quenoy, 2010-2020

Paul du Quenoy

Academica Press
Washington ~ London

Library of Congress Cataloging-in-Publication Data

Names: du Quenoy, Paul (author)
Title: Through the years with prince charming : the collected music
criticism of Paul du Quenoy, 2010-2020 | Paul du Quenoy
Description: Washington : Academica Press, 2021. | Includes references.
Identifiers: LCCN 2020953043 | ISBN 9781680531282 (hardcover) |
ISBN 9781680531299 (paperback) | ISBN 9781680537994 (e-book)

For Charlie, who loves to be entertained

"I am a critic and commentator. I am essential to the theatre."
– Addison DeWitt, *All About Eve*

Contents

Preface

This book is the product of a disaster. In March 2020, I was merrily making my usual rounds of new operatic productions – seeing four in as many days, in fact – when the news suddenly turned dire amid reportage of a terrible virus that originated in China. Leaving New York on March 4, I scarcely realized that, due to the Covid-19 pandemic, the previous evening's Metropolitan Opera performance of Handel's *Agrippina* would be the last I would see for a very long time. Indeed, I have not returned to New York since, in my longest absence from that city in some sixteen years. Within ten days of my departure, the Met and most other theaters around the world were closed, at first for the rest of the season, and then for the entire 2020-2021 season as well. One by one, all of my reviewing commitments around the world were cancelled, leaving radio broadcasts, hastily improvised livestreams, and my old music collection (long since digitized) as the only media through which I could still enjoy the ultimate art form.

Unexpectedly confronted with a *saison manquée*, a cultural catastrophe without parallel in living memory, I surveyed new projects and thought of ways to keep active and engaged. Initially a hobby, classical music criticism had become a professional *métier* in my late twenties and prospered as a welcome diversion alongside a boring academic career that I did not particularly enjoy. Reviewing music had become a large part of my life, taking up forty or fifty days per year.

In my university teaching, I had quickly managed to escape involvement in a dreary and pointless interdisciplinary humanities curriculum by broadening my history appointment to include opera courses offered in the fine arts department. I was also lucky enough to figure out how to move those courses from drab and poorly equipped audio-visual classrooms to one of the university's main assembly halls, where I had a cinema-sized screen, a tremendous sound system, and a dedicated technician. A significant part of my job came to involve the immense pleasure of blasting Verdi, Wagner, and Richard Strauss one afternoon per week. Perhaps twenty-five percent of the students who enrolled were interested and receptive, and, at least until the pandemic, many later dropped notes from cultural capitals about performances they had been fortunate enough to attend. Another twenty-five percent were at least down to party. Telling me of their lives and hopes over Vodka Red Bull and hypnotic bass in the early morning hours, they helped me learn far more about their society and the new generation of international youth than I ever could have gleaned from my ill willed colleagues.

Needless to say, as academia continued its degeneration from a mildly amusing gentlemanly pursuit to a weird, self-abnegating clerisy policed by fanaticized mediocrities, that approach eventually got me into some trouble. But already disappointed, I had wisely cultivated better prospects and was not terribly disappointed to leave my university job shortly after my fortieth birthday. Rossini stopped composing at that age, and if leaving behind a celebrated career was good enough for him, then abandoning a dull and unsatisfying one was certainly good enough for me. Then, less than three weeks after my departure, Lebanon, the country to which professional caprice had led me, collapsed in a massive national revolution that then worsened in a cascade of political, economic, and public health crises from which neither it nor my former university is ever likely to recover, assuming they survive at all.

By the time live performance came to a halt a few months later, I realized that I had accumulated a large enough body of critical work to think about arranging it for this volume. The unavoidable caesura in my active criticism allowed time for review and reflection. The 101 reviews that follow are only a small percentage of the total I have logged over the past ten years, but I chose them to reflect the most interesting performances I recall from that time. Some were good and some were bad. Some are attached to fond memories and others to sour regrets. But all of them were in some way notable for their quality of performance, intellectual engagement, cultural meaning, philosophical musings, or other memorable attributes.

The selection is eclectic and perhaps even eccentric. As a university professor writing on a free-lance basis, I paradoxically had both the broad latitude to review only performances I wanted to review and constraints of time and space that even my lackadaisical attitude toward my job responsibilities compelled me to observe. Following the dates and places of the reviews in this volume could leave the entirely accurate impression that my criticism was occasionally compressed into brief spurts that could, for example, fit in the course of a trip to some stale academic conference that fortuitously abutted an official university holiday. More evenly paced schedules will betray when I was on sabbatical, which was happily quite often, or remind the reader that the three best things about a teaching career are June, July, and August.

I have tried to offer a broad cross-section of the operatic repertoire, but the works chosen for inclusion here inevitably reflect my own tastes, which veer heavily toward the late German Romantic, and trends in international repertoire selection, which strongly favor the so-called "standard repertoire" while cautiously leaving more room for early music, new operas, and rarities from the art form's golden age of creativity. The reader will of course find many well known works under review, but also operas by Handel and Rameau, Adams and Corigliano, and lesser operas by more famous composers. Offenbach's *La Grande Duchesse de Gérolstein* rarely comes up in performance, and for that reason I included it. Verdi's somewhat ridiculous *Giovanna d'Arco* opened La Scala's season in 2015 but had not been heard there since 1865, making it an event of historic significance. Rossini's *La Donna del Lago* has little appreciable modern performance history and was thus unusual enough to add. Massenet's *Cendrillon* – whose charming princely hero gives this book its title with much greater merit than whatever charm I possess, and with only a sly reference to the fictional but delightfully cruel man of letters Sheridan Whiteside – was never at the top of anyone's list but deserved consideration. At the same time, I offer no apology for omitting crowd pleasers like Puccini's *La Bohème* and Mozart's *The Magic Flute*, operas whose inescapable familiarity militates against creative reinterpretation, exceptionally dynamic performance, or virtually any other quality that would make a review of them interesting enough to include.

My peripatetic pre-pandemic life influenced choice of venue as well as repertoire. The standard operatic capitals – New York, London, Paris, Vienna, Berlin, Milan – are all represented, but there are also reviews from the towering festivals of Bayreuth and Salzburg, such outposts of operatic creativity as Santa Fe and Cooperstown, and locales rarely associated with the grand operatic tradition, including Washington, Tokyo, Palm Beach, and even Beirut, which occasionally held some kind of music festival featuring a lone performance of one opera.

Taking these subjective factors into account, one should not conclude that this collection is or pretends to be definitive. I missed or left out more than a few productions important to understanding opera over the turbulent second decade of the twenty-first century. But certain trends do emerge. One can trace career trajectories of renowned artists, some of whom grew with steady predictability, while others inexplicably crashed and burned. Some productions under review reflected the burden of accessibility in a changing and increasingly commodified culture in which free time and leisure have become burdened with ever greater premiums, and in which arts administrators are correspondingly nervous and reactive.

A tendency to throttle culture with politics, usually under the delusion of "relevance," – a sad dictate that emerged within the very same academia that I embraced music to escape – imbued a number of productions with some sort of "message" that was rarely inspiring, often poorly expressed, and frequently unintelligible to audiences who neither needed nor wanted it. The hysteria surrounding the #MeToo movement hoisted tedious and often ridiculous reconsiderations of gender relations upon unmoved audiences, even as the senseless crediting of unproved misconduct allegations offstage devastated careers of enormous achievement, many of which nevertheless continue elsewhere, in societies where innocence is still presumed and the recently renewed Anglo-American Puritanism counts for refreshingly little. As the brief flurry of rage driving sexual politics yielded to equally extreme sensitivities about race, even theaters emptied by Covid-19 busily began to adapt to the nebulous dictates of the new secular holy trinity of "diversity," "equity," and "inclusion," which will undoubtedly cloud the operatic land and soundscape when performances resume.

What I attempt to offer here is a snapshot of opera over the past decade through the lens of a cosmopolitan observer, a *"critique extraordinaire,"* if I may indulge in the admiring words of a friend, fellow critic, and sometime editor. I can only hope that my writing can rise to that soubriquet, which I value as much as an Italian press office's effusively polite salutation of me as *"illustre professore."*

- Palm Beach, December 28, 2020

Chapter One

2010-2011

Richard Wagner, *Tristan und Isolde*
Deutsche Oper Berlin, March 13, 2011

"Concept" productions of Wagner are all the rage, and the race to the composer's bicentenary in 2013 continues to whet the creative appetite. The torrential booing that greeted Graham Vick's new *Tristan und Isolde* at Deutsche Oper Berlin resounded with such fury that a fistfight nearly broke out two rows in front of me. But audience objections seemed to react less to provocation than to this production's dreary mediocrity. Indeed, during the final curtain calls the well deserved applause for the musicians practically ceased in anticipation of the boos people then shouted at the hapless production team.

Following too many recent directors of *Tristan*, Vick views the opera as a commonplace story unfolding among ordinary people. This was a true pity considering the vastly impressive artistic resources at his disposal. Wagner's opera, drawn from medieval epics, is a profound psychological work. The knight Tristan has slain an enemy hero and fallen in love with his betrothed Isolde, who has nursed his wounds. He then betrays her by giving her as a bride to his king and uncle, Marke. Isolde seeks both murderous revenge and suicide in a death potion, for which her servant Brangäne substitutes a love potion. The delirious effects send Tristan and Isolde into a passionate nocturnal love affair despite Isolde's impending marriage. Upon betrayal and discovery, Tristan accepts a mortal wound and flees to his homeland. Isolde joins him to die a transcendent death that will unite them in a way their mortal love never could.

While no one could rightly describe these characters and their story as common, in Vick's production Marke's proud realm is reduced to a dysfunctional modern family household. In all three acts Paul Brown's sets are the interior of a contemporary home, adjusted slightly in each act to shift perspective and, oddly, leaving Tristan with nowhere to flee. The curtain opens on a passive-aggressive Isolde modeling her wedding dress for alterations. Tristan is present for her entire monologue, sullenly positioned on a sofa and taking no part in the action until his music calls for it. The chorus of "sailors" showers Isolde and Marke with floral bouquets. As Isolde nervously prepares for her Act II rendezvous, she cheekily hides her framed wedding photo. It is difficult to imagine anything resembling real passion churning up among these staid individuals in the sweaters they often wear.

Vick's effort is not without bold moments, but they mostly fell flat. Tristan and Isolde do not drink their potion but inject it with a shared needle. The box containing it is visible in the Act II love scene, but the drug paraphernalia do not reappear until Brangäne injects Isolde with it just before the final *Liebestod*, the "love-death" scene in which she expresses her transcendent passion's dissolution of mortal constraints into the wholeness of the universe. Cheapening that passion to a series of delusional heroin rushes drew audible audience hostility.

The effect was far less rewarding than watching these characters, who we know are already in love, fall still more deeply in love when they instead expected death. An omnipresent coffin and cascades of autumnal leaves heavy handedly suggest impending doom, but they are never integrated into the action. A fully naked young woman observes the drama in the first two acts, adding an undertone of innocence, while a naked man appears in Act II, yes, to dig a grave.

These images were distracting only because they were so obvious. Unusually, the third act is set many years after the rest of the opera, with an aged, ailing Tristan encountering a white-haired Isolde and a withered old Marke who must walk with a cane. It is not an uninteresting idea, but one wonders how the obsessive, murderous, and suicidal passions could have survived so long and in such decrepit states. In what is now a rather clichéd presentation of the opera's finale, Isolde remains alive at the end. She simply ambles outside to join passersby, leaving both the content and intensity of her glorious final "love-death" monologue incomprehensible. In short, there is no transcendence, no spiritual union, and ultimately no affirmation that people – especially opera audiences and especially Wagnerians – do in fact aspire to deeper realms of consciousness. What else is the opera about, particularly when it is performed this well? Vick's production only tries to convince us that our lives are banal. Ultimately that probably says more about him, but it is the type of suggestion that makes impassioned audiences boo.

In the first season of Donald Runnicles's music directorship here, Wagnerian talent was abundantly showcased. Warm receptions for singers paired with voluble disapproval of a production is something of a German tradition, but the cast deserved the enthusiasm with which it was greeted. Peter Seiffert has developed fully into the true *Heldentenor* that many have expected him to become. His clarion delivery remained consistently strong throughout the evening, especially in the treacherous third act monologues. Often reduced to raving, Seiffert's Tristan intelligently imparted psychological depth in spite of his bizarre surroundings. Paired with his real-life wife Petra Maria Schnitzer's first ever Isolde added dimensions of passion that might otherwise have been absent. Schnitzer will not go down as one of the great Isoldes, but she sang with an appealing, full bodied sound that she employed with greater energy as the evening went on. In Act I only glimmers of this vast talent shone through, but the second act duet and final *Liebestod* radiated with brilliance. At times, however, Schnitzer's upper register narrowed into metallic tones that failed to capture the effulgent beauty of Isolde's music.

Iceland's best known bass Kristinn Sigmundsson delivered Marke's sad music with a superb line and great pathos. Jane Irwin utilized her fine mezzo impressively as Brangäne. Eike Wilm Schulte's brassy Kurwenal did not earn universal admiration, but contributed a fine representation of the character. Chorus master William Spaulding deserves enormous credit for his work with the Deutsche Oper's choral ensemble, one of the finest in the world today. Runnicles's appointment last year encountered some skepticism, but none of that was in evidence last night. Favoring slower tempi, he led the orchestra in a tight reading of the score that carefully explores its many nuances. Purists who objected to the production also demanded reverence for the music. One couple whispering during the opera's final orchestral strains provoked a nearby spectator to cry out, "*Mein Gott, Ruhe!*" The only misfortune was that this superb musicianship was so underserved by what was happening on stage.

Alban Berg, *Wozzeck*
New York, Metropolitan Opera, April 9, 2011

Alban Berg's only finished opera (*Lulu* was left incomplete at his death in 1935) has returned to the Met for a short run of four performances. Despite this discreet revival, the reappearance of the one hour and forty-minute work has already created a stunning buzz. Met music director James Levine has long championed Berg's *oeuvre* and has now presided over nearly forty performances of *Wozzeck* at the house, about two-thirds of the total since the opera entered the Met's repertoire in 1959. His enthusiasm was very much in evidence last night, although health concerns have continued to make news, cause the cancellation of engagements, and led him to end his tenure as director of the Boston Symphony.

Levine laid those troubles aside as he assailed Berg's intricate score – which balances atonality with moments of romantic sweep and parodic gestures toward such familiar forms as the military march. The Met Orchestra played with some of its greatest delicacy of the season. Indeed, after such a satisfying performance, it is easy to understand why the opera's premiere in Berlin in December 1925 is regarded as a milestone in the history of music.

Levine cast some of the best suited singers working today. Baritone Alan Held, who has grown considerably over the years and now counts a credible Wotan among his parts, took the title role. Capturing all of Wozzeck's insecurities and vulnerabilities, he easily moved from humiliated buffoon to murderous killer. Waltraud Meier's Marie showcases some of this talented artist's best singing. At 55 and on the verge of receiving the Lotte Lehmann Memorial Ring from the Vienna State Opera, she looks young and agile enough for the part – an unfaithful mistress who is tortured by feelings of guilt and fear. Her piercing soprano will not please everyone, but it overcame the difficult orchestration to deliver her music without once descending into shrillness. Tenor Stuart Skelton, in his debut role for the Met, captured the Drum Major's arrogant pride with consummate skill. The seduction scene – an upskirting against a wall – defies Marie's standard luring of him into the house. In the roles of Wozzeck's tormentors, Gerhard Siegel and Walter Fink, cut excellent figures as the captain and the doctor. Siegel's pinched tenor perfectly conveyed the cruel captain, a martinet who abuses Wozzeck while chiding him for the immoral life to which he has no alternative. Fink's baritone rolled out almost too beautifully to allow one to believe that he is an oppressor great enough to pay the impoverished Wozzeck to take part in his medical experiments.

Mark Lamos's stark, stylized production – based on walls placed askew – captures both the degenerated psychology that dominates the opera and the intimacy that we need to understand it well. Gregory Keller's stage direction spares nothing by way of cruelty. Wozzeck's humiliation is egregious yet captures our sympathy. His murder of Marie is not a conventional operatic stabbing, but a full-on throat slashing. The children's mockery that ends the opera packs a full and emotionally disturbing effect.

Giuseppe Verdi, *Otello*
New York, Chicago Symphony Orchestra at Carnegie Hall, April 15, 2011

The Chicago Symphony's residency at Carnegie Hall this season has brought with it a riveting musical treat – a full performance of Verdi's late tragedy adapted from Shakespeare's famous play. The event itself attracted enormous attention, but focus was sharpened by the CSO's music director Riccardo Muti, a stalwart Verdi conductor who has been in the news this year both for poor turns of health and a political display about arts funding in Italy. Muti left behind ailments and politics to deliver a stunning – even authoritative – interpretation of the opera's sophisticated score. It would be a worthy successor to the recorded CSO performances under Sir Georg Solti, but the quality suggests that the Solti recording was merely a predecessor.

Muti's disciplined approach neither underserved the tender moments nor spared anything in the more riveting passages. He knew exactly what he was doing at every moment, and the intense physicality he radiated left no one with any doubt about it. He also assembled a stunning cast, a factor that partially derailed Solti's earlier bet on Luciano Pavarotti's unsuited lyric tenor, which registered poorly in the recording. The title role went to the noteworthy Latvian tenor Anders Antonenko. It was announced that he was unwell and asked for the audience's indulgence, but the talent on display made one wonder how radiant a sound he could produce when well. He lacked nothing all evening and colored the role's *tenore di forza* demands with uncommon strength.

Bulgarian soprano Krassimira Stoyanova proved to New York that she remains one of the world's most accomplished lyrico-spinto sopranos. A pyramid of creamily phrased tonality rose above the audience with no noticeable flaw. Her Willow Song and Ave Maria certainly ranked among the best that could be heard anywhere in the world today. Carlo Guelfi's Iago did not reach the same artistic heights as the other principals, but nevertheless showed improvement over the baritone's earlier New York appearances in the role. A rich stentorian sound complemented a truly outstanding spectacle. Generous supporting cast decisions enriched the overall effort. Eric Owens, fresh from his triumph as Alberich in the Metropolitan Opera's new Ring Cycle, sang an imposing Lodovico. The talented young tenor Juan Francisco Gatell contributed a fine Cassio. With Richard Strauss's *Salome* billed for the Cleveland Orchestra's visit in May 2012, one hopes that the other great Midwestern ensemble may keep up the tradition.

Richard Strauss, *Capriccio*
New York, Metropolitan Opera, April 19, 2011

"An opera," says the theater director La Roche in Richard Strauss's last work in the genre – his so-called "conversation piece in one act – "is an absurd thing." At the heart of *Capriccio* is an impassioned but exquisitely polite debate over what matters most in opera – the music or the words. At stake is the favor of Countess Madeleine, a dilettante dwelling in a country villa outside Paris who balances the musician Flamand against the poet Olivier as they create an opera for her amusement. The artist who makes the better case for his medium will triumph in love as well as in art. After more than two hours of rumination, intrusion, and glorious singing and versification, Madeleine decides that there is no answer to the dilemma that could not be trivial. That Strauss and his librettist – the famed conductor Clemens Krauss – could ask such a question as German armies ground their way to defeat at Stalingrad in the autumn of 1942 alone speaks to the power of art.

The Met's *Capriccio* first appeared in the 1998-1999 season as a vehicle for the leading soprano Kiri Te Kanawa, who was well known for her interpretation of Countess Madeleine's dominant role. This revival, the only one since the premiere season, is also a vehicle – now for the star soprano Renée Fleming. Some critics charge that the voice has lost its luster, particularly in lighter parts if the mixed reviews of her performances in this and last season's production of Rossini's *Armida* are any guide. But the Strauss repertoire remains her ravishing own. Indeed, as the years pass, I only find her more and more at home in Strauss heroine roles and similar parts, such as her triumphant Thaïs in Massenet's opera of the same name. The vocal line is articulated with great care and nuance, while the dramatic personae she delivers have become truly aristocratic creations.

Countess Madeleine demands no less. The finale, a monologue in which she ruminates on the question of which art form matters more, flowed with iconic charm. Fleming maintained her *hauteur* throughout, only playfully letting her guard down during the famous Moonlight Music, when Madeleine basks in the romantic situation she masters, clad in a gorgeous silvery gown while twirling a long-stemmed rose.

The cloying artists can only pale before such a woman, but Joseph Kaiser's Flamand and Russell Braun's Olivier captured their spirit with excellent performances. Peter Rose sang the impresario La Roche, whose monologue about theater reminds us, if in a parodic way, of how important management is to creative magic. In his debut season and role, Morten Frank Larsen played Madeleine's brother, identified only as the Count, as what used to be called a sportsman, a philistine whose interest in art extends only as far as the talented mezzo-soprano Sarah Connolly's Clairon, his actress love interest. Olga Makarina and Barry Banks were well considered additions in the short roles of the Italian singers who serenade the Countess and her party of guests. Sir Andrew Davis may well be the best conductor of the work performing today. He led a well drawn performance that balanced the score's harmonies with dissonant elements that recall the twentieth-century musical milieu Strauss did so much to shape.

With such a talented orchestral reading of this complex yet sublime score, it makes sense that the John Cox's production is updated to the 1920s – nearly the time of the opera's composition – from the original eighteenth-century setting. The dialogue that revolves around Lully, Rameau, and other composers whose memories were more present in the earlier era seemed a bit anachronistic in an era when Wagner was by far the most popular composer in France, but Mauro Pagano's inviting sets place us well at ease in a milieu where the arts are considered both so seriously and so lightly. Having Madeleine served a martini added the perfect touch, or is it a twist?

Richard Wagner, *Götterdämmerung*
Paris Opera, June 3, 2011

This production of the fourth and final installment of Wagner's epic *Ring of the Nibelung* has brought the Opéra de Paris to the conclusion of its first presentation of the full tetralogy since 1957. German director Günter Krämer's unfolding production, which begin with *Das Rheingold* in March 2010, has been a *tour de force* of violent passions, gripping symbolism, and whimsical diversion. The full work is, after all, a story about lust for power – granted by possession of a magic ring – setting in motion events that lead to the end of the world. *Götterdämmerung* brings the tale to its bloody conclusion. The hero Siegfried awakens with his newly liberated bride Brünnhilde, the disgraced daughter of the chief god Wotan, who sends him into the world to do great deeds. He leaves her with the ring as a symbol of his love. Encountering the Gibichungs Gunther and Gutrune and their half-brother Hagen, the son of Wotan's nemesis and competitor Alberich, Siegfried is duped – with the help of an amnesia potion – into betraying Brünnhilde by helping Gunther win her as his bride. Siegfried's reclaiming of the ring from her and the resulting confusion about who is truly her spouse touches off a murder plot that ends with his death. Only then is the true nature of redemption revealed to

Brünnhilde, who in a great sacrificial act ignites a purifying fire that destroys the corrupted world order and allows for its redemption.

Krämer has envisioned the *Ring* as a progression in real time through the middle decades of the twentieth century, an era that has and will long continue to shape the world in which we live. *Rheingold* unfolded in a late industrial age idiom, while *Die Walküre* featured disturbingly clear World War II referents. *Siegfried*, which premiered in March, was set in a campy 1950s, complete with Siegfried's guardian Mime dressed as a beatnik who grows and smokes his own marijuana.

Götterdämmerung introduces a garish 1970s styled with that unfortunate decade's signature fashions. A sleazily mustached Gunther sports an olive-green leisure suit and aviator sunglasses. Siegfried and Hagen bluster about in drab three-piece suits that make them look like Ford administration cabinet members. The Norns and Rhine Maidens appear in identical black cocktail dresses, suggesting that they are creatures of the same corrupting force of nature. Gutrune and Brünnhilde favor dowdy dresses, in the first case to demonstrate how plain the character is, and in the second to illustrate Brünnhilde's cascading fall from divinity into bourgeois ordinariness. With martial orange and red outfits, banners, and garlands, the Act II chorus evokes the empty pageantry of a late Cold War-era communist festival. The hall of the Gibichungs is suggested by picnic tables – oddly set up by male dancers dressed as beer hall girls – and falling paper streamers in every color of the rainbow.

Krämer fills this eccentric universe with vivid imagination. The opera's first moments are filled with the onstage image of the child Hagen, who is confined throughout the opera to a wheelchair and covetously clutches a globe of the world. He is being schooled in his mission by a cloaked Alberich, whose malevolent presence is sharply magnified in this production far beyond his brief and spectral Act II appearance. This pantomime works well with the opening orchestral leitmotifs, which suggest awakening, nature, creation, and death – all concepts connected with Alberich's discovery of the Rhine gold and the consequences of his pursuit of the ring and its power. Presenting Hagen as a paraplegic cleverly facilitates Alberich's domination of the action – he is on stage most of the time and even helps Hagen deliver Siegfried's death blow. At the finale, when Hagen is supposed to admonish the Rhine Maidens to keep away from the ring, it is Alberich who delivers the line. More subtly, in Act II we see that Hagen's spear, which Alberich gives him, is really Wotan's shattered spear from *Siegfried* fastened back into one piece. In one of the production's most striking moments, Brünnhilde recognizes it just as Siegfried is about to swear the oath that he has not betrayed Gunther. And to drive home Alberich's centrality to the plot, the Rhine Maidens vindictively use it to kill him as he pursues the ring at the end.

Krämer's production makes impressive use of digital projection on a vast, bright screen. The waters of the Rhine and the fires that protect Brünnhilde and wreak destruction are its most obvious applications. But we also see Siegfried's spirit ascend illuminated steps to Valhalla to the solemn strains of his Act III funeral music. And in one of the production's more unusual effects, the music signaling Valhalla's destruction is illustrated by a fast-paced video game sequence in which a projected pistol blows away images of Valkyries appearing within a burning palace. This more than anything else probably caused the sound booing that assailed the production team and led one spectator to cry out "*Puant!*" ("It stinks!") when the curtain fell. Nevertheless, along with all the bodies on stage at the end, a glimmer of light on the restored Rhine gold grudgingly suggests the possibility of redemption that is a crucial theme of the larger work.

Krämer's provocative effort certainly benefited from the participation of some of the most outstanding Wagnerian singers available today. Katarina Dalayman's Brünnhilde soared with a fullness of sound that recalled Astrid Varnay's best singing in the role. With the exception of one or two sharp notes in the Immolation Scene, she commanded rapt attention, both vocally and dramatically. Torsten Kerl's more limited and less voluble Siegfried was a disappointment after livelier performances and only reached its full potential in the third act. But it was really the capacious voices of his colleagues that caused his light to seem dim. In his impressive Paris Opéra debut, Hans-Peter König sang a stern and stentorian Hagen whose calculating evil was nevertheless calm and collected. Rapidly becoming a worldwide Wagnerian bass of choice, it is difficult to imagine a voice better suited to the role.

The supporting cast offered Iain Paterson's fine baritone and superior dramatic abilities in the role of Gunther. His portrayal of a weak and easily browbeaten man proved the perfect foil to the strong-willed Hagen who, rather than killing him with his spear as he is meant to do, merely reaches up from his wheelchair to choke him into submission. Sophie Koch delivered Waltraute's music in her scene with Brünnhilde with an incisive mezzo that invites eager anticipation of her planned Venus in Paris's *Tannhäuser* next season. Peter Sidhom's Alberich captured the character's evil to perfection. The Act II scene with Hagen – a deft exploration of the nature of hate and envy – was one of the most riveting I have ever heard. Christiane Libor made a fine dual contribution as Gutrune and the Third Norn. The exciting young conductor Philippe Jordan, the Opéra's music director since 2009, led a magisterial performance that captured much of the score's subtlety with an uncommon clarity while not sparing any effort with the orchestra's rousing brass.

Richard Wagner, *Der Ring des Nibelungen*
San Francisco Opera, June 14-19, 2011

Francesca Zambello's idea of an "American" *Ring* has been unfolding for more than five years, since the *Das Rheingold* installment premiered at Washington National Opera in March 2006. *Die Walküre* followed there a season later, but budget constraints delayed *Siegfried* until the spring of 2009 and limited the presentation of *Götterdämmerung* to just two concert performances that fall. It has fallen to the San Francisco Opera, which co-produced Wagner's epic, to finish the staging and present the first complete cycles of all four operas this summer. Much fanfare preceded the event. Six weeks of lectures, musical events, and public discussions prepared the mood in a scholarly tone. A launch party at the St. Regis Hotel fueled sponsors with a buffet whimsically called "Fafner's Feast." And of course, an international audience assembled from all corners of the globe to display the *outré* eccentricities of devout Wagnerian spectators.

Staging a new *Ring* is undoubtedly the most difficult feat in the world of opera. The tetralogy's sheer length and scale are daunting enough, but its deep philosophical meditations on the nature of power, love, hate, envy, and redemption demand a sophisticated conceptual interpretation. Only superb artists of enormous talent and great stamina can fully address its massive demands

Zambello's "American" interpretation follows the trend in other productions that develop the plot in linear time over a recognizably recent past. *Rheingold* opens in a 1920s milieu with gods who resemble F. Scott Fitzgerald characters preparing to move into a skyscraper Valhalla. Their immediate nemeses, the giants Fasolt and Fafner, who demand payment for building the gods' castle, are cartoonish construction workers who make their entrance on a lowered beam. Alberich, the greater existential threat, whose theft of the Rhine gold sets the whole bloody tale in motion, is a prospector in a river bed that evokes the California gold rush.

Walküre takes the action forward a generation, to a 1950s blossoming of American industrial capitalism. Wotan is now styled as the chief executive of a vast manufacturing concern, presiding over his empire from a sky-high office that looks down over a gray city silhouette. His Valkyries are aviatrixes who cleverly parachute in during their famous Act III "Ride." Hunding is a cabin-dwelling backwoodsman whose life is brutalized by the developments around him. Siegmund and Sieglinde play out their scene of doom beneath the construction site of a highway overpass. Valhalla's heroes are depicted in black and white photo slides of actual American soldiers killed in the country's wars.

In *Siegfried* we find a decaying industrial idiom that evokes the malaise of the 1970s. Mime inhabits a broken down trailer in a squalid trash dump by a power station that ominously emits green smoke. Fafner's transformation into a dragon is explained by the character's operation of an armored vehicle that looks like a cross between a tank and a trash compactor. He dies when its vital power cords are severed. Siegfried liberates Brünnhilde in surroundings that look bleaker than those in which Wotan had left her in the previous opera.

By the time we enter the gloomy universe of *Götterdämmerung*, environmental despoliation and social atomization are complete. The Norns, whose rope of fate contains all the knowledge of the world, are antiseptic technicians who tend cables inside a vast computer motherboard. Where else is our knowledge stored today, if not in computer servers? The obliteration of their wisdom by spiraling fate results in a hardware crash. The Rhine Maidens are reduced to bag ladies who desperately try to clear the garbage from their aquatic abode. They ultimately kill Hagen by snuffing him out – tastelessly – with a yellow garbage bag. Gunther, Gutrune, and their evil half-brother Hagen appear in louchely decorated digs within a glass and steel structure that could have been designed by Philippe Starck. Their realm is a zone of hopelessness tended by a gruff private army of wage slaves. The only weak suggestion of the tetralogy's redemption theme comes in the form of a child planting a sapling ash tree – the source of the world's blossoming wisdom before Wotan corrupted it – for the amusement of the blasé denizens of Gunther's realm.

No one can accuse Zambello of lacking imagination, though I did wonder what provocations this *Ring* made that Patrice Chéreau missed in his centennial production in Bayreuth 35 years ago, based as it was on the destructive evolution of industrial society. Günter Krämer's recently completed Paris production of the *Ring* also embeds the work deeply in the pitfalls of industrial modernity. The impressive technical execution of Zambellos's effort relied on innovative video projections to convey landscapes – from the flowing Rhine to the mountain heights to blighted urban districts. Old fashioned smoke and mirrors – aided by ample amounts of liquid nitrogen – gestured toward magic. It seemed incongruous to include these elements, however, when the production's bleak idiom suggests a thorough de-mythologizing of the work. If we are meant to see the *Ring* as an all too human progression from hubris to ruin, then who needs divinity or enchantment? The larger philosophical suggestion seems to be that there is none.

With imaginative power thus undermined, a pervasive tension evolves between what the tetralogy really is and what Zambello wants it to be. I am uncertain she succeeded in resolving it. To take a central example from her development of the characters, her characterization of Brünnhilde rises on the stated idea that she is herself the hero Wotan needs to restore harmony to the world. But for as well as Nina Stemme sang the role, the dramatic interpretation suggested nothing more than a rambunctious preteen who jumps on Wotan's back in her first scene, reacts as though she is being grounded when Wotan decrees her divine punishment for disobeying him, and succumbs to puppy love when Siegfried awakens her. Her morphing into a vicious wronged woman in *Götterdämmerung* implies a level of emotional sophistication she simply does not have; this Brünnhilde should be crying herself to sleep rather than plotting murderous revenge. And nowhere does the progressively bleak production allow her or anyone else to emerge as heroic. The Immolation Scene, in which Brünnhilde reveals her newly acquired knowledge of the world and appreciation for what is needed for its redemption before embracing her end, is eviscerated by a soapy reconciliation with the hapless Gutrune (who ever cared about her?) and the Rhine Maidens, who make an unscripted appearance to lead the action as the end nears (again in questionable taste by dousing Siegfried's funeral pyre with gasoline). If this immature Brünnhilde is really so heroic, why is she not the dramatic center?

Excellent voices can imbue even the most troubled production concepts with aesthetic appeal, but despite all the fanfare only two of the principals rose to the challenge. Stemme, who sang her first Brünnhilde only last year, made an exciting debut in her first full Cycle performances of the role. Her cool Scandinavian tones recall the best efforts of her Swedish countrywomen Birgit Nilsson and Astrid Varnay two generations ago. Her technique is at its best in the middle register, where creamily delivered Bs and Gs pollinated the score with a delicious musicality one can only savor. Her top notes were not perfect – the final "Heil" in the prologue of *Götterdämmerung* warbled and she sang a touch sharp in the Immolation Scene – but this is a Brünnhilde the world needs and will long remember.

Another star ascended in Brandon Jovanovich's excellent Siegmund. The voice's fine baritonal coloring conveyed a union of nobility and authority. These dynamic performances overshadowed the other principals. Mark Delavan has the necessary legato and vocal color for Wotan, but in all three incarnations of the role he sounded underpowered. Act III of *Walküre* and his scenes in *Siegfried* were the only places suggesting the effulgence readily encountered in other performers of the role today.

Anja Kampe's Sieglinde showed flashes of power, but the voice has room to grow. The role of Siegfried was divided between Jay Hunter Morris and Ian Storey. Morris was the more severely parted. In Act I of *Siegfried* he at times lapsed into inaudibility. Although the voice possesses a fine lyrical quality, it is simply – and obviously – not right for a Heldentenor role. Storey fared rather better in *Götterdämmerung*, though the voice's throaty qualities made the hero sound more gravelly than the brilliant music needs to soar. A "vocal indisposition," moreover, caused his singing to collapse late in Act II. After treatment during intermission he continued through Act III with noticeable caution.

Gordon Hawkins's Alberich made a stir when he first sang the role in Washington five years ago, but this time the voice betrayed a curiously listless quality through much of the role and only fluttered decision in the delivery of the curse in *Rheingold*. Andrea Silvestrelli blustered through Hagen's malevolent music and the lesser part of Fasolt. The Italianate basso was not unappealing but seemed out of place, especially when accompanied by a mischievous dimension that we rarely encounter in this grim role. It was nevertheless a clever touch to put him in bed with Gutrune at the spectral opening of Act II of *Götterdämmerung*. Daniel Sumegi's Fafner and Hunding both emerged with rough edges. The supporting cast offered few standouts. David Cangelosi's energetic Mime – complete with cartwheels – captured the character's vices and in vocal terms even rivaled Morris's unfortunate Siegfried in power. Stefan Margita's Loge and Ronnita Miller's Erda were skillfully executed. Gerd Grochowski, who sang Donner and Gunther, sounded serviceable if not more. Melissa Citro's Freia and Gutrune were rather weak, though her slutty interpretation of the latter role enlivened this usually dull part.

San Francisco's former music director Donald Runnicles returned to the podium for the *Ring* Festival. He led a pedestrian orchestral effort. While efficient and technically correct, it disappointed listeners intrigued by the score's great subtlety and possibilities for deeper exploration. Although Runnicles's rendering of *Götterdämmerung* occasionally reached into that realm, too many of the great moments lacked emotional charge and dramatic power.

There will be two more Cycles, with the last concluding on July 3. Zambello's effort leaves the impression of a work in progress. More careful casting decisions and a refinement of the production concept could make this *Ring* worth hearing again.

Giuseppe Verdi, *Macbeth*
Salzburg Festival, August 19, 2011

Salzburg's new productions continue to unroll with Verdi's first Shakespearean opera, once astonishingly absent from the repertoire. Indeed, even director Peter Stein confessed that he has long disliked the opera and only approached it partly because his Italian wife has a higher opinion of it. The unique environment of Salzburg's Felsenreitschule (Cliff Riding School) opened up unusual creative possibilities. The back wall of the theater is the face of a sheer cliff that ascends far above the festival city. Tiers of carved passageways allow movement within the wall, and open passages between the audience and orchestra pit create additional performance space. The cliff's dark shadows are appealing for works with a spooky dimension, which *Macbeth*'s witches, nocturnal murders, and mad scene amply supply.

Stein's effort is for the most part traditional. There is no egregiously forced political message beyond the usual axiomatic comment on the pursuit of power. No attempt is made to update the action from the Middle Ages. The major innovations arise from the director resolving what he identifies as his own pet peeves. Shakespeare's original three witches replace Verdi's exaggeration of them into three choruses. We still have the choruses singing, but the dramatic action falls to three (male) dancers in grotesque costumes that accentuate pallid female nudity. The choruses may not have enjoyed it, but they were reduced to trees and stumps in what is meant to foreshadow Birnam Wood and its fated but improbable advance to Dunsinane Castle. The same effect appears in the scene of Banquo's murder – here there are only four assassins, two of whom Banquo slays in allowing his son to escape, while the large chorus is disguised. It is not the most imaginative effect, but it does dispense with the logical puzzle of how a Verdian chorus of thirty cannot kill a man and a boy.

More successful was Stein's use of the Felsenreitschule's passageways to make way for Lady Macbeth's mad wandering in the final act. No other theater could have allowed this to happen so naturally. The passage before the orchestra pit was also a useful conduit for King Duncan's procession – with its long pantomime – and for the sullen refugees as they flee Macbeth's oppressive tyranny.

In the witches' presentation of Banquo's future progeny, we see the standard nondescript figures of kings processing before Macbeth, but the mirror held by Banquo's ghost then cleverly projects images of real British monarchs – including Charles I, George III, Victoria, and Queen Elizabeth – all presumably descended from Banquo's line via Charles I's grandmother, Mary, Queen of Scots. The large choreographed battle in the final act also suited the production's traditional milieu.

Macbeth went through multiple revisions, leaving its exact scoring the subject of perennial surprise. Stein, in consultation with conductor Riccardo Muti, not unwisely placed the often discarded ballet music as an introduction to Act III and replaced Verdi's strident and rather incongruously upbeat later choral ending with the composer's abbreviated original finale, preceded by Macbeth's psychologically self-pitying arioso "Mal per me."

Muti's presence in the pit marked a historic occasion, for the 70-year old conductor has announced that this will be his last production for Salzburg.[1] It is for that reason that all performances were long sold out and more people than usual could be observed outside advertising for last minute tickets. Muti's reputation with Verdi is unsurpassed among his contemporaries, and he led the Vienna Philharmonic and the Vienna State Opera's chorus in a disciplined performance that captured the score with energy and verve.

Željko Lučić's powerful baritone had some rough edges but served the title role well. His Act I piano singing and delivery of the great regret aria "Pietà, rispetto, amore" registered improvement over his Metropolitan Opera performances of the role in the 2007-2008 season. Tatiana Serjan's Lady Macbeth frequently succumbed to the shrill tones

---

[1] Muti has returned for concerts, most recently in August 2020 despite restrictions caused by the Covid-19 pandemic.

and awkward interpolations that the role's difficult range can generate. The death aria and its final D-flat soared into what might be called an aesthetically excellent performance, but this was really the only highlight in Serjan's singing. Both leads radiated little dramatic insight into what are, at least in Shakespeare, among the most vivid characters in literature. Dmitry Belosselskiy's Banquo likewise sang without much verve, though the lower notes were not beyond his appealing bass voice. The best vocal performance came from rising star tenor Giuseppe Filianoti, a luxuriously fine singer for the lesser role of Macduff. The character's only aria "O figli," an apostrophe to the bodies of his murdered children, resounded with a chilling insistence that I have never heard injected into the role.

Richard Strauss, *Die Frau ohne Schatten*
Salzburg Festival, August 21, 2011

The Salzburg Festival's first new production this year boldly takes on what avid Strauss fans regard as the composer's greatest work. *Die Frau ohne Schatten*, a fairy tale adapted from sources as varied as Norse mythology, *The Arabian Nights*, and Goethe, addresses marital love by dwelling heavily on guilt, manipulation, jealousy, anger, and reconciliation.

The Emperor of the mythical realm of the South Seas has taken as his Empress the divine daughter of the god Keikobad. She is barren, a condition illustrated by her inability to cast a shadow. A messenger from Keikobad announces that if she casts no shadow soon, Keikobad will reclaim her and turn the Emperor to stone. The Empress's nurse schemes to acquire the shadow (and thus childbearing ability) of a mortal woman, the downtrodden wife of the poor dyer Barak, offering in exchange a life of riches and pleasure. The dyer's unnamed wife, who is of little interest to her abusive husband, agrees and nearly betrays him with a more appealing man conjured by the nurse. When the dyer's wife deceitfully tells Barak that she has succumbed to temptation, his righteous fury convinces her that he loves her after all. She then confesses that she really had been faithful, placing their relationship on a new plane of honest devotion. Observing this moving commitment, the Empress decides that her place is among humanity and renounces the shadow the nurse has acquired for her. The opera ends happily, with both couples rejoicing in the ecstasy of marital bliss and with both women casting shadows.

Christof Loy has dispensed with the fairy tale elements to reimagine the action unfolding during a 1950s-era commercial studio recording session of the opera itself. Johannes Leiacker's only set for the entire performance is recognizably Vienna's *Sofiensaal*, a concert venue that served as the chief recording studio of Decca records until the hall was destroyed by fire in 2001 (according to 2006 report the premises are to be redeveloped as condos[2]). The characters appear as first-rate Straussian singers charged with performing the opera's roles for the recording. The recreated *Sofiensaal* is dominated by an elevated stage with recording equipment that silent technicians, including a young John Culshaw-like character, frequently adjust to add the sense of depth and reality that earlier recordings lacked.

This could easily be taken as simply a bad approach or a jaded lack of imagination. Studio recording inherently suggests dramatic stasis – the singers are merely there to do a job managed by others. The prospect of attending a performance staged in this manner sounds like going to concert opera or, worse, merely observing professionals in the doldrums of their work. There threatens to be no room for the raw emotions or deep psychology of Strauss's immense characters.

In their vintage 1950s street clothes, the singers could have walked off the set of Alfred Hitchcock's *North By Northwest*. Yet Loy subtly manages to address the opera's themes and make its drama resonate. In the course of the evening, all of the principals come to inhabit the roles with their own complexes and neuroses while ostensibly just performing the music. The effect is not unlike *Pagliacci's* murderous play-within-the-opera or the psychologically revealing opera act set within Strauss's earlier work *Ariadne auf Naxos*.

Indeed, the emotions and antagonisms quickly become apparent despite the setting. The baritone and soprano performing the roles of Barak and his nameless wife are presented as a married couple who also seem to be plagued by childlessness. Their unhappy relationship suggests the

---

[2] These plans were later adjusted to allow the original hall to be reconstructed.

failed marriage of Christa Ludwig and Walter Berry, much of which coincided with their memorable performances in those roles (often together, both before and after divorce) two generations ago. Barak's costume is distinguished by the square, heavy rimmed glasses and combed back hair remembered from Berry's publicity photographs. The two singers' interaction closely mimics the opera's plot. When Barak is indifferent to his wife, the baritone is indifferent to the soprano. When Barak is meant to go off and get drunk, the baritone leaves the studio and returns overserved and undersupervised. The gut-wrenching scene over the wife's pretended infidelity in the opera screams out real marital problems in the lives of the singers. When the couple reconcile at the end, it is as much the reconciliation of a mid-twentieth artistic couple as of the mythical characters whose music they are singing. The hidden analogies emerge in a more rarefied version of the troubled Richard Burton-Elizabeth Taylor marriage(s) on display in their synergetic joint films, whether they were Antony and Cleopatra or Edward Albee's fractured professor and housewife.

The Empress, or rather the soprano portraying her, is described as a young singer – easily Leonie Rysanek, who first performed the role at age twenty-nine. Loy's reinterpretation of the plot suggests that her struggle to relate to her colleagues' adoption of their characters mirrors the Empress's descent from the pedestal of divinity to real empathy for mortals. It is less clear who the Emperor is ("a tenor performing in Europe for the first time," as the program notes tell us – perhaps James King), and the character spends much time nervously observing and reacting to the others. This substitutes in a way for the Emperor's less vivid character in the opera. The older mezzo singing the nurse is every bit as nasty and manipulative as the character she portrays. The opera's final scene – the set's only alteration throughout the evening – is staged as a Christmas concert for children, but the milieu does allow the two couples to luxuriate in bliss while the nurse is reduced to the petty schoolmarm people as manipulative as she is usually are at heart.

Loy suggests that since the archetypes and psychoses of mythology are ultimately projections of human feelings and frail mortal needs, humans can experience and explore these imperatives as easily as imagined gods and heroes. Reality, in other words, substitutes for myth in a provocative inversion of the conventional understanding – so important to Strauss and his librettist Hugo von Hofmannsthal while surviving the horror of the First World War – that myth is necessary to escape reality.

The production might have suffered under the weight of its abstraction had the musical effort been less outstanding. The clear star of the evening was the Vienna Philharmonic under Christian Thielemann, who will soon take over Dresden's Staatskapelle Orchestra. Taking an appealingly slower tempo than Karl Böhm's memorable recordings, Thielemann drew a plush, ravishing sound that soared into a transcendent realm of delight. Anne Schwanewilms sang a splendidly vulnerable Empress, especially in the role's gorgeous middle register. Evelyn Herlitzius surpassed her with stratospheric ascents that captured all the existential angst and emotional confusion of the Dyer's Wife. In the role of the Emperor, Stephen Gould resonated with a strong, clarion tone that has made him a rising Heldentenor. Wolfgang Koch's Barak was rather more subdued than it should have been, but still emerged with confidence and nobility. Michaela Schuster's smoky lower register imparted real malevolence as both the Empress's nurse and the seasoned but mean mezzo-soprano this production has singing the role. The excellent baritone Thomas Johannes Mayer, who sings Wotan internationally, was a welcome addition as the spirit messenger of Keikobad.

Chapter Two

2011-2012

Charles Gounod, *Faust*
Paris Opera, October 22, 2011

The Paris Opera has not unveiled a new production of Charles Gounod's masterpiece since 1975. This season's impressive effort has been a troubled affair. Shortly after rehearsals began in September, a *contretemps* between superstar tenor Roberto Alagna and veteran conductor Alain Lombard resulted in Lombard's withdrawal from the production. Star power is very much alive, but to prove that it is not the only thing that can derail an opera, a continuing labor dispute disrupted the staging of some of the production's early run performances. Fortunately, these inauspicious beginnings have been overcome and the magic unfolds with deceptive ease.

Gounod's opera adapts Johann Wolfgang von Goethe's philosophical Renaissance tale of an elderly scholar who sells his soul to the devil to regain his youth and enjoy sensual pleasures in which he had never delighted. With the devil's help, he seduces and abandons the peasant girl Marguerite, who bears their child. After she is condemned and imprisoned for killing it, Marguerite rejects Faust's attempt to rescue her with the devil's help. Instead she is declared saved by a chorus of angels while Faust is doomed.

Jean-Louis Martinoty's production updates the action to a colorful late nineteenth century. Johan Engels's sets are dominated by vast pale white bookshelves flanked by spiral staircases. A large crucifix hangs in the middle. The message that Faust curses faith as much as he curses knowledge looms over the entire staging. When necessary, the bookshelves break up into four sections to allow entrances and lighting effects. Creative use of the Opera Bastille's stage elevator answers the opera's challenge of quick changes in scene and mood. Faust seduces Marguerite in a verdant garden that rises from below. When he returns to her in the third act, it becomes a desiccated park in front of her house. Another swift movement introduces the Walpurgis Night scene, raising the heathen queens of antiquity into place amid much billowing smoke.

The overall visual effect is stunning, and Martinoty's dramatic innovations are for the most part tasteful. In an unorthodox take on the first act, Faust's first lines are not sung by Alagna but by the tenor Rémy Corrazza, listed in the program as "Faust II." His croaking qualities evoked the cantankerous older version of the character, who orders about medical students and writes the part's first word, "*Rien*," ("Nothing," meaning "In my life of scholarship, I have learned nothing") as he expresses suicidal despair. Only after Méphistophélès appears do we see and hear Alagna, who rises into place inside a life-size crystal ball. The devil normally tempts Faust with a vision of the fresh Marguerite, but here the real temptation is this vision of his younger and more beautiful self. The metaphor sits well in our narcissistic age. Alagna takes over upon this unconventional entrance, enthusiastically embracing Faust's renewed life while, perhaps gratuitously, stripping down to his bare chest.

Another fine iteration on the plot occurs in the third act, when Marguerite finds the jewel box that the rejuvenated Faust has left for her and sings an entrancing aria (the famous "Jewel Song"), rejoicing in its dazzling contents. Martinoty has Méphistophélès silently help her put on the jewels and voluptuously embrace her. It is unclear whether he is invisible or she is too enraptured to notice him, but literally as well as metaphorically, the devil's hands are all over the seduction. In a less pleasing moment, we see the abandoned Marguerite tormented by Méphistophélès in church while still holding her living child. She stabs it to death in front of horrified parishioners. The effect was provocative but unnecessary. The finale is traditional enough to allow Marguerite to be saved and, more unusually, to restore her murdered brother Valentin to life. Faust, however, is not dragged down to hell, but runs off stage in Méphistophélès's company, chasing chorus girls. As the curtain falls, we can surmise that his final damnation lies in the future, though the emptiness of his amoral life could be punishment enough.

Alagna's star power made him the victor over Lombard in the production dispute, and he did not disappoint. The voice's soaring metallic qualities recalled glorious, clarion French tenor singing of ages past while still imparting the tenderness that the role demands. His part of the seduction duet was a ravishing combination of sensitivity and sensuality. No one could have expected Marguerite to resist. Nevertheless, the upper register betrayed a few strained moments of vocal tightness that prevented Alagna from delivering a uniformly stellar performance. His singing was still rousing, however, and it was encouraging to see him approach the drama with greater care than he has in previous performances. When he sang the role in the Metropolitan Opera's last production, which premiered in 2005, he famously broke character to acknowledge the applause after "Salut, demeure chaste et pure." There was no evidence of that here.

The Albanian soprano Inva Mula's supple voice radiated a sweetness that captured Marguerite's vulnerability with an uncommon beauty of tone. The more passionate scenes did not reflect the full-bodied power of a Mirella Freni, but it is clear that this talented singer has what it takes to develop the role in the future. Méphistophélès is a tricky part that calls for a *basso cantante* who can also sing with a firm baritonal line. Paul Gay admirably showcased elements of both, though the essential low notes that color the part's menacing evil tended to elude him. Tassis Christoyannis took few chances with Valentin. He began the evening with a certain dryness in "Avant de quitter ces lieux" but seemed to overcome it in time for his seminal fourth act scene, in which Méphistophélès helps Faust murder Valentin in a duel over Marguerite's sullied honor.

Alain Altinoglu took the podium after Lombard's departure. He demonstrated an admirable mastery of the work and drew a steady orchestral performance often marked by moving Gallic subtlety.

Philippe Fénelon, *La Cerisaie*
Paris Opera, February 5, 2012

Russia's rich literary heritage has inspired many operas. Tchaikovsky, Mussorgsky, Shostakovich, and Prokofiev drew on the works of Pushkin (*Eugene Onegin, The Queen of Spades, Boris Godunov*), Tolstoy (*War and Peace*), Dostoevsky (*The Nose*), and less well known writers such as

Valery Briusov (*The Fiery Angel*) and Nikolai Leskov (*Lady Macbeth of Mtsensk*) to produce enduring masterpieces. Somehow the intense psychological dramas of Anton Chekhov have not translated as well into the musical realm. Philippe Fénelon's new opera seeks to address this gap, adapting Chekhov's last and perhaps most famous play, *The Cherry Orchard* (*La Cerisaie*), commissioned by the Paris Opera in cooperation with Moscow's Bolshoi Theater.

Fénelon, who lived close to Paris's Russian Orthodox Cathedral on Rue Daru and drew inspiration from its Sunday services, has tried to merge his French musical training with a Russian text by Alexei Parine. Dramatically, he caves to the current fashion of deconstructing the narrative tale into a series of twelve scenes, bracketed by a prologue and epilogue. The scenes unfold in the context of the original play's incidental ball, accompanied by a stage band and a solo ballet dancer who add nothing of great interest to the performance.

It was not a particularly successful effort. Chekhov's play depicts a hapless landowning family forced to auction off its estate to pay debts. At the climax of the play, the family's former serf turned *nouveau riche* merchant Lopakhin triumphantly announces that he was the successful bidder and that after his former owners depart he will cut down their precious cherry orchard to build profitable country cottages to rent to urbanites.

Incomprehensibly, Fénelon advances this scene to the prologue, denuding his opera of dramatic effect and allowing the rest of it to unfold in the disparate scenes. In these short vignettes, the estate's owner Madame Ranevskaia sings of a voluptuous love affair in Paris, her brother Gayev gives an impression of his dissolute existence, her daughter Anna wonders whether she will ever marry, the servants dwell on the problems of their lives, and so on. But they are for the most part disconnected from each other and from the larger plot. In a case of dramatic license, Fénelon adds scenes for the ghostly character of Grisha, Madame Ranevskaia's long dead son, who had drowned on the estate in childhood but whose memory still haunts her. To make the work more confusing, Grisha and the elderly servant Firs are cast as trouser parts for female singers, while the part of the nurse Charlotta is distractingly written for a bass. I doubt I could have followed the work or divined the story had I not previously read Chekhov's play.

If the dramatic presentation was weak, Fénelon's score demonstrated little originality. Its dissonances and episodic harmonies more strongly evoked the early twentieth century music familiar to Chekhov's era (he died in 1904) than of anything much since. I was reminded of Richard Strauss's exclamation about Debussy's *Pélleas et Mélisande*: "*Mais c'est tout Parsifal*," that is, essentially derivative of Wagner's music. It could likewise be said that Fénelon's opera is "*tout Richard Strauss*" with some Alban Berg mixed in (one of the dance sequences copies the festive music in the first scene of Verdi's *Un Ballo in Maschera*, but who knows why?).

Unfortunate staging choices by Georges Lavaudant further impeded Fénelon's effort. Jean-Pierre Vergier's sets are dominated by gigantic gnarled roots and branches that rise above the stage and merge into each other to form a kind of roof. It immediately suggested the first act of Wagner's *Die Walküre*, though it was obvious and intrusive even on its own. The costumes turned the characters into spectral caricatures perhaps meant to evoke Russia's faded nobility, but the effect was more comic than tragic.

Despite the poor presentation and derivative score, the young cast should be congratulated on a fine musical performance. Mostly hailing from the former Soviet Union and making their Opéra debuts in this production, they brought a spirit and fine musicianship that at least enlivened the incongruous scenes. The program identifies most characters by the Russian diminutives of their first names. Elena Kelessidi sang a strident Madame Ranevskaia, or Liouba. The fine tenor Marat Gali contributed a fine Gayev, or Lionia. The lithe soprano of Alexandra Kadurina added a haunting resonance to Grisha's otherworldly music. Ulyana Aleksyuk's sturdy interpretation of Anna (Ania) stood among the most memorable performances of the evening, as did Igor Golovatenko's strong willed but not insouciant Lopakhin.[3] Ksenia Vyaznikova as Firs and

---

[3] Golovatenko has now progressed to major baritone parts.

Mischa Schelomianski as Charlotta performed their opposite sex parts with a mirth that made up for the confusion.

Tito Ceccherini led a well paced performance of Fénelon's score, even if the music could have been more imaginative. Staging the opera in the more intimate Palais Garnier rather than the cavernous Opera Bastille suggests that more works could successfully be returned to the French capital's traditional operatic stage.

Wolfgang Amadeus Mozart, *Così fan tutte*
London, Royal Opera, February 7, 2012

The Royal Opera's winter season includes all three of Mozart's great Italian operas with libretti by his most fruitful collaborator, Lorenzo da Ponte. *Così fan tutte*, the least famous of the three, rounds out the effort in this revival of Jonathan Miller's production. In one respect Miller's effort recalls his Metropolitan Opera production of one of the other Mozart-da Ponte collaborations, *The Marriage of Figaro*, still in repertoire there. As in that production, the backdrop here is an unfinished interior in a mild state of disorder. I still wonder what this sedate effect is supposed to represent, but it cannot be accused of distracting the audience, even if it is in an unattractive shade of yellow.

Otherwise, the production updates the action to contemporary times. When Ferrando and Guglielmo go off to war, they wear standard European military fatigues and blue UN helmets. Their "Albanian" alter egos, which they must adopt to seduce each other's betrothed in order to fulfill the conditions of their bet with the cynical Don Alfonso, look like bikers. For most of the evening, Fiordiligi and Dorabella sport casual outfits that just scream "casual Friday." At the end, when they seem ready to marry the "Albanians," they predictably appear as biker chicks. Their secretarial and bespectacled maid Despina looks slightly more officious. Alfonso is a bit better turned out. The wagered "zecchini" of the original libretto become "euros" in the supertitles. And in case no one has seen enough mobile phones in London lately, the entire cast uses them, with Alfonso cleverly delivering one of his asides into one as though he is complaining to a confidant about the prospect of losing his bet. Despite this one twenty-first-century innovation, there was really nothing about this *Così* that Peter Sellars did not do in his famously updated production of the opera twenty years ago.

A glorious vocal performance of Mozart's music can make up for a lackluster production, but this was only partially in evidence. Michèle Losier's rich mezzo drew out Dorabella's part with great distinction and was well paired with the talented young American tenor Charles Castronovo, whose more tenuous start as Ferrando developed confidently into virtuoso lyric tenor singing in the second act. Baritone Nikolay Borchev's Guglielmo produced some solid sounds and was well acted, but lacked a more than typical quality. Malin Byström's edgy soprano underserved the beautiful role of Fiordiligi. The most active dramatic part in the opera falls to Despina; mezzo Rosemary Joshua acquitted herself rather well, contributing a fine if perhaps by necessity wiry quality to the role while hitting the essential comic notes. Now in his fifth decade of performing at Covent Garden, veteran baritone Sir Thomas Allen added a charismatic stage presence as Don Alfonso, even if the voice shows some weathered signs. Sir Colin Davis led a faultless orchestral performance.

Modest Mussorgsky, *Khovanshchina*
New York, Metropolitan Opera, February 27, 2012

The specter of Peter the Great haunts Mussorgsky's less well known historical opera. Begun in the year of the bicentennial of Peter's birth (1872), its plot reflects weightily on the important turn in Russian history with which the tsar is identified. Will Russia modernize or hold fast to its medieval Muscovite traditions? Will its great nobles become tame servitors, or will they displace the autocratic monarchy in their own interest? Will Peter survive, or will he be sidelined by his willful half-sister, the Regent Sophia, and her favorite, Prince Golitsyn? It takes a sophisticated knowledge of Russian history even to begin to understand this complex work and the dynamic forces behind the leading characters.

To make it all the more abstruse, tsarist censorship restrictions prevented either Peter or his half-sister from appearing as characters in the opera, and they are only alluded to (in the Mariinsky Theater's current production, however, a mute Peter appears in Scene 3 to pardon the defeated *streltsy*, or musketeers, after their failed rising). If I lacked graduate training in Russian history, I would find it beyond distracting to make sense of who the Old Believers were, why they were so angered by the liturgical reforms of Patriarch Nikon (another big name of the era who is mentioned in the opera but never appears), or the political nature of the Khovansky/Shaklovity conspiracies.

Even then, the work's grasp of history itself is far from perfect. Mussorgsky, guided by the critic and publicist Vladimir Stasov, conflated two separate incidents in Peter's early reign into one intricate plot. The actual "Khovansky episode" (referred to in Russian by the opera's title, the "*shchina*" suffix meaning "era of," but usually in a negative sense) occurred in 1689 and resulted in Peter's undisputed arrival in power. The episode involving Shaklovity, the *streltsy* commander whose operatic incarnation arranges and gloats over Khovansky's murder, had occurred seven years earlier, in 1682, and resulted in the younger Peter's temporary subordination to Regent Sophia. The Old Believer phenomenon, which was merely incidental to these power struggles, had developed as the result of contested church reforms in earlier decades.

This engrossing and rather unwieldy political drama, dressed up with a conventional operatic love triangle, has not enjoyed wide popularity outside Russia. The Met first produced it in the 1949-1950 season, but it vanished from the repertory after only four performances and did not return until August Everding's production premiered in 1985. Sparing revivals last brought it to the Met stage in 1999.

Ming Cho Lee's sets lose vitality in the public scenes, set on Moscow's Red Square and in the Kremlin. The backdrops rest uneasily over the action and look mainly like wooden tracings of the original buildings. The internal scenes in Prince Golitsyn's Westernized household (complete with harpsichord) and Prince Khovansky's more Muscovite abode (for some reason imagined as red) convey greater intimacy. It was a pity that the final immolation scene did not feature more pyrotechnics, but there was smoke and fire. The costumes, by John Conklin, are laudable museum-quality reproductions of sumptuous seventeenth-century Russian dress. The lackluster scenes and the Met's penchant for introducing more Russian operas over the past two decades suggest that it might be time for a fresh look.

Part of the Met's great strength in the Russian repertoire is the immense vocal talent that has come to its disposal in the twenty years following the collapse of the Soviet Union. Virtually the entire cast consists of distinguished singers from St. Petersburg's Mariinsky Theater, long familiar to New York audiences because of the Met's sometime association with the Mariinsky's artistic director Valery Gergiev. Gergiev's appearances at the Met have been infrequent in recent seasons and anyone who ever heard him conduct *Khovanshchina* in Russia will miss his raw energy and emotional power in the pit. Kirill Petrenko, however, demonstrated fine musicianship in leading the complex score. Left unfinished at Mussorgsky's death, its professional premiere only took place in 1911. The score was then reorchestrated by Shostakovich, and Stravinsky added a choral ending for the self-immolating Old Believers that is now frequently used.

The Ukrainian bass Anatoli Kotscherga made his long overdue Met debut in the title role. He captured the wily old prince's machinations and gruffness in a superb study only slightly undermined by an aging voice. The tenor Misha Didyk, another Ukrainian debuting in the house, sang the role of Khovansky's son Andrei with the light lyricism often demanded in Russian tenor parts. Olga Borodina sang as beautifully as I can recall her singing, reaching lustrously into the saintly role of Marfa's deep mezzo range. The fortune teller scene and final aria were models of singing that Met audiences should long cherish. Her husband, the bass Ildar Abdrazakov, sang his first Russian role in the house as the Old Believer priest Dosifei with a profound and appealing clarity. George Gagnidze's Shaklovity showcased an especially splendid yet sinister contribution. And the redoubtable tenor Vladimir Galouzine, the world's leading Ghermann in Tchaikovsky's *The Queen of Spades*, was in fine voice as the well intentioned but ill starred Prince Golitsyn. The Met's chorus stood on a level nearly equaling the best Russian ensembles. The choreographer Benjamin Millepied, known for his work in the film *Black Swan*, made his Met debut in arranging the dance of Khovansky's Persian slave girls.[4] The effort avoided kitsch in favor of an engaging sensuality.

---

[4] Millepied later became director of the Paris Opera but left after a brief and reportedly stormy tenure.

Alban Berg, *Lulu*
Berlin State Opera, April 11, 2012

The Berlin State Opera continues its residency in West Berlin's Schiller Theater, principally a drama venue adapted for opera, while the company's original home on Unter-den-Linden undergoes a multi-season renovation. The Staatsoper's work remains prodigious. On March 31 it opened a new production of *Lulu*, Alban Berg's fairy tale of decadence *non plus ultra*.

The opera traces a debauched woman's sex-propelled descent from respectable bourgeois marriage to a Bohemian life among unstable artists to the utter degradation of a streetwalker's demise. In three short hours we witness the villainous heroine cause one husband to die of fright, drive another to suicide, and murder a third after seducing his son, whose throat is slashed before the final curtain descends. In the end she and her lesbian paramour Countess Geschwitz are done in by Jack the Ripper, Lulu's last client as a prostitute living among London's down and out. The infamous serial killer traditionally stabs them to death, but in Andrea Breth's production he douses his victims with gasoline instead. They perish in a blazing fire Lulu herself ignites with a lighter Jack hands her, accompanied by a heavily amplified, blood curdling death scream projected off stage. The effect is no less stunning for its ambiguous brutality, which leaves us with the provocative question of whether Lulu is punished by a corrupt society or whether she is her own judge and executioner. It is hardly a coincidence that Berg intended the same baritone to sing Lulu's last husband Dr. Schön, whom she murders, and Jack, who murders her in what seems like karmic justice.

Lulu is fundamentally an ensemble piece with one starring role, the title character herself. The gorgeous young German soprano Mojca Erdmann could easily have had another career as a sought-after fashion model. A cool, slender blonde, she looked, acted, and sang the part to near perfection. Clad throughout the performance in a slight, shimmering silver gown, her visage betrayed the fixed, expressionless stare of a psychopath whose actions and inactions fall beyond the pale of simple amorality. The voice is equally attractive, with artful soubrette qualities easily shed for lustrous highs. Challenging stage directions had her deliver the part in a variety of awkward contortions (and more than once on her back), but whether she was carried in the arms of one of her lovers, tilted sideways, or forcing her doomed third husband Dr. Schön to dump his more respectable fiancée while riding him piggy back with a crop, the notes were all there.

Among the large ensemble, the graceful baritone Michael Volle stood out in the dual role of Dr. Schön and Jack the Ripper. He alternated deftly between the doctor's weak willed desperation and the killer's cold blooded cruelty. Tenor Thomas Piffka handled Schön's even more feckless son Alwa with a pinched tenor that never wafted into agitated shrillness. Veteran dramatic soprano Deborah Polaski took the mezzo role of Geschwitz with lithe tones that captured the character's ethereal qualities. Thomas J. Mayer contributed a fine vocalization of the character known simply as "the Athlete," a lowlife admirer of Lulu's.

It is a pity that Erich Wonder's set was not more expressive. With no change of décor, the opera unfolds entirely within a bleak industrial site enclosed by bare factory walls. A pile of full-sized wrecked cars looms at stage right. It is not completely ridiculous for Lulu's painter second husband's atelier (especially in Berlin, where such spaces are an artist's preferred environment) or the miserable abode Lulu and her remaining hangers-on inhabit at the end. It was much harder to accept as the bourgeois drawing rooms of Lulu's first and third husbands or as the theater where she dances between fatal marriages.

Moidele Bickel's costumes work well for Lulu and for Geschwitz, whose draping dark blue gown recalls the dreamy symbolist age *femmes fragiles* the character evokes. Unfortunately, the male characters were almost identically dressed in drab and tattered 1930s-style suits and fedoras. Sometimes it was difficult to tell them apart. True to the Brechtian theatrical milieu in which the work had its genesis, aggressive background action comments on the seediness of the characters and their surroundings. We have the obligatory casual fornication, a pantomime of Jack killing a double of Lulu while the very much alive original is still committing her misdeeds a few paces away, a cameraman on roller skates filming some of the more lurid scenes, and so on. The distractions seemed a bit overdone.

Berg left the score unfinished at his death in 1935, and his widow refused others permission to complete it for the remaining four decades of her life. As a result, the full three-act version now in general use was only unveiled in 1979. The Staatsoper uses this version, but cuts were abundant. Notably, the opera's prologue, in which an animal tamer tantalizes our voyeuristic love for humanity's beastly nature, is replaced by Lulu's elderly and perhaps dying pimp/father figure Schigolch lying flat and reflecting ironically on the wonders of life and how grateful he is for them. This short and less effective alternative concludes with a foreshadowing of Lulu's final death scream. The lively Paris gaming house scene normally found in Act III also disappears. It is not strictly necessary to the plot as it unfolds in the course of the opera's self-sufficient scenes, but it is one of the opera's more active and energetic sequences. And it would have been amusing to meet the freakish characters who appear only in it.

The production's most interesting innovation was David Robert Coleman's new orchestration of the final scene, the refugee's London of degradation, despair, and death. Coleman claimed to be "shocked" when the Staatsoper's general music director Daniel Barenboim suggested the task to him, but he has admirably reworked the score with elements of jazz that Berg appears to have intended to include. Coleman's livelier version employs steel drums, a xylophone, a glockenspiel, and a marimbaphone (an antiquated steel bar and tuner instrument) to produce a brassier and more automated sound. It goes saucily well with the depravities of the final scene. Barenboim led the orchestra with admirable precision and finesse, essential qualities that might not immediately suggest themselves for interpreting an opera of *Lulu*'s frantic debauchery.

Jean-Philippe Rameau, *Hippolyte et Aricie*
Paris Opera, June 9, 2012

As the Paris Opéra approaches the end of an unusually dynamic season, its last new production revives Rameau's first opera. Unknown to audiences in the nineteenth century, fresh looks at *Hippolyte et Aricie* in more recent times have been infrequent. The last Opéra production was in 1996, replacing the previous effort, which dated back to 1908. The sparse attention has not done this important work justice. Its premiere in 1733 represented an evolutionary step in French opera, from the staid classicism of Jean-Baptiste Lully to a more accessible idiom. Its lyric qualities are far stronger than those of the earlier French repertoire, and the harmonies so much more sophisticated that musicians of Rameau's day reportedly had trouble playing them. Voltaire even quipped that the composer had the misfortune of knowing more about music than Lully did.

Rameau composed to a libretto by the *abbé* Simon-Joseph Pellegrin, who drew from both ancient tragedy – Euripides's *Hippolyte* – and its greatest adaptation in the tradition of French classicism – Racine's *Phèdre*. Neither work dominates the opera's plot. After an homage to the goddess Diana, the lovers Hippolyte and Aricie nearly fall victim to the jealous Phèdre, Hippolyte's wicked stepmother, who takes advantage of her husband Thésée's absence in Hades to vie for Hippolyte's affections. Thésée, however, triumphs over the underworld's furies and returns to discover the situation, for which he mistakenly blames Hippolyte. After calling upon Neptune for his son's death and seeing him devoured by a sea monster, Thésée learns the truth from the guilty Phèdre, who then kills herself. In the end Diana saves Hippolyte and ensures his happiness with Aricie. Thésée knows of the happy outcome but is punished by never being allowed to see his son again.

Ivan Alexandre originally created this new production for Toulouse's Théâtre du Capitole in 2009. The effort could be called old fashioned, but its drop sets and extensive use of traditional theatrical machinery make for seamless transitions between the operas five acts. Antoine Fontaine's appealing neo-classical decors rely on pastel colors that complement the passions at work on stage. Only the fourth act appearance of the sea monster (which actually does devour Hippolyte) bordered on camp. Costumes by Jean-Daniel Vuillermoz approximated the era of Rameau's later life as an opera composer (he was fifty and a well known church organist when *Hippolyte et Aricie* premiered) in the early reign of Louis XV.

No effort was spared in casting the leading roles. Sarah Connolly, best known now as an internationally accomplished Straussian mezzo, delivered Phèdre with a well centered middle range and full bodied clarity of tone. The part's seminal third act aria "Cruelle mère des amours" strikingly prefigured the pathos heard in eighteenth-century music up to

Mozart. In the role of Thésée, Stéphane Degout lived up to his reputation as perhaps the finest lyric baritone singing today. The part flowed with a rich ease and fluency that would be difficult to parallel in any genre. Although those two characters have arguably the opera's best vocal music, it was a slight disappointment to find the title roles somewhat under cast. Australian-born Finnish tenor Topi Lehtipuu's Hippolyte projected light warmth in a part that required more ardor. The youthfulness of Anne-Catherine Gillet's Aricie, though attractive, was rather too thin to command the stage. François Lis doubled in the bass roles of Jupiter and Pluto, but lacked the requisite low notes for the parts to find their greatest effect. The exquisitely sung Diana of mezzo-soprano Andrea Hill, however, added a plush luster to the pantheon of deities. Rameau's *oeuvre* falls outside the "opera-ballet" genre that dominated much of eighteenth-century French music, but it would be an oversight not to praise the dancers of the Opéra's ballet, who executed Natalie van Parys's choreography with precision and charm.

Perhaps the most rewarding contribution to the performance came from the orchestra and chorus of the Concert d'Astrée baroque ensemble, led by its artistic director Emanuelle Haïm. Having recently celebrated its tenth anniversary, the ensemble played Rameau's score with a virtuoso authenticity that is making itself increasingly welcome in the great musical capitals of Europe.

Richard Wagner, *Parsifal*
Bayreuth Festival, August 5, 2012

Since its premiere, Stefan Herheim's production of Wagner's last and most spiritual opera (which the composer called a "sacred stage festival play") has stood as Bayreuth's best answer to critics of the festival, who charge that its stagings are too outlandish, dull, or otherwise flawed to be admired or taken seriously. Herheim responded with a *mise-en-scène* so infused with symbolism, meaning, and pure poetic beauty that it is hard to grasp everything he meant to say, even in a second viewing. The difficult path of Germany's recent history intertwines with the opera's intense Christian mysticism to address all manner of questions about faith and redemption.

Discussing the Herheim production's entire content in full could fill an entire volume. There is, in fact, such a book, by Antonia Goldhammer, which runs to 168 pages. But to summarize briefly, Herheim uses each of the opera's three acts to show Germany's progression from imperial times in Act I to doomed Weimar Germany in Act II to a traumatized postwar Federal Republic in Act III. The director has publicly described the darker parts of this progression as a trip to hell. The action unfolds in the milieu of Wagner's villa, Wahnfried, his Bayreuth home. Atop the historicism rests the opera's quest for redemption through suffering, a trope that Herheim interpolates as universal. Since Wagner apologists passionately argue for the human universality of his music, the statement is a profound one.

If *Parsifal* is about achieving wisdom through compassion and compassion through suffering, then in this production Germany moves through its own suffering in war to a democracy that contributes to the universal culture of mankind. Indeed, the third act finale culminates in a projected globe of the world over a gigantic circular mirror that reflects the audience. The image of a dove then shines above the proscenium. Wagner originally intended for a real dove to descend into the temple of the Holy Grail, but Herheim uses it here to resolve his general theme: it replaces the double-headed Hohenzollern eagle that rests above Act I and the Nazi eagle that menaces the action at the end of Act II.

As for *Parsifal's* inescapable mysticism, the entire first act is interpolated through the Rosicrucian myth, which held that Jesus's second coming would become manifest in the biological descendant of a child born to Mary Magdalene. Here we see Parsifal as that child. Stage action during the ethereal prelude, which unites sentiments of faith, suffering, and hope, shows the child hero at his mother's death bed, ignorant of her pain and suffering. When he is transported to the Grail temple, the myth unfolds in full, with the Grail rite centering around the new Christ child's birth, an event connected with the unhealed Amfortas, who is presented as an unredeemed Jesus. The chorus of knights emerges clad in First World War uniforms, completing the rite with a regimental mass on the eve of the war to end all wars.

In the opera's intense second act Klingsor's realm appears as a military hospital in which the wounded knights are tended by his flower maidens, done up like cabaret girls of the 1920s. The introductory music, which inverts the music of the knights, is accompanied by video projections of harsh battlefield scenes. Kundry struts in wearing a tuxedo and top hat with a blond wig, an undeniable reference to Marlene Dietrich in Josef von Sternberg's pre-Hays Code film *Morocco*. In keeping with the mysticism, she transforms into the ailing Herzeleide, thus becoming both Parsifal's mother and the Magdalene whose womb will give the world its redeemer. By the end of the failed seduction scene, when the spurned Kundry angrily calls upon Klingsor to destroy Parsifal, the Weimar fantasy yields to machine gun-wielding Nazi storm troopers and a brown shirted Hitler Youth – a hint of what Parsifal could become – who parade under swastika flags. The stage effect combined with Klingsor's music produces visceral revulsion. Parsifal's purity enables him to withstand their assault, not only catching the Holy Spear as convention dictates, but causing the whole edifice of Nazism to crash down around him. In a hint of Kundry's conversion and third act penance, she spreads her arms to shield him as the machine guns fire away.

Act III shows the aftermath of the battle, a metaphor for the Second World War. Gurnemanz emerges from the ruins of Wahnfried (which actually was bombed in an April 1945 air raid) to find a repentant Kundry, still clad as Parsifal's mother. The anointing scene unfolds traditionally, but the Grail temple has now become the Bundestag, the West German legislature, as it appeared in 1951, the year of the first postwar Bayreuth Festival. The scene's angry choruses of knights, which begin as a conversation, are presented in the manner of a parliamentary debate. Amfortas appears in ministerial guise; his inability to perform the rite unites all factions against him. Parsifal appears, heals the wound, and takes charge of the order as the orchestra resolves all the harmonies. Gurnemanz, Kundry, and the child Parsifal stand at stage front as a reconciled "holy family," while the projected globe and mirror declare human universality.

Hearing Wagner in Bayreuth may be the greatest pleasure for any serious enthusiast, and the musical performance was a truly stunning achievement. Burkhard Fritz lacked charisma, but his steady vocal performance in the title role was nevertheless an inspired work of art. Susan Maclean's Kundry rightly received the loudest ovation. An engaging actress as well as a superb *Zwischenfach* singer, she endowed the role with superb musicianship and a dramatic sensibility that mixed its essential eroticism with intriguing dimensions of guilt and self-loathing. The bass role of Gurnemanz requires enormous resilience. Kwangchul Youn imbued the part with a superb line, gorgeous low notes, and an uncommon lyricism. The fine baritone Detlef Roth was an effecting Amfortas. Thomas Jesatko carried off Klingsor's role with a fascinating perversion that positively made one enjoy a role that is rarely if ever costumed in fishnet stockings.

The dynamic young conductor Philippe Jordan brought a lighter touch and somewhat faster pace to the score than Daniele Gatti had in the production's presentation in earlier years. The chromatic effect was not always as emotionally pronounced, but the lyrical touches to the Grail temple scenes that end Acts I and III were a wonder to hear. Both visually and musically, it is a welcome sign that the opera will be Bayreuth's first international broadcast, with the August 11 performance beamed into movie theaters around Europe. And every Wagnerian in the world should buy, savor, and relish the forthcoming DVD.

Richard Wagner, *Der Fliegende Holländer*
Bayreuth Festival, August 6, 2012

A new production in Bayreuth is always fertile ground for controversy, usually because of some weird element in the staging. This year's new production, of Wagner's earliest "mature" work, was dogged by scandal even before the curtain went up. Just days before the premiere, the long announced star baritone Evgeny Nikitin suddenly withdrew under administrative pressure after it was revealed that youthful internet videos showed him sporting a swastika tattoo on his chest. Nevertheless, the questionable tattoo, as publicity photos reveal, had long been covered by another one, and the Dutchman's costume would not have revealed any tattoos had he gone on in the production. Stefan Herheim's currently running production of *Parsifal*, moreover, uses swastika flags quite vividly. But none of this mattered. Nikitin was out. He did not help his side of the story by changing his reaction from a simple apology to a doubtful claim that he did not know the swastika was offensive to an even more dubious assertion that the tattoo was not a swastika at all. Regardless, the controversy really was much ado about nothing, and for the record Nikitin is a fine Dutchman (he has sung the role in St. Petersburg's Mariinsky Theater). We can hope he returns to Bayreuth one day, no matter what tattoos he may once have had.[5]

It was fortunate that Bayreuth had the excellent German-trained Korean bass-baritone Samuel Youn on hand to replace the hapless Nikitin. Possessing a cool, rich legato, Youn achieved a considerable success for which he deserves much praise. There were a few rough edges to be sure, but the character almost demands them if the Dutchman's spectral despair is to come through convincingly. Adrianne Pieczonka's Senta was less fortunate. The essential ballad, which introduces the girl's obsession with the legendary and damned captain, sounded thin and at times rather forced. She floated a few sublime notes in the duet, but inconsistent ascents left the overall effort uneven. Franz-Josef Selig was a stentorian Daland, though his low notes came out a bit muddy. Benjamin Bruns and Michael König ably rounded out the cast as the Steersman and Senta's hapless suitor Erik.

Christian Thielemann led a superb orchestral performance, displaying enormous energy and an electric vitality along with an almost superhuman aptitude for keeping the sound plush throughout nearly two and a half hours of continuous music.

The young director Jan Philip Gloger cannot be credited with tremendous inspiration in his presentation of this stormy tale. Like so many productions of this opera, he has reduced it to a modern legend of soulless capitalist materialism. The tortured Dutchman makes his entrance in the *de rigueur* business suit, toting a carry-on suitcase and a disposable coffee. As he so often does in houses in Germany and elsewhere, he looked like any poor white-collar stiff trudging through the Frankfurt airport. His suitcase is of course filled with US dollars.

---

[5] Nikitin sang the role without controversy in François Gerard's new production at the Metropolitan Opera when it premiered in March 2020.

Senta's father Daland is the predictable corporate executive, attended by a puppy dog-like Steersman, whose short aria about his beloved involves him producing a chic dress with a visible price tag instead of the golden band his song tells us he wants to give his sweetheart. Daland's office worker "sailors" repeat this action *en masse* when they sail off.

Senta and the Act II maiden's chorus pack and ship cardboard boxes carrying electric fans. This is almost clever since their chorus calls for "spinning," but the major dramatic effect was to make spectators in the hot and stuffy Festspielhaus wish they had one. The stage action of the third act chorus looks like a corporate pep talk, in which the lickspittle Steersman smilingly extols the simple fan's virtues. At the end of the opera, the factory switches over to making and packaging a new corporate product: table lamps with figurines of the presumably redeemed (or just dead) Dutchman and Senta in their final suicidal embrace, which comes after Senta stabs herself with a pair of scissors. At least she does not slash her throat with them, as in other German productions, but the method was again disappointingly predictable.

The production was not totally devoid of originality. Christof Hetzer's set opens the action with a blazingly illuminated computer mainframe that dominates the stage. When the mood is stormy, its neon lights sputter along and display blinking zeroes on screens that recall modern stock exchanges. When the action is moving forward, however, the installation hums along with steadily rising figures in the register. It seemed that so much more could have been done with this, but Gloger's confined and rather clichéd concept may not have allowed for much else.

Chapter Three

2012-2013

Richard Wagner, *Lohengrin*
Milan, La Scala, December 7, 2012

With attention focused on the forthcoming bicentennial year, the big question on the Italian cultural scene has been: Whose bicentennial? Wagner's or Verdi's? Both composers were born in 1813, and answering this question has been a very delicate matter for Italy's impresarios. The venerable La Scala's solution seems to be to celebrate both. All but two works in its new season are by the bicentennial composers. Wagner is honored with Claus Guth's opening night new production of *Lohengrin*.

December 7 – Saint Ambrose's Day – is always dramatic in Milan. This year was no exception. Arguably Europe's most important annual cultural event, La Scala's annual opening night always draws leading political and cultural figures from Italy and elsewhere, as well as the paparazzi who love them and the riot police who protect them. Audience members could rub elbows with cabinet ministers, famous actors, and glamorous socialites and look with bemusement or trepidation at the small anti-austerity protest across the piazza. The young actress Tea Falco appeared in a swan headdress and white feather boa. Wagner's unsmiling great-granddaughter Eva, co-director of the Bayreuth Festival, looked formidable. Prime Minister Mario Monti made an impassive entrance, despite sudden political machinations that imperiled his government. Despite his cool front, he announced he would resign the next day.

Alas, December 7's other performance lacked the power to stun the gilded audience. Wagner's opera is supposed to be a tale of divine heroism, in which a knight of the Holy Grail arrives to champion a young girl, Elsa, accused of murdering her brother, the rightful heir to the throne of Brabant. Guth has reduced this quintessentially Romantic work to a claustrophobic tale of youth repressed to the point of neurosis by a burdensome but empty society. The milieu suggested by Christian Schmidt's sets and costumes is approximately Wagner's own time and place – a dark mid nineteenth-century German nowhere entrapped within high enclosed walls lined with three levels of closed doors. The only stage decorations are a simple table and an upright piano with heavy Gothic letters telling us it was made in Berlin. Are we in a mental institution? A prison? An army barracks? We can only guess, but the answer is not likely to be appealing.

The direction made the principals into a dysfunctional bourgeois family. Lohengrin and Elsa were shorn of their usual heroic proportions and appeared as innocent schoolchildren. They tick nervously whenever they are in the intimidating surroundings of King Henry's court. Lohengrin's disappointing entrance places him lying on his side facing away from the audience. His jumpy movements around the stage for much of the rest of the evening suggested a desire to escape. It reminded me of the suicidal student characters in Frank Wedekind's expressionist play *Spring Awakening*. The opera's rousing choruses give the nobles of the realm a chance to buck up Lohengrin's courage, but this only suggests that they thirst for leadership he does not have and cannot offer. Only in the third act is there some relief. The marriage scene, in which the ever-present walls now loom over a pond with tall reeds, allow Lohengrin and Elsa to escape their social constraints and seem genuinely at ease with each other and themselves. They kick off their shoes, splash around in the water, and for the first-time act like somewhat adjusted people. But this moment comes too late in the evening to settle our minds. That Wagner prefigured expressionism is an interesting academic point, but it does not really make for good theater.

Telramund and Ortrud lurk somberly in black outfits, acting as Elsa's tutors. This odd idea could be entertaining when they indulged in their base insinuations about Lohengrin's character and origins. Ortrud at one point slams a piano shut on Elsa's hands during a bonkers piano lesson. But their antics did not match the depth of their characters or the nature of their grievance. In Wagner's libretto, Telramund is the next heir to the throne and Ortrud's family once ruled the land. It is hard to imagine the petty schoolmasters they have become ferociously invoking pagan gods and pure evil to destroy their neurotic charges. Why would they need to? This stunted Lohengrin and Elsa pairing is already on its way to ruin without any magic spells.

As often happens in *Regietheater*, glorious music accompanied a stale production concept.

Jonas Kaufmann is so supercharged a Heldentenor that it seems cliché to offer the usual praise for his immense talent. Possessing firm baritonal qualities, he delivered the title part with seasoned sensuality and, when he needed to, well centered gravitas. His Elsa, Annette Dasch, arrived at the last minute to replace the announced Anja Harteros and her understudy, both of whom were indisposed. Dasch sang with voluptuously creamy tones that recalled her fine Bayreuth performances in the role.

Evelyn Herlitzius unrolled a superbly menacing Ortrud, though she did not always resist the role's temptation sharp on some of the high notes. Icelandic Tómas Tómasson sang serviceably but not more as Telramund. I expected a richer sound from bass René Pape in the role of King Henry. His fine legato was there to enjoy, but the voice occasionally sounded thin in the passages that call for real authority. Baritone Željko Lučić is having a major Verdi career around the world. His casting in the lesser role of the King's Herald was a luxury, indeed.

Maestro Daniel Barenboim can be hit or miss in his Wagner conducting. This evening was a definite hit. Sometimes he drove the brass a bit too forcefully, but Wagner did say he would gladly compose only for the horn if he could. Throughout the performance, both the orchestra and chorus brought the music into its full grandeur, indeed, to heights that allowed the audience to overlook the visual weaknesses in the production.

Giuseppe Verdi, *Nabucco*
Milan, La Scala, February 1, 2013

Controversy swirled in the Italian press last fall, when Italy's leading opera house greeted the joint Verdi-Wagner bicentennial season by opening with Wagner's *Lohengrin*. Was the great national composer to be ignored in favor of the Germanic titan? Lest anyone think so, La Scala has decisively entered the Verdi phase of its commemorations. This season the house will present five new Verdi productions and then revive two additional ones. *Nabucco*, his third opera and the work he identified as the true beginning of his artistic career, opened on February 1.

In Daniele Abbado's production, *Nabucco* cast a pall of gloom over the opening of La Scala's Verdi festivities. The opera abbreviates the Biblical story of the ancient Hebrews' Babylonian captivity, confining its events to the reign of Nebudchanezzar, who enslaves the Israelites and then releases them after his prayers to their god deliver him from madness brought on by his own sacrilegious pride.

Advancing the action to a dismal modern milieu, Alison Chitty's gray sets and prosaic costumes suggest a depressing European 1940s nowhere, in which the opera's ancient Hebrews become persecuted modern Jews. She did not take the analogous step of making Nabucco and his bad Babylonians into recognizable Nazis, but this merely left the persecutors' identity and motivations a frustratingly unanswered question.

The Temple of Solomon is minimally suggested by a series of disappointing concrete slabs, which the Babylonians topple when Nabucco orders its destruction. His descent into madness – divine punishment for proclaiming himself a god – is not the standard thunderbolt, but a black out from which he emerges with his suit jacket pulled down to constrain his arms. Were it not for the horrified look on his face, it would have been hard to shake the image of Humphrey Bogart doing this to disarm the embarrassed hoodlum played by Elisha Cook, Jr. in *The Maltese Falcon*. Until Jehovah restores Nabucco's sanity toward the end of the opera, he wanders the stage in his undershirt. Abigaille burns the documents proving her slave birth in a worrisome pyrotechnic display. The graven image of the Babylonian god Baal is hinted at by wire mesh knight figures that could have been brought to the stage from the modern art installation accompanying any minor European city's Renaissance exhibit.

A degree of innovation came in Luca Scarzella's video effects, which haphazardly project a bird's eye view of the action in black and white on a giant screen at stage rear. While the video added the unnerving viewpoint of a security camera, it was not enough to make Abbado's production a success.

Leo Nucci will turn 71 in April, but he shows no sign of slowing down.[6] Some dry patches notwithstanding, his technique and range remain an almost fully intact reminder of his mid-career triumphs in Verdi baritone parts. Despite the lackluster surroundings, his stentorian Nabucco was simply riveting. The younger cast showcased rising Verdian talent. As Abigaille, Ukrainian soprano Liudmyla Monastyrska contributed full, voluptuous tones through her purring middle and lower registers. They recall her recent international success as Aida, a role in which she will return to La Scala in October. The bel canto ascents demanded by this early Verdi piece proved more challenging, however, with the occasional sharp notes infiltrating an otherwise solid performance. Monastyrska's dramatic abilities also seemed somewhat constrained, though the signature aria "Anch'io dischiuso un giorno," in which Abigaille confesses an emotional vulnerability she has long since buried, unfolded with an alluring intimacy. Bass Vitalij Kowaljow delivered a solid interpretation of the prophet Zaccaria, though the part's very lowest notes sounded muddy.

The fine Latvian tenor Aleksandrs Antonenko and Italian mezzo Veronica Simeoni rounded out the cast as Ismaele and Fenena, who carry on a forbidden love affair across the opera's political divide. *Nabucco*'s most famous music by far is the "Va, pensiero" chorus – an anthem for Italian national ambitions, – and this and the opera's other expertly sung choral pieces won much deserved praise. Nicola Luisotti's conducting moved the action along rapidly without losing track of the opera's introspection and sensitivity.

Giuseppe Verdi, *Falstaff*
Milan, La Scala, February 2, 2013

This production of Verdi's final opera is paired at La Scala this season with *Nabucco*, which was composed more than half a century before and could hardly have presented a better occasion to observe an artist's evolution over a lifetime. The laurels for inaugurating Verdi's bicentennial season fell to the Canadian director Robert Carsen, whose *Falstaff* has

---

[6] Nucci sang for another six years, only retiring in 2019.

already appeared to critical acclaim at Covent Garden. Based on Shakespeare's *The Merry Wives of Windsor*, the opera follows the escapades of the impossibly fat Sir John Falstaff, who tries to replenish his shaky finances by seducing the wives of prosperous burghers, first Alice Ford and then Meg Page. He lazily sends the two ladies the same letter, allowing them to see through the ruse and make a fool of him. Alice's husband Ford only gradually clues in after a fit of jealousy over the situation and unrelated outrage that his daughter Nanetta is scheming to avoid an arranged marriage to elope with the sympathetic but unsuitable Fenton. The opera ends happily, with Falstaff humiliated, Nanetta and Fenton married, and the whole cast declaring that all the world is folly and that he who laughs last laughs best.

Carsen has imaginatively updated the setting from Tudor times to a frowzy post-World War II Britain, a milieu where Falstaff's ne'er-do-well aristocratic habits clash mightily with the twin adversaries of austerity and middle-class morality. It was hard to imagine the other characters embracing the opera's rambunctious frivolity instead of giving Falstaff a stern lecture on the virtues of gainful employment and sober professionalism.

The production opens in Falstaff's room at the Garter Inn, where he is perched in a massive bed set before very English wood-paneled walls and surrounded by soiled room service trolleys. When his retainers Pistol and Bardolph (Pistola and Bardolfo) refuse to go along with his plans to deceive the wives, at least not without proper payment, he chases from the room by defacing the ceiling with a couple of rifle shots. The wives receive his letters and plot their revenge in a dining room that looks to be part of the same establishment. The Nanetta-Fenton romance unfolds there as well, with Fenton cast somewhat predictably as a waiter. The dessert cart allows him to carry out the thrusts and parries called for in the libretto in place of swordplay. Ford approaches Falstaff disguised, again predictably, as an American clad in a lamentable Southwestern-style outfit carrying a suitcase full of greenbacks. The setting for their meeting and Ford's jealousy monologue is the Garter Inn's smoking room, where Falstaff's jovial outbursts comically disturb the reserved newspaper readers. His outsized tweed suit added a Sydney Greenstreet-like hilarity, but his change into a red riding coat meant for a fox hunt reminded us that he may once have been dapper. Whatever pretense of that is demolished in the would-be seduction scene, set in a 1950s-style kitchen that recalls a sitcom of the early television era. Falstaff is tossed into the Thames via a window set above the kitchen sink. Licking his wounded pride in Act III, we see him holed up in a barn, which he shares with a crowd-pleasing real-life horse who munches hay while the fat knight curses the cruel world. The final scene in Royal Park is suggested by a starry sky with a table that eventually sets the banquet of the finale.

La Scala has cast the two leading Falstaffs of our time: Ambrogio Maestri sang early in the run and Bryn Terfel took over the remaining performances, beginning with this one. It is hard not to rain down superlatives on Terfel's performance. It was a *tour de force* in every sense –vocally, dramatically, and comedically. His distinctive baritone's warm resonance endowed the character with plucky, avuncular charm. Even the displays of arrogance came off with heartfelt allure. Terfel simply dominated the stage, physically as well as musically, and will certainly enter posterity as one of the role's leading interpreters.

Massimo Cavalletti may need a few more years to grow into the role of Ford, but his talent and musicianship were strongly in evidence. In the role of Alice Ford, Carmen Giannattasio sang with an admirable middle voice solidity that did not impede her skilled exploration of the role's comic dimensions. Manuela Custer's Meg Page and Marie-Nicole Lemieux's Mistress Quickly were fine complements to the female roster. The charming young tenor Antonio Poli sang an endearing Fenton who was every bit worthy of Ekaterina Sadovnikova's delectable Nanetta. Daniel Harding led a spirited performance that may have occasionally moved too fast to allow the audience to drink in all the comedic tricks.

Gioachino Rossini, *La Cenerentola*
Paris Opera, March 1, 2013

Rossini's "other" comic masterpiece of 1817 came into the world only a few weeks after the much better known *The Barber of Seville* but has had a place in the repertoire since its premiere. A version of the enduringly popular Cinderella tale, it famously sheds much of the magic. There is no pumpkin or glass slipper. A fairy godfather takes the place of a fairy godmother. A buffoonish wicked stepfather fills in for a simply evil wicked stepmother. Still, the opera soared in popularity all over the world (it was the first opera presented in Australia, for example). Nevertheless, it was a relative latecomer to the Paris Opéra, only arriving here only in 1977. The current production, by the late Jean-Pierre Ponnelle, is even older, dating back to its 1968 premiere at the Bavarian State Opera. Paris audiences only saw this version for the first time when it entered the repertoire last season.

Lately, *Cenerentola* has enjoyed a renaissance in operatic capitals, with the principal roles going to such stars as Cecilia Bartoli, Joyce DiDonato, Juan Diego Florez, and Lawrence Brownlee. Paris's effort is more subdued, though the great *basso buffo* Simone Alaimo, now a bit worn of voice, shares the role of Don Magnifico. His nephew, baritone Nicola Alaimo, is the alternate cast's Dandini, leading us to wonder what synergies these operatic relatives might have radiated if paired on stage and why they were not. The question lingered in my mind, but the older Alaimo was a *tour de force*, impossible not to watch in his boorish physical comedy.

It is the title role that really sparkles, however, and in the promising young mezzo Serena Malfi the Opéra made a fortunate casting decision. Lithe lyricism and a purring lower register, together with crystal clear coloratura runs, evoked a young Bartoli. Already scheduled for her Metropolitan Opera debut, the public has much to look forward to in this exciting new artist, who only made her stage debut in 2009 and has some room to grow.

Tenor Antonio Siragusa has nothing to answer for in a *Cenerentola* universe dominated by Florez and Brownlee. A fine lyric tenor, he scaled the role's difficult ascents with admirable confidence and enjoyable flair. "Si, ritrovarla io giuro" was easily the evening's highlight among the male singing. Riccardo Novaro's Dandini accomplished this difficult role with zeal – a servant, Dandini must impersonate his master and then switch back again. François Lis's less well articulated legato eviscerated the charm of the fairy godfather Alidoro. Jeannette Fischer and Cornelia Oncioiu played up the comic notes in the stepsister roles of

Clorinda and Tisbe. Riccardo Frizza led a delicate and well balanced performance that took appreciable advantage of the Palais Garnier's intimacy. The time may have come for heavier works to be staged there again.

Ponnelle's production, for which he also designed the sets and costumes, looks like a giant dollhouse, with individual rooms in Don Magnifico's rundown manor and Don Ramiro's palace emerging from behind sliding screens. It is a bit quaint, but tells the story most effectively and avoids the current preoccupation with overdirecting classic opera.

Vincenzo Bellini, *Norma*
Washington National Opera, March 9, 2013

After an absence of ten years, *Norma* has returned to the stage of the Washington National Opera in a new production by theater director Anne Bogart. Bellini's opera is a melodramatic rollercoaster of emotion, and the production's star attraction is the ample soprano Angela Meade, who has sung the title role at the Caramoor Festival and impressed New York audiences in such Verdi roles as Elvira in *Ernani* and Leonora in *Il Trovatore*. This production marks her Washington National debut. Blessed with a powerful chest voice, Meade delivers the title role – that of a Druid priestess betrayed in love by Pollione, the secret Roman father of her two children – with an uncommon dynamism. When the score required it, as it does in Norma's signature entrance aria "Casta diva," Meade adeptly floated gorgeous, crystalline pianos. The coloratura ascents were less stellar, however, and at times her dramatic reading was flat. One of Norma's great challenges is to harness, at short notice, a rage that approaches murderous ferocity – at one point she actually stands over her sleeping children with a dagger. It may have been the fault of the direction, but Meade consistently treaded the route of dignity and *hauteur*. The effect struck me as too cool and collected to produce the most sublime insight into this tempestuous character.

Dolora Zajick has been a dramatic mezzo of choice for more than two decades now, and remains at the height of her powers. Bellini originally wrote the role of Adalgisa, the new flame of Norma's love, for a soprano, with a higher vocal line than many mezzos can credibly perform. Zajick accepted this challenge with vigor and easily equaled Meade in her superb technique. Their duet "Mira, o Norma," the evening's highlight, bathed in a delicious synergy of vocal power.

The Pollione of tenor Rafael Davila, also in his Washington National debut, was the odd man out in this love triangle. Davila had an easy time with the drama, but his vocal projection betrayed weakness and strained alongside those of his love interests. He sounded especially pallid in the great confrontation trio "O! Di qual sei tu vittima," which unfolds after Norma has learned of his betrayal and Adalgisa has sworn to persuade him to return to his original love. A more successful company debut was that of the stentorian Ukrainian bass Dmitry Belosselskiy, whose performance as Norma's stoic father Oroveso was solid and heartfelt. Daniele Rustioni, who has yet to turn thirty, conducted the performance in what was his debut as well. He brought speedier tempos than one often finds in this relatively static piece, but his enthusiastic reception was well deserved.

Bogart's production, yet another debut effort for Washington National, features one rather bland stylized set of neutral beiges and grays. The Druid temple is suggested – awkwardly – by a wooden wall held up by an irregular bunch of poles and curved stone wall opposite. A circular opening lies between, occasionally allowing curtains to shelter the more intimate scenes. A lunar backdrop allows the Druid moon goddess (the "chaste goddess" of "Casta diva") to dominate the action, almost inescapably so. James Schuette's traditional costumes (robes and gowns for Druids, armor and helmets for Romans) introduce descriptive period ambiance. At the very end, when Norma spares Adalgisa and condemns herself to death by fire, in which she is joined by a repentant Pollione, there is no fire. Norma and Pollione simply stride off into glowing red light. Bogart's program note stresses the conflict between Norma's matriarchal Gaullic sphere and Pollione's patriarchal Roman world, and what she believes to be the importance of restraint in human relations, but the sets do little to draw these pictures. Perhaps their greatest advantage is that they allow the fine vocal talents of Mmes Meade and Zajick to emerge without much visual distraction.

Giuseppe Verdi, *Un Ballo in Maschera*
Milan, La Scala, July 22, 2013

Celebrations of Verdi's bicentennial year continue unabated at La Scala, where the last of five new productions of the composer's operas was unveiled here on July 9. *Un Ballo in Maschera* is one of Verdi's fiery middle period masterpieces – a standard operatic love triangle wrapped up in a vicious political intrigue that results in the ruling tenor's assassination by his closest friend Renato, a baritone husband who believes he has been cuckolded even though the tenor's love for his wife Amelia is never consummated. At the time of *Ballo*'s composition, its royal assassination plot was so politically controversial that the censors forced Verdi to change the setting from royal Sweden to colonial Boston in order to avoid the spectacle of a king being killed on stage. A governor of Massachusetts who was merely an earl (*conte*, in Italian) was fairer game.

True to form, the intrepid young Italian director Damiano Michelietto has reimagined the drama for our times. Although this version follows the non-royal tradition, in which the opera's tragic hero is Governor Riccardo rather than King Gustavo, here he is a populist politician up for reelection in what his campaign posters tell us is a super-contemporary 2013. Apart from wondering whether that year will be advanced if the production is revived in the future,[7] a nod to contemporary scandal-ridden Europolitics follows in posters that announce Riccardo's mandate as one of "uncorrupted glory" ("*incorrotta gloria*"). Since his unconsummated affair with Amelia drives the romantic plot, this could be a clever play on words.

However one takes it, this production was an energetic *tour de force* that exhibited Verdi's dramatic flair to the fullest and luxuriated in the rich symbolism that imparts modern relevance to lasting repertoire favorites. Paolo Fantin's sets place the action in starkly modern political settings. Riccardo's "court" is, naturally, his campaign headquarters, reproduced in excruciatingly functional detail, right down to the insipid water cooler. When he hears of the sorceress Ulrica, who will fatefully predict his assassination upon his incognito visit to her, she is illustrated

---

[7] Note: The production was never revived but rather replaced by a new production.

in a series of screen-projected photos as a faith healing televangelist. Her lair is a garish show set where she cures the afflicted and is overwhelmed by the outpouring of paparazzi who appear when Riccardo's identity is revealed.

The second act's vile locale, where Ulrica has counseled Amelia to partake of an herb to cure her illicit love, is not the traditional execution site but rather a haunt of downtrodden streetwalkers. When Amelia imagines a spectral vision approaching her, she is literally mugged by a prostitute, who relieves her of her fur coat and pearl necklace. Riccardo then arrives in a black luxury sedan to solicit her declaration of love. Only Act III suffered a bit too much from the *Regie* approach. Rather than a modern take on the actual masked ball at which Riccardo is killed, we are treated to a political rally that ends in a sort of hide and seek among life-size cardboard cutouts of the governor giving a thumbs up. Renato finally emerges from them to fire the fatal shot. His dying words, however, are more creatively presented as the observations of his ghost. Rather than telling everyone of his plan to send Amelia away with her husband to preserve her virtue, the other characters find his letter ordering it and mime the expected reactions without hearing him deliver his lines from the great beyond. This does avoid the awkwardness of a man who has just been mortally wounded having to sing beautifully.

The starry cast added to the evening's raw energy. Sondra Radvanovsky sang Amelia to critical acclaim in the Metropolitan Opera's new production earlier this season, and La Scala's notoriously critical audience cheered her to the rafters. There is a metallic edge to the voice that does not appeal to everyone, but soaring ascents and delicate pianos assured a triumph. Her Met Riccardo Marcelo Alvarez rejoined her here. There is much to praise in the voice, though the heft needed to ascend into the higher range occasionally drew an unattractive bark. La Scala cast a fine Renato in the talented baritone Željko Lučić. Smooth tones and fine upper range singing accompanied a well studied dramatic characterization that never descended into caricature. The talented young baritone Alessio Arduini made a fine impression in the small role of Silvano. Soprano Serena Gamberoni admirably sang the role of Oscar, usually a trouser part for a male page, but recast here as Riccardo's female personal assistant.

The young conductor Daniele Rustioni led a fast-paced performance that brought Michelietto's energetic production to life.

Gioachino Rossini, *La Donna del Lago*
Santa Fe Opera, August 6, 2013

Beethoven famously – and presciently – praised Rossini's comedies as his lasting contribution to opera, but in recent decades the Italian composer's more serious works have received greater consideration. *La Donna del Lago* is one of the more recent, with productions in the past few years in London, Paris, and Milan. Paul Curran's undemanding traditional approach, which brings the work to Santa Fe for the first time, is shared with the Metropolitan Opera.

This opera is not, as the title might suggest, an Arthurian story of power and fate, but rather a soapy romance that strains credulity even in the notoriously fanciful world of opera. The first of Sir Walter Scott's works to receive an operatic treatment, it presents a heroine, Elena, who is torn at by three suitors: her true love Malcolm, her politically expedient fiancé Rodrigo, and finally King James V (Giacomo) of Scotland, Rodrigo's enemy whom she happens to meet disguised under the name Uberto. They all love her, but in the end happiness brings her to the man of her choice. After three hours of wrestling with the dilemma and many cadenzas to express how difficult this resolution is, Rodrigo conveniently dies in battle. The King decides to reveal his identity and behave magnanimously, uniting Malcolm with Elena to live happily ever after.

Operas such as this are often a vehicle for a star singer, and Santa Fe certainly had one on hand in Joyce DiDonato, the coloratura mezzo of our time. Lilting ascents and flawless technique brought florid power and grace to what is essentially a soprano role. Allusions to cut glass may be tiresome, but no amount of praise can overstate the raw talent and insight in DiDonato's delivery. It is tenor Lawrence Brownlee's misfortune to have gained a reputation as the lyric tenor opera companies hire when they cannot book Juan Diego Florez (who has sung Giacomo/Uberto and other roles in the same *Fach* around the world). The voice is a talented one all the same, though some of the ornamented runs sounded too jumpy and effortful. Mezzo Marianna Pizzolato had a better night as Malcolm, a trouser role, even if costuming her in baggy male clothes made for some awkward love scenes. Wayne Tigges added his fine baritone in the role of Elena's father Douglas, an enemy of the king, and René Barbera's brawn contributed some fitting pomp to his rebellious role as chief of the Highlanders.

Stephen Lord took few chances with the score. Slow tempos and competent playing did little to enliven the dramatic moments, though several of the ensembles and the martial *strette* were well worth hearing.

Curran's production offered few surprises. A patch of Highland earth dominates Kevin Knight's set design and separates when necessary to allow for other representational sets to emerge for population by traditionally clad Scotsmen, including Highlander warriors with the traditional blue face paint. The only set that betrayed some imagination was Giacomo's gilded court, a superb setting for DiDonato to let loose with her *rondo* finale "Tanti affetti." Still, Santa Fe's unique stage allowed for the patch of earth to blend appealingly with the natural background of mountains and sky visible in the long first act.

Jacques Offenbach, *La Grande Duchesse de Gérolstein*
Santa Fe Opera, August 7, 2013

Offenbach scored a smash hit with this delightful comedy about a debauched Grand Duchess who promotes a simple soldier to general in a gauche attempt to seduce him away from his true love. Its premiere in 1867 enjoyed immense popular and commercial success and drew the attention of many of Europe's statesmen and crowned heads. No less a mover and shaker than Otto von Bismarck declared its military fripperies the picture of warfare in his time. After France's defeat by him just three years later, the new French government banned the opera for a time, associating its satires too closely with military disaster.

Santa Fe first mounted Offenbach's less known smash hit as long ago as 1971. Lee Blakeley reimagines the work this year as what he hopes will be an accessible commentary on modern American sensibilities. For starters, he takes the action out of a militaristic and vaguely Germanic nowhere and resettles in early twentieth-century America. Adrian Linford's sets do not exactly evoke a milieu of grand duchesses and flashy court nobles, but do allow for a lively culture of honor, political intrigue, and scandalous romance. The frenetic overture accompanies a hilariously vigorous army calisthenics routine. Our Grand Duchess is reborn as (or reduced to) contemporary pop culture's "cougar," a woman of a certain age who delights in younger men. And to give it a fully American flavor, the spoken dialogue is delivered in a modern vernacular text written by Blakeley himself, replete with amusing *double-entendres* for which the "privates" of the Grand Duchess's army provide a frequent target. And, set in America or not, what would Offenbach be without a show stopping dance? A riotous can-can closes the second act.

Star mezzo-soprano Susan Graham has taken to the lighter nineteenth-century repertoire lately, having appeared to great acclaim in Lehar's *The Merry Widow* in Paris last season. These types of roles do not allow her extraordinarily rich lyric qualities to expand to their fullest extent, but her statuesque stage presence and the devilish dramatic charm made her absolutely perfect for the role. The young tenor Paul Appleby countered her with ebullient charm and a voice of rosy warmth. As his true love Wanda, Anya Matanovic captured innocence at its fullest. A robust supporting cast of soldiers, politicians, conspirators, dancers, and party guests filled the stage with the kind of dynamism that reminds us what theater truly is. Emmanuel Villaume led an energetic performance that never flagged in energy and left the audience walking on air in the New Mexican desert.

Chapter Four

2013-2014

Giuseppe Verdi, *Rigoletto*
New York, Metropolitan Opera, November 20, 2014

Michael Mayer's "Las Vegas" production of Verdi's tale of revenge has returned to the Met the season after it premiered. A colorful, clever effort, it tries hard to fit the opera's themes of sexual outrage and vindictive, if unsuccessful, revenge taking. Going after a kind of mob boss/lounge singer who has raped the daughter of one of his acolytes could easily splash across the era's Rat Pack-filled headlines. But on some levels, the opera is left underserved. Verdi's court, based on the royal court in Victor Hugo's play *Le roi s'amuse*, is a place of refined Renaissance pleasure and traditional European codes of honor that have nothing to do with Vegas. Only extraordinarily creative reinterpretations of the libretto could give us a milieu where Countess Ceprano's "movie star looks" can "really light up a room."

The title role went to the venerable Russian baritone Dmitri Hvorostovsky, who has publicly stated his intention of becoming the greatest Verdi baritone in the world.[8] The pretensions are not misplaced. His voice has thickened somewhat over the years, but his superb legato and skilled high tessitura singing wielded rapier-sharp excitement. Costumed with a wig that suggested the thinning hair of a middle-aged man may have gone a bit too far to stop him from playing essentially himself, but every scene in which he appeared commanded imperturbable attention.

The other revelation of the evening was the Bulgarian soprano Sonya Yoncheva, who made her Met debut as Gilda. The voice was limpid

---

[8] He achieved it, only to die prematurely in 2017.

and articulate and delivered a finely nuanced reading of the signature aria "Caro nome." She had every reason to be proud when spotted celebrating after the show.

Matthew Polenzani has come a long way since his early *comprimario* singing at the Met, and his voice occasionally rose to the challenge of Verdi's lascivious Duke. "Parmi veder le lagrime," for example, radiated a generous warmth of tone to match the character's evolving emotions. The part's more challenging singing – "La donna è mobile" notably – suggested room for growth.

Štefan Kocán and Oksana Volkova were a diabolically murderous duo in the roles of the assassin Sparafucile and his sister and bait Maddalena. Kocán's superb legato gave the part a scary gravitas. Combined with Volkova's gravely mezzo, the final scene and its notoriously difficult quartet imparted a special resonance.

Richard Strauss, *Der Rosenkavalier*
New York, Metropolitan Opera, November 22, 2013

As New York's silvery autumn approaches its end, the Met has once again revived its beloved production of this bittersweet comedy of errors. This is a *Rosenkavalier* that takes us into the past. Nathaniel Merrill's storybook production dates back to 1969, old enough to have given the operatic world the bizarre verb "to Rosenkavalier," meaning to keep a successful production in a company's repertoire for so long that the idea of replacing it defies logic and reason.

As the Met's great 1980s-vintage Franco Zeffirelli productions are replaced one by one, there are rumors that Peter Gelb's reign as general manager may not spare the house's venerable old *Rosenkavalier*. And after nearly twenty years of attending its frequent revivals (the last in the 2009-2010 season), Robert O'Hearn's sets are in my estimation beginning to look a bit tired, even if the costumes sparkled as brilliantly as ever.[9]

Nevertheless, the opening night of this season's revival proved that even an old production of a repertoire favorite can come alive with a breath of fresh air. Strauss's opera explores many dimensions of love: an

---

[9] The production was replaced with a decidedly lesser effort in 2017.

older woman faced with the inevitability of losing her young lover, the young lover's balance between fidelity and mutual infatuation with an innocent and even younger girl, and the innocent girl's earnest desire to escape an arranged marriage an odious older man. What a delicate balance of emotion it all requires.

With Martina Serafin, the Met may have found its new Marschallin. In a role long associated in the house with the superstar soprano Renée Fleming, the native Austrian inhabited the part with an aching delicacy. Gorgeous round tones delivered the Marschallin's sweetness, regret, resignation, and wisdom turn by exquisite turn.

Paired with the Octavian of the talented British mezzo Alice Coote, the ensembles came alive with shimmering tones. Coote perfectly captured the delicate balance between animus and anima that any great Octavian demands.

It was unfortunate that the rising young German soprano Mojca Erdmann failed to appear as announced. Her shimmering tones would have made an excellent Sophie. But the talented American soprano Erin Morley admirably stepped in with youth and a natural innocence matched by a sweet voice that enlivened every scene in which she appeared.

Peter Rose, a veteran Baron Ochs, was in full form last night. Some of the part's signature lower notes came out a bit muted, however, and he could have acted less the ham. The third act inn scene would have succeeded just as well without the simulated fellatio.

Among the supporting cast, Wolfgang Ablinger-Sperrhacke made an entertaining Met debut as Valzacchi, one of the "Italian intriguers" who foils Baron Ochs's embarrassing assignation with Octavian in the guise of the Marschallin's maid. James Courtney's wheezing notary and Tony Stevenson's stentorian police commissar remain house favorites. And what a treat it was to have the rising tenor Eric Cutler in the small but vivid role of the Italian tenor, whose love song livens up the Marschallin's first act *lever*. His robust reading provoked one of the rare outbursts of applause the part has received since Luciano Pavarotti sang it long ago.

The English National Opera's music director Edward Gardner led an energetic performance overall, though the ensembles, especially the Act

III trio, unfolded a bit more slowly and with greater restraint than one might hope for.

Vincenzo Bellini, *I Puritani*
Paris Opera, November 25, 2013

Bellini's last opera – a masterpiece of the bel canto repertoire - premiered in Paris but has not had much recent history here. By repertoire standards, the work is a bit slow moving. Set during the English Civil War, *I Puritani* tells of the troubled nuptials of Elvira, whose family is battling against the Stuart dynasty, and the young royalist Arturo. When Arturo feels honor-bound to rescue the disguised queen Henrietta Maria (Enrichetta) on the eve of his wedding, Elvira concludes that he has run away with a strange woman and throws the expected mad scene. When all is explained, the emotional effect fortuitously restores her sanity just as the Puritan leader Oliver Cromwell declares a general pardon. The marriage can then go happily forward as the austere Commonwealth continues.

The Opéra's only previous production premiered in 1987 but was never revived. The task has now fallen to Laurent Pelly to place *Puritani* more firmly into the repertoire. Unhappily, the visual effort was not much of a success. Pelly is known for productions that might be described as "stylized traditional," with nothing too outrageous to cause offense but nothing too starkly representational, either. But this approach often accomplishes little. The production's only set is a large rotating (sometimes dizzyingly rapid) black steel frame that depicts the Puritan-controlled fortress near Plymouth where the action takes place. Elvira inhabits a barred chamber within it. The unnecessarily depressing suggestion is that no matter what happens, her whole existence is one of inescapable imprisonment. Just in case anyone missed the point, the image of a weeping woman is occasionally projected against the back wall. The rest of the time the other cast members and large choruses of soldiers and ladies in waiting march around it, resembling ants toiling in some kind of supersized insect farm. Pale light effects indicate changes in mood, but the opera's plot is so somber for so much of the evening that there is little room for bright spots. Indeed, although certainly unintentional, the lighting's most effective use was at the curtain calls.

The Opéra fielded some impressive vocal talent for Bellini's intricate score. In her house debut, the rising Italian soprano Maria Agresta sang the central role of Elvira with an effecting and almost dreamy delicacy. Cool, round tones conquered the part's challenging coloratura roulades, though occasionally the cadenzas were too abbreviated to impart much thrill. Her voice is one to be heard, but she took few chances. Perhaps she will in future performances.

Mariusz Kwieceń's accomplishments include opening the current season at the Metropolitan Opera in the title role of Tchaikovsky's *Eugene Onegin*. As the outraged lover Riccardo, he delivered a smooth reading of the part's smoldering passion. Michele Pertusi's deeper tones and rich legato in the part of Elvira's uncle Giorgio riveted the audience all evening and drew the most applause. His synergy with made the rather pedestrian duet "Suoni la tromba" downright exciting. Only the tenor Dmitri Korchak, who sang the role of Elvira's true love Arturo, seemed out of place. The voice is not without a certain sweetness, as was in evidence in the Act III duet "Nel mirarti un solo istante," but the part demands greater heft. Too often he evoked a petulant adolescent rather than a dashing hero.

The very young Michele Mariotti, just thirty-four years old, made his debut at the Opéra with this performance. He led a robust reading, with especially clarion brass bringing out the score's martial qualities.

Giuseppe Verdi, *La Traviata*
Milan, La Scala, December 7, 2013

Every December 7 – St. Ambrose's Day – is a hallowed holiday in Milan. In addition to celebrating the city's patron saint, it also marks the beginning of a new season at Italy's premiere musical theater. This year's occasion was no different from any other. The rich and powerful of Italy, Europe, and the world assembled in black and, in a few cases, even white tie. Italian President Giorgio Napolitano's entrance into what used to be called the royal box (now the "central box") drew a standing ovation from an audience fretting over the country's chronic political instability. The paparazzi's cameras flashed blinding lights to capture images of arriving celebrities, occasionally against their will. Unusually for an opera premiere, a cordon of riot police protected the surroundings as anticapitalist protestors jeered across the piazza. And just before the performance began, Maestro Daniele Gatti observed the death of Nelson Mandela and called for a moment of silence to honor the South African leader.

Last season controversially opened here with Wagner's *Lohengrin*, a much criticized choice to celebrate the German composer's shared bicentennial year with Giuseppe Verdi. The controversy faded quickly enough, but last night Italian patriots could console themselves with a new Verdi premiere in the actual anniversary year itself.

La Traviata is undoubtedly the composer's best known opera, a tragic tale of romance in which the courtesan Violetta believes she has found true love with her suitor Alfredo. After three months of domestic bliss in the countryside, Alfredo's father cajoles her into abandoning the young man on false pretenses because their scandalous association threatens his daughter's reputation and marital prospects. When the deceived but outraged Alfredo publicly denounces Violetta, only her terminal illness and the revelation of her noble sacrifice leads to a deathbed reconciliation.

Responsibility for La Scala's new production went to the Russian director Dmitri Tcherniakov, long considered an *enfant terrible*. Among other concepts, he has staged Wagner's *Tristan and Isolde* in a submarine and hotel room and designed a production of Rimsky-Korsakov's *The Tsar's Bride* (opening at La Scala in March) in which Ivan the Terrible's various marital candidates are introduced with giant projections of online computer files.

Tcherniakov was roundly booed at the curtain calls, but his radical artistic tendencies were only slightly in evidence. In most ways the sets are downright traditional – spacious drawing rooms for the party scenes, a well stocked country kitchen for Alfredo and Violetta's love nest, and a return to the drawing room for Violetta's death scene finale. Innovation was limited to an updating of the action to a composite "present," which the costumes suggest could fall anywhere between the 1950s and today.

Sporting a mixture of bobbed haircuts, 1970s-vintage leisure suits, and formal attire that would not have been out of place in the La Scala audience, the champagne-popping chorus added the dimension of a postmodern nowhere. There may have been a message in this, but if so it quite escaped me and its glib postmodernity rather undermined the plot. It was hard to imagine this collection of lounge lizards caring so much about a young rake mixed up with a woman with a past that it would threaten his sister's marriage. The Act II gambling scene was obfuscated by ungainly spotlights that flashed on Violetta as she delivered her asides commenting on the rising tension. The first one disoriented the performers enough that she either missed or was not given a cue, causing several lines to go unsung. Another oddity was the uselessly magnified role of Violetta's maid Annina. Normally a humble servant with a handful of unmemorable lines, here she appeared as a sort of guardian and confidante. In Act I Violetta sings her deeply introspective aria "Ah, fors'è lui" to her rather than in the more psychologically effective soliloquy. In the final scene Annina chases out Alfredo, his father, and the doctor so that Violetta might die alone. In both cases the distraction was heavy handed and unwelcome.

La Scala openings aim to showcase major international vocal talent, and this year did not disappoint. The title role went to the German soprano Diana Damrau. Her technique has improved over the years, and the awkward ascents that once characterized the voice have been considerably tamed. Full, rich tones delivered an impassioned Violetta of convincing elegance, though the pitch occasionally wavered in the Act I coloratura runs. The accomplished Polish tenor Piotr Beczała is rapidly working his way to superstar status. Scintillating and clarion, he brilliantly captured Alfredo's ardor. Some interpolations in the Act II cabaletta "O mio rimorso" seemed outsized, but the overall effect was charged and exciting. Baritone Željko Lučić performed admirably as Giorgio Germont, Alfredo's meddlesome father. Blessed with a strong, stable legato, he brought the role to life with the necessary gravitas tempered by compassion.

Daniele Gatti led La Scala's orchestra in a vivid performance, though the touch was occasionally too heavy on the strings. He should be credited not only with fine musicianship but also with the wise decision to perform the score without some of the usual cuts. The rarely heard *duettino* that follows Act III's "Gran' Dio, morir si giovane" allowed Alfredo and Violetta to explore their feelings more deeply.

Gaetano Donizetti, *L'Elisir d'Amore*
New York, Metropolitan Opera, January 21, 2014

Donizetti's comic talents reached their heights in this lighthearted farce of love and romance. Poor Nemorino loves the wealthy and book learned Adina, but she scorns him as a simpleton and nearly falls for the brash bluster of the visiting Sergeant Belcore. Help comes in the form of the quack Doctor Dulcamara's cure-all that passes for a love potion but is in reality a bottle of cheap wine. Nemorino gets drunk on it, and his antics drive the Adina-Belcore marriage forward, with him left abused and in despair. Unknown to him, however, his wealthy uncle has died and bequeathed him everything, a change in fate that suddenly makes him immensely attractive to all the local women except Adina, who is instead drawn by his new popularity and apparent happiness. A confession of love resolves the romance, with Dulcamara taking all the credit and selling his elixir far and wide.

Bartlett Sher's production premiered to tepid reviews on the opening night of last season. The picturesque sets and costumes are appropriate to the opera's time and place and not without color. But the tendency toward cool shades of blue dilute the work's intrinsic warmth in a way that could be less satisfying to those who treasured the old John Copley production, in which the great Luciano Pavarotti took storied bows. There is a surprisingly dark streak of cruelty in this presentation, with Nemorino's abuse at the end of Act I taking on rough physicality at the hands of Belcore's men.

Nevertheless, the vocal fireworks more than filled the stage before an audience diluted by the serious snow storm that blanketed New York. Anna Netrebko sang Adina to the usual star-level acclaim after having earlier in the day posted a public Facebook photo of herself in a bathing suit enjoying the snow as it covered her balcony. The tenacious look on her face was only surpassed by her stunning singing and beguiling acting. A few early sharps yielded to the round, warm tones that have won her well deserved international reputation for vocal excellence unharmed by exuberance. Her mastery of gesture, expression, and stage movement made it impossible to remove one's eyes from her all evening.

Tenor Ramon Vargas could be forgiven for not reaching Pavarotti's iconic stature in the role of Nemorino. But his voice has not lost its alluring sweetness, and the portrayal was gifted without losing the much needed light touch. Nicola Alaimo's stentorian baritone was at home in the role of the blustering Belcore. And Erwin Schrott delivered a comical Dulcamara without the voice failing to remind us what a superb bass-baritone he is and how well he can tackle Don Giovanni and the heavier repertoire that undoubtedly awaits him.

Maurizio Benini is a ubiquitous wonder in the ranks of the Met's regular conductors, a tireless and energetic musician who has mastered the Italian comic repertoire. He led a fun and eager performance.[10]

Antonín Dvořak, *Rusalka*
New York, Metropolitan Opera, January 23, 2014

The title role in Dvořak's only famous opera has become intimately associated with the reigning diva Renee Fleming. Hearing her live has become nearly a surreal experience, a Parnassus of the operatic world now made all the more majestic by the soprano's invitation to sing the National Anthem at this year's Superbowl (a first for an opera singer) on February 2. Fleming, herself of Czech origin, has publicly declared her wish for Rusalka to be her signature role, and indeed her grand Met portrait features her in the part. She did not disappoint. The sumptuous "Song to the Moon," the Act I aria in which Rusalka begs the lustrous moon to tell the handsome prince of her love, resounded with sparkling lines that danced like moonlight over the grateful audience. One should well remember that it was this piece that Fleming credits with building her career – she sang it as her Met National Council Auditions in 1988. Here and in the Act III, aria, however, the voice betrays some wear. Some, but not too many, of the low and middle register notes sounded muted or swallowed in the cavernous Met. Nevertheless, the triumph continues and Fleming certainly added to it in last night's revival opening.

---

[10] Benini's ubiquity is almost a joke. When I traveled to Argentina in 2019 and saw a totally unfamiliar cast in Verdi's *Rigoletto* at the Teatro Colón, the conductor was none other than Maurizo Benini. I did not review it.

Fleming was fortunate to have as her prince the star tenor Piotr Beczała, who opened La Scala this season to much acclaim. He brought a bright, clarion sound to the role that lacked nothing in drive and power. The portrayal, by turns triumphant and despairing, was solid and effecting. The achingly beautiful final duet, in which the lovers enter eternity, could not have unfolded in better voice. John Relyea's Wood Gnome was authoritative and matched well with veteran mezzo Dolora Zajick's Ježibaba. Emily Magee debuted as the Foreign Princess, who diverts the prince's affections only to spurn him when she realizes how easily they were won. The vocal effort was underwhelming, but the characterization strong.

The Met's orchestra resonated with an uncommon intensity under the baton of Yannick Nézet-Séguin, though at times Dvořak's sumptuous late Romantic score may have been too loud to coordinate in the best way with the principals. Avid fans unable to come to New York may judge for themselves in the February 8 high definition telecast, available in movie theatres all over the world.

Alexander Borodin, *Prince Igor*
New York, Metropolitan Opera, February 24, 2014

February has been a bad month for Russian President Vladimir Putin. Despite Russia's impressive Olympic victories, the Sochi Games turned out to be a $51 billion showcase of graft and corruption that even the Kremlin's deftest apologists cannot explain away without sounding embarrassingly Soviet in their mendacity. Then, as the vulgar Potemkin-village closing ceremony bored the world, Putin's obedient satrap in Ukraine, former president Viktor Yanukovych, decisively lost his two-month battle against an energized national opposition angered by his clumsy, Kremlin-influenced decision to reject closer economic ties with the European Union. Over the weekend, Lenin statues across Ukraine bit the dust as the rebels turned Yanukovych into a fugitive from revolutionary justice whose current whereabouts are unknown but whose private pleasure compound and zoo are now open to the general public.

On February 24, Putin maintained a stony silence as his country observed a holiday weekend for "Defender of the Fatherland Day."

Formerly known as "Red Army Day," it commemorates the anniversary of Lev Trotsky's 1918 decree drafting soldiers to defend the incipient Soviet regime against its many internal enemies.

It was a pure but striking coincidence that both the gaudy Olympic display and the dramatic denouement of the Ukrainian Revolution should accompany an ambitious American foray into Russian culture. Just as the Olympics began, the Metropolitan Opera opened its new production of Alexander Borodin's only work in the operatic genre, *Prince Igor*. Absent from the company's repertory for nearly a century, it last appeared (in Italian translation) in 1917. This year, I celebrated Defender of the Fatherland Day by attending a late-run performance before jetting off to Hawaii to give an academic lecture on the complementary subject of Russia and the Middle East.

Borodin was a surgeon and then a research chemist who composed music in his spare time. He worked on *Prince Igor* for eighteen years before he died suddenly at a ball in 1887, aged 53. Borodin left the opera incomplete, but sympathetic colleagues, the famous composers Nikolai Rimsky-Korsakov and Alexander Glazunov, patched together what they could from Borodin's various notes and fragments and used their intuition to complete the score and fill out the orchestration. According to one estimate, about 20 percent of the final product was written by others, including the overture (strangely dropped in the Met's new production), which was composed by Glazunov.

Steeped in Russian history and based on the first known Russian epic tale, *Prince Igor* takes us back to the Middle Ages, when Kiev was the political and economic epicenter of what we now know as "Russia" instead of a rebellious national capital on the periphery of an empire that continues to decay. Kiev stood atop a loose confederation of principalities ruled by a dynasty claiming descent from Viking warriors who mastered the Eastern Slav lands around the year 860. Among them was the minor realm of Putivl, located today in northeastern Ukraine close to the Russian border. In the late twelfth century its ruler, Igor Svyatoslavovich, led a campaign against the Polovtsians, a nomadic Turkic tribe that dominated the arid steppe borderlands to the east and raided Slavic settlements and trade routes.

In the course of events, Igor is defeated and captured, only to find that the Polovtsian ruler, Khan Konchak, treats him as an honored guest and offers him his freedom if he will lay down his arms. Igor is too proud and tormented by guilt to accept, even though his son and the Khan's daughter have taken the opportunity to fall in love. At home, meanwhile, Igor's roguish brother-in-law, Vladimir, Prince Galitsky, terrorizes Putivl and tries to seize power but is felicitously killed as the Polovtsians attack and devastate the city. Having escaped captivity, Igor returns to his ravaged domain to surprising popular acclaim, defiantly exhorting his people to crush Russia's enemies.

When Borodin's opera premiered posthumously in 1890, its strident celebration of Russian patriotism struck powerful chords, not only with chauvinistic Russian nationalists but also with "Eurasianist" Russians who took pride in their country's Asian heritage and viewed their culture as an appealingly exotic fusion of East and West. As the illegitimate son of a Georgian prince and Russian peasant woman, Borodin himself strode that divide.

The Met's new production is by Dmitri Tcherniakov, who makes his company debut. Tcherniakov has a reputation as an *enfant terrible* for such creative reimaginations as setting the claustrophobic first act of Wagner's *Tristan und Isolde* in a modern submarine and introducing prospective brides for Ivan the Terrible in Rimsky-Korsakov's *The Tsar's Bride* with projections of online dating profiles.

In *Prince Igor*, he dismisses much of the cross-cultural content in favor of politicized psychodrama. Indeed, the entire act featuring Igor's captivity and rosy reception by the Polovtsian Khan is reduced to a fantasy or hallucination. A giant video projection of the grievously wounded prince yields to an imagined field of flowers, where he and the other characters explore his subconscious longings and fears. The effect is not unimpressive, though the famous Polovtsian Dances, sequences choreographed to Borodin's driving Oriental rhythms by Itzik Galili, looked like "jazzercise" for stressed baby boomers working out at a prudently moderate pace.

Greater emphasis fell on the psychodrama at home. Putivl emerges as a metaphor for all Russia, elaborated by sets and costumes that suggest an early twentieth-century society teetering on the brink of war and revolution. When the action returns to the beleaguered principality, we find Igor's brother-in-law Vladimir running amok. He and his security services push around Igor's wife Yaroslavna (sung by the ravishing Ukrainian soprano Oksana Dyka in her Met debut role) and her law abiding subjects. Surprise! – they must pay bribes to get things accomplished and can do nothing when they and their loved ones are abused and violated by the ruling thugocracy. In the middle of a drunken debauche, this ne'er do well, performed with exquisite brutality by the talented bass Mikhail Petrenko, cries out that he will "restructure" the government and, naturally, seize the treasury. "What else is power for?," he snarls in a rhetorical flourish that would not astonish anyone if the character's lines came from the pouting lips of another famous Vladimir.

Igor finally regains his realm, still haunted by his failures as a leader and a man. In what could only have been a directorial coincidence, his once proud city hall now looks remarkably like Evromaidan after the pitched battle that routed Yanukovych. Defying logic, Igor's downtrodden people emerge from the ruins to celebrate his return to the strains of triumphant music.

In this production, Tcherniakov and conductor Gianandrea Noseda decided to end the opera with a plaintive and virtually unknown Borodin orchestral melody as a sort of coda to the final act. As it plays, Igor wrests himself away from the crowd's misplaced adulation to lead them in the prosaic task of clearing rubble. Tcherniakov insists that Igor's people are giving him a touchy-feely pass for having recognized his weaknesses and courageously moved on. But the greater temptation is to stare in disbelief as the shell-shocked populace slavishly praise and obey their leader no matter how disastrous he is.

A stellar musical performance allowed these messages to resound in profound relief. One of the luxuries of the post-1991 world is that the Met could field an extraordinarily talented cast drawn almost entirely from former Soviet republics and led by the authoritative Russian bass-baritone Ildar Abdrazakov in the title role.

Putin has called the collapse of the Soviet Union "the greatest geopolitical catastrophe of the twentieth century." Yet ironically, without that very "catastrophe" and the consequent end of the Soviet system's oppressive travel restrictions, the American public might well have had to wait another 97 years to devour with such authenticity these searing psychological insights into his hateful regime. Intermission eavesdropping suggests that the New York audience is drawing the right conclusions, but Tcherniakov should probably be careful when he goes home.

Georges Bizet, *Carmen*
Santa Fe Opera, August 11, 2014

Carmen is the famous tale of the weak willed soldier Don José, who is ruined by the passing fancy of a seductive gypsy whom he later murders in a fit of passionate rage. Stephen Lawless's production updates the opera from its original setting in nineteenth-century Spain to a late 1940s Mexico. Zoot-suited criminals keep the town garrison high on cocaine, while the cigarette factory girls strut their stuff in various states of undress. Carmen's smuggler chums congregate at Lillas Pastia's, here a desert cantina, and traffic in illegal immigrants who must get past an ominous U.S. Border Control point.

The idiom is not always successful and vitiates the opera's emotional effect. The famous "Habanera," the seductive aria in which Carmen warns of her fickle affections, is over-illustrated by her coworkers, who revolve around her in a circle while delivering the aria's choral refrains. When she admonishes any would-be lover to "*prends garde*," they collectively point at the ogling soldiers, who raise their hands in a campy gesture of mock surrender. This wincing distraction only got worse when soldiers hose down the randy girls to stop them from acting out more lustily. The contemporary immigration debate may be pressing in the American Southwest, but the gesture toward the issue in Act III adds nothing to the plot. Instead, it yields an ungainly border fence that awkwardly confines all of the act's intense interpersonal drama. Cole Porter's song "Don't Fence Me In" begs us not to confine passion; this unfortunate set shows us the consequences of doing so.

Lawless's directorial notes posit his production as a *Carmen* "possibly recognizable to the *Breaking Bad* generation." Yet it is hard to see how his laborious reset serves either Bizet's viscerally psychosexual melodrama or the contemporary politics of immigration and the drug trade. A modern Carmen seducing a more obvious Walter White type may have benefited the opera while also adding something to the politics. In any case, very few members of the *"Breaking Bad* generation" seemed to be in the audience.

Intelligent casting redeemed this contrived production. Ana María Martínez shone brightly as Carmen, with a purring lower register that swelled like waves in a sea of lava that never quite erupts. Sometimes the approach sounded a little too restrained, but it nevertheless suited a character whose brutal frankness rarely allows for rabid emotional outbursts.

Roberto De Biasio brought robust, forceful tones to the role of Don José. While perfectly well suited to the character's indulgence in passion and despair, they did not always elide well with his modulations to quieter expressions. As Escamillo, bass Kostas Smoriginas tended to muddy the part's lower notes, but still made a fine dramatic impression, with the character staggering through most of his scenes inebriated. Joyce El-Khoury's frail voice matched the limited possibilities of Micaëla, the village girl José abandons for his life of crime. Rory Macdonald led a spirited performance, yet not one that could overcome the score's hackneyed *espagnolerie*.

Ludwig van Beethoven, *Fidelio*
Santa Fe Opera, August 12, 2014

Director Stephen Wadsworth has updated of Beethoven's only from its own original Spanish setting to a Nazi prison at the very end of World War II. *Fidelio* is a paean to liberty in which the honest Florestan has been unjustly imprisoned by a cruel rival. His faithful wife Leonore disguises herself as a young man – named "Fidelio" in reference to her most admirable quality – and takes a humble job at his prison to find an opportunity to rescue him. Evading the fatherly oversight of the jailer Rocco and the misplaced romantic attentions of Rocco's daughter Marzelline, she rescues Florestan just as he is about to be executed. At that very moment merciful higher authorities arrive to free the prisoners and punish their persecutors.

Updating operas to a Nazi milieu can invite more than controversy. Often they are offensive, irrelevant, and, especially in Europe nowadays, even a bit cliché. Wadsworth's production escapes these categories. By focusing on Rocco and his modest family, who inhabit a simple two-level house that sits above the subterranean prison, it asks the enduring philosophical question of whether humanity is still possible in even the most bestial circumstances. As so many Third Reich memoirs relate about Hitler's jailers, we see Rocco only as a humble man and loving father – until he puts on his SS uniform. A character who is in his own words "only following orders," he is plagued by doubt, falling into sincere prayer, relenting when urged to show mercy to the prisoners, even facilitating (if unwittingly) Leonore's entry into Florestan's cell.

Fresh from work on theatrical pieces of the French Revolutionary era, Wadsworth's deft exploration of moral ambiguity warped by tyranny resonated strongly. The cruel prison governor Don Pizarro, Florestan's nemesis, fits the idiom perfectly as a Nazi commandant. The young officer Jaquino, who seeks Marzelline's hand, is obsessed with doing on the right thing to advance his life within a system he is too naive to understand. The suffering of the prisoners, dressed as concentration camp inmates, is ennobled to a whole different dimension by Beethoven's powerful choruses. The "liberators" who appear at the end are not the high state officials the composer envisioned, but British troops who bring the same hopeful message of the power of justice and unity of mankind.

Solid vocal performances enlivened this successful reimagining. Paul Groves's Florestan offered an attractive *Heldentenor* quality that lacked only a few of the role's top notes. As Rocco, Manfred Hemm's lavish, round tones rewardingly confirmed his transition from the lyric baritone parts he sang earlier in his career. Greer Grimsley's cavernous lower timbres roared Pizarro's menacing threats.

The role of Leonore requires a strong dramatic soprano for a part that prefigured Wagner's most demanding female roles. Alex Penda (the soprano formerly known as Alexandra Pendatchanska) is, alas, gifted with a lighter voice that struggled through the role's most challenging moments. In the ensembles, however, the blend of voices rose to sublime heights. As in *Carmen*, the Santa Fe Opera chorus delivered a resounding performance. Under the steady hand of the company's new music director Harry Bicket, this is not a production to be missed.

Chapter Five

2014-2015

Richard Wagner, *Parsifal*
Tokyo, New National Theater, October 10, 2014

Japan's New National Theatre opened its seventeenth season by completing its presentation of Wagner's mature works with this original new production of his last opera, *Parsifal*. The honor of staging this milestone fell to veteran German director Harry Kupfer. His third exploration of the work could be expected to owe something – perhaps even much – to his first two stagings, but in fact the influence is rather limited. All that seems to have been taken from his early 1990s Berlin Staastoper production is a giant swiveling crane that hovers close enough to the stage to move people and objects on and off set. Most of the visual concept is dominated by a jagged illuminated pathway. Segments of it descend to remove characters or bar the paths of others. Most of the time it radiates a pale white light, though at certain moments it reflects the elements in demand. Hence, when Parsifal enters Klingsor's magic garden, it turns green and sprouts flowers. The device recalls the light projections onto the aluminum "machine" that dominates Robert Lepage's unfortunate and burdensome Metropolitan Opera *Ring* production, but the effect here is far less cumbersome.

A uniquely Japanese embellishment tackles the opera's religious connotations. *Parsifal* unfolds in a descriptively Christian milieu – the realm of the Holy Grail knights who defend the sacred chalice and seek to recover the Holy Spear. Yet the opera's spiritual and psychological elements – attaining wisdom through compassion, enlightenment through renunciation, and so on – originate in Buddhist ideals that Wagner encountered through the prism of Schopenhauer. Kupfer embraces this more enthusiastically than any other producer probably has by placing a trio of silent Buddhist monks on stage for most of the first and third acts. In Act I they merely observe the action, but by Act III they are drawn into it, behaving more or less as spiritual gurus as Parsifal explores the realm of enlightenment. At the end of the opera, he is wearing their robes and, together with the redeemed Kundry, invites the grail knights to follow the jagged illuminated path toward them. The crane, meanwhile, slowly sweeps the uncovered Holy Grail offstage. "Has the Western God fallen?," we are provocatively left to wonder.

Any good performance of *Parsifal* requires stamina, and the New National Theatre rose to a high standard by recruiting a solid international cast familiar to any devoted Wagnerian. Christian Franz took on the title role with a brilliant alacrity that resonated in virtually every phrase. One wonders why Bayreuth and the Berlin houses do not avail themselves more of this extraordinarily talented *Heldentenor* in their Wagner productions, though he is often seen elsewhere. Evelyn Herlitzius likewise delivered an impassioned Kundry with gentle subtleties that seemed to be lacking even in her Deutsche Oper performance in the role two years ago. The veteran British bass Sir John Tomlinson is nearing the end of his prime. The notes were solid and stentorian in Gurnemanz's long narrations, but the Good Friday scene betrayed patches of age and strain as he attempted its challenging high notes. Egils Silins's Amfortas and Robert Bork's Klingsor rounded out the cast with steady portrayals.

Under the New National's recently appointed artistic director Iimori Taijiro, a Bayreuth assistant conductor for two decades, the Tokyo Philharmonic gave a disciplined reading of Wagner's score. The tendency was toward slower tempos, which brought the music into moving relief, even if the playing sounded a bit brassier than some tastes would appreciate. It is Taijiro's ambition to make his house one of the world's leading opera companies. With Wagner productions of this caliber, he may well succeed.

John Adams, *The Death of Klinghoffer*
New York, Metropolitan Opera, November 8, 2014

"See it, then decide," boldly announces a Metropolitan Opera advertisement for its most newsworthy production in recent memory. John

Adams's controversial *The Death of Klinghoffer* attempts to explore the human dimensions of the October 1985 hijacking of the Italian cruise ship *Achille Lauro* by Palestinian terrorists and the murder of one of its passengers, the elderly, wheelchair-bound Jewish American tourist Leon Klinghoffer. Angry criticism has descended on the opera since its world premiere in Brussels in 1991. Its opponents have long argued that it contains offensive anti-Semitic content and "explains" or even "glorifies" terrorism to such a degree that it should be proscribed and struck from public performance. But the volume of invective has never vaulted to the heights it reached in New York this fall. Indeed, when this very production, by Tom Morris, opened at the English National Opera in London in February 2012 (the Met and ENO share it), the controversy drew just one protestor who seemed to be ignored by everyone else.

Months before the Met's current season even opened, however, an unexpected barrage of outrage caused General Manager Peter Gelb, then under enormous unrelated pressure in contract negotiations with the Met's labor unions, to cancel the opera's planned radio and HDTV cinema broadcasts. The stage show nevertheless went on when the company presented its production premiere on October 20. This time several hundred protestors gathered to deride the work. Signs screaming "Metropolitan Nazi Opera" and "Propaganda Masquerading as Art" greeted a nervous first-night audience. Leon Klinghoffer's daughters Lisa and Ilsa denounced the opera in a printed statement that the Met included in the program, stating that the work "sullies the memory" and "rationalizes, romanticizes, and legitimizes the terrorist murder of our father." Hecklers had to be removed by security personnel. Even three weeks later, a couple of protestors were still seen distributing leaflets to curious passersby under the watchful eye of the NYPD. Neither the premiere nor any other performance was stopped, but all the negative attention seems to have been a boon for the Met's suffering box office. Less well known contemporary operas like *Klinghoffer* tend to sell poorly, yet this nearly sold out performance teemed with an unfamiliar audience of earth-tone clad bourgeois bohemians trying hard to look socially conscious.

Lisa and Ilsa Klinghoffer's feelings notwithstanding, many *Klinghoffer* haters have by their own admission remained ignorant of what they stand so vehemently against. Since they feel that *Klinghoffer* should not be performed, most obviously have not and will not attend a performance, listen to the music, read the libretto, or engage the opera in any other way beyond blindly objecting to it. If they did, they would surely realize that the work glorifies nothing and no one, not even art (more below). The terrorist characters are completely unsympathetic. Their leader is a cruel, vengeful tyrant ruled by anger. His men are naive and easily led youths who end the evening complicit in the murder of an innocent old man. It is true that the libretto gives them "back stories" that "explain" their rage, but to explain is not to excuse. What antagonist lacks a back story, especially in opera? When the captain of the *Achille Lauro* suggests to one of the terrorists that he might engage in dialogue with his Israeli enemies to find a peaceful solution, the latter replies that for him dialogue would mean the end of hope and the end of life.

Is this really rational, romantic, and legitimate? As the character of Leon Klinghoffer himself declares in an Act II monologue addressed to his captors, such implacable hatred can never rationalize, romanticize, or legitimize. To any sane person, especially one who is about to be killed, it merely horrifies. That is the whole point of terrorism. And the characters who indulge in it in *The Death of Klinghoffer* are absolute and unmistakable villains, from beginning to end.

As for the opera's supposed "anti-Semitic" character, both the Anti-Defamation League and Supreme Court Justice Ruth Bader Ginsburg (seen in the premiere's audience) have publicly stated that *Klinghoffer* is not anti-Semitic. The ADL merely noted that the opera could "enflame" anti-Semitism in places where it already exists. In my experience of the work, first at the ENO and now at the Met, this was limited to a couple of lines in which murderous, gun-toting terrorist madmen mindlessly spout tired old anti-Semitic stereotypes (that Jews are "avaricious" and "control America"). As the ADL clarifies on its website, it is the characters who are anti-Semitic, not the work. I wondered how their extreme brutality and unapologetic violence could recommend their prejudice as valid, understandable, or worthy of emulation by anyone, especially members of an opera audience. Does the *auto-da-fé* scene in Verdi's *Don Carlo* (returning to the Met later this season) rationalize burning heretics and glorify the Spanish Inquisition? Of course not. It does exactly what *Klinghoffer* does to the terrorists: it makes the perpetrators look cruel and despicable. When *Don Carlo* appeared at the Met in the 1950s, it was criticized by Catholic groups for giving their faith bad press, not by non-Catholics who argued that it endorsed the burning of heretics simply by presenting it on stage. Indeed, with *Klinghoffer*, it is actually the *Palestinians* who could credibly play the "I'm offended" card. After all, this their sole depiction in the entire world of opera reduces them to terrorists and, in their opening chorus, a hateful mob bent on revenge.

If people do legitimately wish to protest anti-Semitism on the operatic stage, it is curious that the same groups who protested Klinghoffer are not planning similar demonstrations against Wagner's *Die Meistersinger von Nürnberg*, which opens in a Met revival only a few weeks from now and arguably *does* contain real anti-Semitic content. But at present there is no sign of any planned protest, and it seems that Wagner's opera will go on without incident and be broadcast on the radio and at the movies.

The real problem with *Klinghoffer* is common to most political art. Rather than exploring human drama and feeling for what they really are, it reduces action to pantomime and characters to puppets. Their sole and often painfully obvious purpose is to indicate some urgent problem with a variation of "See this? This is bad. And you should agree!" In *Klinghoffer's* case the problem is terrorism. But I did not leave the theater feeling provoked to greater contemplation or more emotionally moved to oppose terrorism than I already did. Adams's score only highlighted the weakness of this facile approach. Subordinating musical expression to the political message, it is dominated by the kind of outdated 1980s minimalism and low range orchestral undulations that make so many contemporary opera scores sound like movie soundtracks or, perhaps worse, alike. In *Klinghoffer* the problem is unfortunately so acute that at times the opera can only be advanced through plot narrations projected on an on-stage screen, the functional and equally awkward equivalent of intertitles in silent film. Beyond the many *longueurs*, in moments where the drama could be profound, the orchestra is banal. In moments where the drama is banal, the orchestra tries to be profound.

Fine casting of what might be called an ensemble piece did reveal some vocal talent, even if it had to work within the limitations of the score and libretto. The title role itself indicated both this strength and these limitations. Alan Opie's resonant baritone served Leon Klinghoffer so well that I doubted it was really a good idea to have the character remain silent through the entire first half of the opera, a device spared virtually all other operatic title characters apart from Turandot. Paulo Szot's Captain and Sean Panikkar's terrorist character Molqi were the other strongest standouts. The Met's chorus delivered its music with consistent power. Morris's production relied heavily on video and other digital abstractions that were technically well executed but suppressed the music and drama into even paler relief. David Robertson's conducting did what it needed to do on a professional level, though it was hard to call the evening enjoyable.

Dmitrii Shostakovich, *Lady Macbeth of Mtsensk*
New York, Metropolitan Opera, November 10, 2014

It seems almost irritatingly *de rigueur* to begin a discussion of Shostakovich's second and final opera with a reference to its troubled history in Stalin's Soviet Union, where the dictator's visible displeasure at its 1936 Moscow premiere led to its condemnation. Enough has been said about that elsewhere. More interesting is the composer's adaptation of Nikolai Leskov's story of warped family intrigue and gratuitous sexual violence. Raped or ravished (depending on the production) by her feckless husband Zinovy's farmhand Sergei, the bored housewife Katerina falls for the rapist/seducer. She then poisons her boorish father-in-law and, helped by Sergei, kills her husband, too. Arrested at their own wedding after the town drunk tips off the police about Sergei's rotting corpse, the devilish couple is exiled to Siberia. On the way Sergei abandons Katerina for the tramp Sonyetka, who surrenders herself to him fully when he manages to appropriate Katerina's last pair of stockings for her. Driven mad by Sergei's betrayal, Katerina drowns herself and Sonyetka as the column of prisoners sullenly trudges on. Alongside these maudlin scenes, the opera's tragic plot is offset by funny satires of Russian provincial life. Its score embraces sharp dissonance to illustrate fractured personalities, frenzied circus-like music to depict extremities of sexuality, grotesques of traditional and popular musical forms to mock the characters, and occasional harmonic passages to develop sympathy for Katerina and her predicaments.

Lady Macbeth returns to the Met for the first time since 2000 and exactly 20 years to the day it first entered the company's repertoire in 1994. Graham Vick's production updates the story from its original setting in the 1860s to a garish late Soviet-era nowhere. Attributes of the sets and costumes suggest both the 1950s and the 1980s. Action in the troubled Izmailov household revolves around an old-fashioned television and refrigerator. Zinovy makes his exit and entrance in a boxy little Soviet car. After his murder, his corpse ends up in its trunk. Katerina and Sergei's wedding is dominated by a giant disco ball that casts obnoxious neon colors all over the stage. The police and prisoners are stiff products of stale institutional Soviet officialdom. Instead of the Siberian river in which Katerina drowns Sonyetka, the final scene places the murder-suicide in a ditch where the convicts empty their excrement.

When this production first premiered, it was widely taken as a forceful comment on the dislocation of the troubled post-Soviet Russia then painfully emerging from communism. Twenty years later, with the chaotic edge of 1990s Russia now worn into the staid bludgeoning of Putinism, it looks a bit outdated, more a historical comment on that moment in time than a piece with any contemporary relevance. This is only the production's second revival, but it is one clear case of a production that should legitimately fall on Peter Gelb's chopping block.

With so much native Russian talent emerging in the post-Soviet world, staging a Russian opera with non-Russian principals could be a potential hazard. Yet in Eva-Maria Westbroek, the Met found a superb Katerina, chilling when she needed to be (which is often) and pensive and lyrical when the drama called for that affect. The study was nothing less than superb, the dramatic highlight being her scream when the orchestra blasts her shock at the full extent of Sergei's betrayal. Along with Brandon Jovanovich's bright and ebullient Sergei, their excellent Russian diction helped the evening along. Anatoli Kotscherga's Boris anchored this superb principal cast with snarling bass tones. In an opera with many small character roles, it was a special pleasure to see so many fine Russian repertoire singers deployed to maximum effect. Most noteworthy was Vladimir Ognovenko's police sergeant, who barked out his corrupt orders with the authority of Boris Godunov, another role he sings. Dmitri Belosselskiy's old convict captured the character's philosophical song with deep pathos. The talented mezzo Oksana Volkova made the trashy Sonyetka easy to despise.

James Conlon delivered a solid and technically meticulous performance, though there were patches when the action slowed more than it should have. The most thrilling orchestral moment – in an opera with so many – was the repetitive brassy music of the scene in which Zinovy's body was discovered. Otherwise the orchestra seemed to focus on the eerier qualities of the piece in a way that passed over much of its excitement.

Ludwig van Beethoven, *Fidelio*
Milan, La Scala, December 7, 2014

St. Ambrose's Day - December 7 - always brings a flurry of festivity to Milan. Pre-Christmas celebrations of the city's patron saint culminate in what is arguably Europe's most prestigious annual cultural event: opening night at the famed La Scala. In these uncertain times, however, there was more at work than just the art. Exceptionally virulent political demonstrations against Italy's economic austerity measures brought out a much stronger than usual police presence of over a thousand officers. Several roadblocks forced even pedestrian traffic to approach the theater through unfamiliar alleys as red flag-waving demonstrators stood nose to nose with helmeted riot police protecting themselves with bulletproof shields. Two officers were injured by Molotov cocktails as demonstrators tried to rush the theater. Police wagons and ambulances stood abundantly at the ready.

To make it to this year's opening, I had to show my ticket to both the riot police and the *carabinieri* (in a normal year it would have been one or the other, but not both). The atmosphere inside the theater was palpably tense as police and La Scala security officials rigorously profiled the crowd for suspicious characters. Strict controls and unfamiliar restrictions governed movement through the theater's honeycomb of narrow corridors. With few exceptions – including Milan's mayor Giuliano Pisapia, IMF chief Christine Lagarde, and fashion designer Giorgio Armani – the usual bevy of A-list politicians and celebrities stayed away.

How ironic that the performance should have been Beethoven's only opera, the uplifting tale of the unjustly imprisoned Florestan, who ends the work delivered from tyranny amid an outpouring of universal joy. At the heart of *Fidelio* is Florestan's nobly devoted wife Leonore, who has disguised herself as a man ("Fidelio") and taken a servant's job in his prison in order to free him. Meanwhile she has attracted the attention of the modest jailer Rocco's daughter Marzelline, who is in turn coveted by another young servant, Jaquino. This could be a comedy of errors were it not for the murderous cruelty of the prison warden Don Pizarro, who wants to do away with Florestan before the government minister Don Fernando arrives to free him. At the crucial moment, Leonore reveals herself and confounds Pizarro by challenging him to kill Florestan's wife first, just as horns proudly herald Fernando's arrival to liberate the prisoners.

This new production marks the end of the illustrious conductor Daniel Barenboim's nine-year tenure as La Scala's music director. Riccardo Chailly assumes the post next year. Barenboim wasted no energy embracing his swan song. The orchestra, which opened the opera with Beethoven's improved *Leonore* No. 2 overture instead of the original, delivered the score's final 1814 version with polished intensity. There were moments when the maestro's baton may have lingered ponderously over a phrase, but the commanding sound revealed the ferocious concentration and superb attentiveness that marks Barenboim at his best. The choral singing also emerged in splendid relief, headily transporting us from the darkness of imprisonment to the light of life and liberation.

Opening night at La Scala is always a display of world class vocal talent, and the effort here looked promising. But the results were rather mixed. Anja Kampe got off to a shaky start in the role of Leonore, a notoriously treacherous part for even the most capable dramatic soprano. The voice seemed curiously underpowered for much of the first act and, in the difficult "Abscheulicher" aria, even a bit listless. By the second act, however, she seemed more focused and delivered the steadier creamy tones that have made her an accomplished Sieglinde among other roles of similar timbre. As Florestan, who only enters in the second act, tenor Klaus Florian Vogt deployed his sweetly balanced vocal line to great effect, even if it tended at times to sound a touch nasally and perhaps too high for the part. Falk Struckmann's Don Pizarro resonated with power and authority, though the "scare factor" did not always make itself felt. Kwangchul Youn's Rocco enjoyed a promising start before falling into muddied low notes that occasionally had trouble competing with the orchestra.

As for the opera's younger couple, tenor Florian Hoffmann's Jaquino was light of voice but not without merit. Mojca Erdmann's luster seems to have worn off. Her Marzelline hinted at the piquant soubrette soprano she once commanded so admirably, but she often sounded edgy and under voiced. It is far from a compliment to say that her best singing was in the ensembles, though even here other voices seemed to be a bit muted so as not to overwhelm hers. The fine baritone Peter Mattei contributed a memorable performance in the small but important role of Don Fernando.

Deborah Warner's production relies on *Fidelio*'s easy adaptability to almost any place in any era. Since we do not know either the exact details of Florestan's offense against Pizarro or the nature of the police state that allows for his predicament, the boundaries of time and geography are few. But rather than seize onto a truly creative theme that might explore the work's psychological and political depths, Warner moves the action to a bland and all too familiar present. Florestan's prison is a vast dilapidated industrial building that resembles a broken down factory undergoing renovations. A single flashing orange prison light and makeshift barbed wire fence atop a wall suggest its improvised purpose. Part of it serves as the frowzy quarters of Rocco's household. Chloe Obolensky's costumes clothe the entire cast in the common street dress of any modern city's sullen downtrodden. The effect may have been unintentional, but the massed chorus looked a lot like the protestors staking out the theater. Marzelline and Jaquino are petulant kids in hoodies. Jaquino's covers a t-shirt that screams "Wow!," an obvious and rather gangly reference to his naive infatuation with Marzelline. Rocco sports a frayed cardigan over his simple work clothes. Pizarro and his guards look like goons from the world of organized crime.

Does Warner mean to offer the stunningly obvious observation that petty tyranny is alive and well in the twenty-first century? If so, is deliverance from it possible or even desirable? And with Molotov cocktails flying a few yards down the street, did we really need or want to be told? Her *mise-en-scène* neither offered much of an answer nor asked many deeper questions. Even if she intended to subordinate the work to shallow considerations of "relevance," it is hard to conclude that she succeeded.

Some hints of our self-referential culture did penetrate the staging. Leonore uses a toy gun to hold off a knife-wielding Pizarro from killing Florestan. The tyrant eventually wrests it from her and angrily breaks it apart, only to find that is then too late to follow through with the murder. It reminded me of Cary Grant realizing he is being held by a woman armed with a harmless starter pistol at the end of *North by Northwest*, but I sorely missed the Alfred Hitchcock film's elegant whimsy. When Marzelline learns that "Fidelio," the object of her affection, is really a woman very much in love with her husband, she spends the lively choral finale pouting in self-indulgent disappointment, finally giving poor Jaquino a dismissive peck on the cheek before scurrying away. But these touches did not succeed in imparting as much meaning as Warner could have done with such an immense opportunity. "The danger of gala night is that people will see on TV that the opera is full of people wearing evening dress," she commented in an expression of what might have been behind her conceptual approach. But she still went to the after party with them at Milan's exclusive Società del Giardino.

Wolfgang Amadeus Mozart, *Le Nozze di Figaro*
New York, Metropolitan Opera, December 8, 2014

Sir Richard Eyre's new production of this Mozart classic opened the Met's season this year, replacing the faint effort of Jonathan Miller, which had endured since 1998. Eyre has had a successful career of producing crowd pleasing favorites, and this *Figaro* was no exception. Rob Howell's sets and costumes update the action to a kind of decadent 1930s – the eve of a violent era that easily parallels the opera (and play's) original pre-French Revolution Old Regime setting, which also teetered on the edge of doom. Here the clever servants sport recent fashions while Count and Countess Almaviva end the day in the elegant formal wear and dressing gowns of a Fred Astaire movie. Hints of modernity and of the changing world the characters inhabit intrude on the action. Count Almaviva gets ready for what he thinks is his garden rendezvous with Susanna by (perhaps unwisely for those in the know) snorting a bump of cocaine. Figaro, also taken in by the ruse, jealously stalks him with a camera equipped with one of those massive old-style flashes. Throughout, the art deco stylings are deployed to their full usefulness to suggest abrupt social change to this unbalanced world.

While the atmospheric effects work well, the overall staging is more problematic. The set makes heavy use of the Met's rotating stage to situate most of the action within and around a cylinder that occupies only about one-third of the space. This does allow for faster scene changes and amusing visual effects as the evening goes by, but too often – indeed, for most of the first three acts – it has the unfortunate consequence of confining the action within its narrow sliver. The remainder of the stage is either underutilized or lost altogether.

Opening night Met productions are a vocal feast. How pleasant that this second cast largely equaled the original in stature. Erwin Schrott's Figaro is internationally famous, and it easy to see and hear why – he is by turns naive and cunning, outraged and amused. The technique is solid in delivering the part's challenging arias as well as in carrying on its extensive recitative. The characterization could be more original, but here the direction could be at fault - much of the production's comedic antics will be familiar and even predictable to those who frequently see the work.

Another leading baritone, the talented Mariusz Kwieceń, commanded the role of the Count with an equally impressive voice. His drama was likewise constrained, but he had some excellent physical comedy in his seduction scenes. It was terribly amusing to see him appear during the overture to pantomime the afterglow of his conquest of Ashley Emerson's pert Barbarina, who scurries from his presence once he has had his way with her. Danielle de Niese may have too light a voice to be an ideal Susanna, but she captured hearts. Rachel Willis-Sørenson, who debuts as the Countess this season, took few chances and came off as rather bland. John Del Carlo's Bartolo and Suzanne Mentzer's Marcellina proved the wisdom of giving these smaller but still very important roles to experienced repertoire singers.

Edo de Waart led a balanced reading of the score.

Richard Wagner, *Die Meistersinger von Nürnberg*
New York, Metropolitan Opera, December 9, 2014

James Levine's triumphant return to the Met podium after prolonged health problems could find no finer expression than in his beloved Wagner conducting. His first work with the composer since returning is this seven-performance revival of Otto Schenk's engrossing storybook production of the only comedy among Wagner's mature works. Unhappily, this is the end of the road for the Schenk production. Tentative reports suggest that it will fall under Peter Gelb's axe to be replaced a few seasons hence by a new production imported from the Salzburg Festival.[11] Replacing crowd pleasing favorites may not be the best strategy for a house that no longer commands 70 percent capacity, but it is the course the management has chosen to take. The loss can only be endured. For more than two decades, we have had a luxuriously depicted Nuremberg laid out in exquisite detail. Now we may be condemned to move on.

Meistersinger works so well in traditional productions because the opera is a powerful allegory about the nature of art itself. The young nobleman Walther von Stolzing has left the boredom of his estates to seek aesthetic pleasure and romance among the mercantile middle class of bustling Nuremberg. At stake is Eva, daughter of the wealthy goldsmith Veit Pogner. Her hand in marriage is pledged to whichever champion can triumph in a song contest governed by the rules of the town's master singers' guild, a voluntary association devoted to maintaining exacting traditional standards of vocal art. Within this rarefied milieu, the town clerk Beckmesser thinks he has an edge. Pogner has promised to intercede

---

[11] It has yet to happen. A planned new production scheduled in 2020-2021 was cancelled along with the rest of that *saison manqué*.

for him to win Eva's legitimate affection. Walther's arrival – handsome, dashing, and formed outside the traditional "master" system through his private study of the writings of a different Walther, Walther von der Vogelweide (a character in Wagner's earlier opera *Tannhäuser*) – threatens to upset Beckmesser's plans. Beckmesser does all he can to cast doubt on Walther and his suitability. At the end of Act I, he appears to dispose of him through a rigid application of the singers' rules to Walther's audition song, an audacious piece that strikes the most respected of the masters, Hans Sachs, as something that sounds so old but is so new, a song that does not follow the rules yet contains no error. Inspired to help the young man when he fails to run off with Eva, Sachs moves past his and Eva's own mutual attraction and instead cultivates a dream Walther has had to compose the winning "Prize Song." Beckmesser tries to steal it, only to have Sachs catch him in the act. Sachs nevertheless invites him to take it, knowing that a mind and spirit as limited as the town clerk's will never express it as heartfully as Walther will. Beckmesser humiliates himself at the contest, leaving Walther to perform the song with unassailable beauty. Triumphant, he scorns the honor of the master singers, only to have Sachs upbraid him for his refusal to honor tradition and its importance in preserving "holy German art."

The major allegory is to Wagner's own troubled career. Espousing and producing a new sound in opera, he found himself readily and frequently dismissed by doubters, critics, rivals, and others who neither understood nor wanted to understand his obvious genius. And naturally, it is Wagner's self-idealization as Walther who triumphs in the end and the critics who are confounded. His id, represented by Hans Sachs, still compels him to respect and honor tradition, but the future of that tradition is now for him to define. For such a self-referential work by a man who was in all personal accounts an egomaniac, it is only to be expected that *Meistersinger* should be Wagner's longest opera. Clocking in at six hours, including intermissions, one patron was overheard comparing it to a transcontinental flight, though one hopes her aesthetic experience was more enjoyable.

The Met's revival had a troubled start in its casting of the leading role of Hans Sachs. The excellent baritone Johan Reuter, memorable from his performances as Barak in Richard Strauss's *Die Frau ohne Schatten* last season, had been scheduled but yielded the role in most performances to the veteran Wagnerian bass-baritone James Morris, who performed it regally in the last revivals of 2001 and 2007. In two performances – including the one under review and the broadcast of December 13 – the role went to the fresher voice of Michael Volle, known for his excellent debut as Mandryka in Strauss's *Arabella* last season. Possessing a fine, rich legato and superb line, Volle had all the stamina he needed to move decisively through the longest Wagner baritone part.

Johan Botha's Walther resonated with a strong clarion tone, though by the end of the evening he seemed to fade under the strain.[12] As Eva, Annette Dasch may have been out of her league. A warm, soft voice that has served her well in smaller European houses seemed lost in the cavernous Met, forcing a shriller tone at times. Johannes Martin Kränzle captured Beckmesser as an annoying person rather than a crude anti-Semitic stereotype or shrill ham. Pogner should be sung by a stentorian bass of true authority and Hans-Peter König fit the bill, though not in as round a way as he has done in his other Wagnerian singing. Paul Appleby and Karen Cargill did well as David and Magdalene, but one could not escape how unnecessary these characters are to the work. The evening's true stars were the orchestra and chorus under Levine's authoritative baton. Some object to his slower tempos, but the sound was plush and every note in the score received marvelous pollination from the practiced hand of the Met's own master.

Franz Lehár, *The Merry Widow*
New York, Metropolitan Opera, January 13, 2015

This New Years' Eve, the Met audience was treated to the Met's retake on the repertoire's other great operetta, Franz Lehár's *The Merry Widow*. Presented entirely in English with an original book by Jeremy Sams, it still delivers the basic outline of the comic tale of the poor fictional Balkan nation of Pontevedro and its attempt to save its tottering finances by arranging the marriage of its richest citizen, the young widow Hanna

---

[12] Botha died less than two years later, at age 51.

Glawari, to the fading playboy diplomat Count Danilo, who happens to be her old flame. A comedy of errors reunites them as a true love match accompanied by a fortuitous financial boon for Danilo and, perhaps, for Pontevedro as well.

Traditionally, the Met has presented at least the spoken dialogue of its operetta and light opera productions in English, sometimes preserving the native language for the sung score. This has rarely been a fortunate choice, and this rather corny new *Merry Widow*, which the company has only ever done in English, is no exception. Sams delivers a cliché-ridden ramble of bad puns, cloying metaphors, dumb jokes, tedious malaproprisms, and hackneyed quips that make one wince far too often to enjoy the better aspects of the performance. Susan Stroman's production, her Met debut, delivered a Disneyfied version of *Belle Époque* Paris with all the expected attributes. Its most creative edge was the transition from Act II to Act III, when inventive use of the Met's sliding stage transforms Hanna Glawari's garden into Chez Maxim's. Originally a choreographer, Stroman's talent shined most strongly in the production's finely executed and truly glittering waltzes and can-cans.

The cast promised a blockbuster evening. In taking on the role of Hanna Glawari, Renée Fleming's first foray into the operetta genre promised much amusement. Yet the voice often sounded too large and too heavy for the role. At times she seemed to try to hold back enough to deliver the lines in the style of the work. But despite her physical allure and undeniably strong stage presence, the result often led to devoiced lines that betrayed overcompensation. The opposite was true for Broadway star Kelli O'Hara, who brought her vivacious music theater voice to the operatic stage for the first time in the role of Valencienne. As her lover Camille de Rosillon, Alek Shrader seemed more in his element in this lighter tenor part than he does in his opera roles. Baritone Nathan Gunn's Danilo also fared well, with crisp diction and strong comic acting despite the utter banality of his lyrics. Veteran baritone Sir Thomas Allen's Baron Mirko Zeta added a fine comic presence. Carson Elrod's ham performance as Njegus, a spoken role in this production, was too annoying to demand much attention.

The Met orchestra and chorus acquitted themselves with a superb performance under the baton of Sir Andrew Davis.

Giuseppe Verdi, *Aida*
Milan, La Scala, February 15, 2015

Any new production of Verdi's *Aida* at La Scala is bound to capture worldwide musical headlines. Veteran director Peter Stein had quite a legacy to overcome: Italy's principal opera theater has fielded only two other productions over the last half century, both of them sumptuously traditional efforts by Franco Zeffirelli. Caught in a love triangle with the king's daughter Amneris and her Ethiopian slave girl Aida, the warrior Radamès must reconcile his feelings with duty. Duped into betraying his country, he ends the opera sealed in a tomb, where Aida joins him, true to the last.

A major challenge in staging *Aida* is its distinctive musical and dramatic affects: the work is hard to place in any setting other than the Egypt of the Pharaohs. Stein thus had almost no choice but to keep the Egyptian idiom. Yet as seen at the production's premiere on February 15, he cleverly managed to unload the opera's usual weighty opulence in favor of a stylized concept featuring minimalist sets and basic yet evocative costumes. Purists may object (and some did leave in a huff after the first act) that the production lacks the usual visual accoutrements: there are no temples, pyramids, hieroglyphics, elephants, or horses. There is a Nile Scene but no Nile.

Most structures are suggested by neutrally colored archways that are recognizably Egyptian in style but basic in design. Act I unfolds before a simple doorway set against a black backdrop. Amneris's quarters are backlit by a projected wall of cool blue. The famous triumphal procession – here regrettably shorn of its famous ballet sequence – passes before a simple raised dais that accommodates the pharaoh's court. A large retaining wall suggests the Nile. The trial scene happens behind an archway at the bottom of confined staircase illuminated by fluorescent light. The scene set in the Temple of Vulcan, in which Radamès is chosen to lead the Egyptian army, does billow the standard clouds of incense, but this is one of the very few visual referents that remain.

For the most part, Stein's effort intriguingly diverted attention away from the setting and instead allowed the audience to focus on the characters and their emotions. Aida's perpetual sadness grew more and more expansive over the course of the evening in the American soprano Kristin Lewis's fine performance. After a reticent start, she displayed an outstandingly disciplined *spinto* technique that allowed her rise to many of the part's vocal challenges. There were moments when her ascents lacked the bloom that a true Aida needs, but the potential for growth was audible and admirable.

The extraordinarily talented young Georgian mezzo Anita Rachvelishvili stood out as the evening's true star in her performance as Amneris, the king's daughter who rivals Aida for Radamès's affection. The character undergoes more psychological development than any other, from adoring love to raging jealousy to anguished regret, and the skill on display commanded attention in every scene in which she appeared. Muscular ascents and purring low notes delivered highly charged emotional content rarely seen on any operatic stage these days. The portrayal recalled the famous performances of the recently departed Elena Obraztsova.

Massimiliano Pisapia (no relation of Milan's mayor Giuliano Pisapia) replaced an ailing Fabio Sartori in the role of Radamès. At times he capably rose to the challenge, producing some weighty top notes. But more often his performance was uneven and suggested that the voice might be better suited to lighter parts. George Gagnidze, another very talented Georgian singer, sang a stentorian yet sensitive Amonasro. He captured the baritone register in tones that evoked the part's Golden Age singers. The legendary bass Matti Salminen bravely took the part of Ramfis, the high priest, but the voice betrayed age and wear. Carlo Colombara's King of Egypt resounded more comfortably in its element, with fine round vowels. Zubin Mehta led a superbly energetic performance with a firm command of La Scala's orchestra and chorus.

Any premiere in this exquisite house generates palpable excitement from Milan's discriminating audience. But like the production's values on stage, the reactions this time were surprisingly muted. Not even the feared *loggionisti* – the diehard fans who occupy the upper balconies – registered their usual disapproval.

Chapter Six

2015-2016

Giuseppe Verdi, *Otello*
New York, Metropolitan Opera, September 21, 2015

Verdi's penultimate opera – the second of his three works adapted from Shakespeare – rages with such intensity that any fresh interpretation should demand the opera world's undivided attention. Opening the Met's 2015-2016 season, Bartlett Sher's new production only heightened the sense of expectation. A prize-winning Broadway director now making his sixth effort for the Met, Sher's new *Otello* assembled a promising young cast of singers who have only recently arrived at the top of the operatic world. Latvian tenor Aleksandrs Antonenko's authority in the title role is known to New York audiences from his 2011 concert performance with the Chicago Symphony at Carnegie Hall. Bulgarian soprano Sonya Yoncheva debuted to stellar reviews just two seasons ago after starting her career in Europe. The older baritone Željko Lučić has delivered commanding performances of several progressively more challenging Verdi baritone parts over the past decade; his Iago was much anticipated. After a string of triumphs in some of the repertoire's most demanding works, the 40-year old French-Canadian conductor Yannick Nézet-Séguin is widely rumored to be a possible successor to Met music director James Levine.[13]

On paper this should have been a thrilling evening. Unhappily it was not. The excitement was already eviscerated by a distracting and

---

[13] The rumors were true. In June 2016, the Met announced that Nézet-Séguin would become its music director in the 2020-2021 season, with the title "music director-designate" from the 2017-2018 season. In February 2018, however, his appointment as music director was accelerated to the 2018-2019 season following James Levine's suspension amid sexual harassment allegations.

unnecessary two-month media discussion of the Met's decision to feature Otello without the usual dark makeup, an empty and pandering political gesture trivial to aesthetic considerations, which otherwise received almost no attention.

This is not to say that the vast bulk of Sher's production concept deserved much praise. Perhaps after looking too closely at the intellectual career of Verdi's librettist Arrigo Boito, the director decided that it would be a good idea to derive a production concept from the Italian writer's interest in the plays of the Norwegian dramatist Henrik Ibsen. Instead of a colorful Renaissance Cyprus, his *Otello* strangely unfolds in a bleak nineteenth-century northern European nowhere. Es Devlin's disappointing sets deliver icy, translucent structures that slide awkwardly around the stage for no apparent reason other than to give the characters shifting places to hide. Catherine Zuber's stuffy costumes confine everyone but Desdemona – improbably clad in a brilliant red dress much of the time – to boring shades of gray.

It is unclear whether this lack of dynamism was contagious or whether the stage direction lacked inspiration per se. Either way, throughout the evening movement and action languished in an odd torpor. In the opera's crushing concertante scenes principals and chorus alike were herded into vapid front-facing "park and bark" poses that seemed almost deliberately deprived of energy.

Antonenko had a few moments of requisite pique, but too few to deliver a convincing interpretation of the emotional maelstrom that so exquisitely tortures his character. Despite occasionally brilliant high notes, he was not helped by a generally underpowered voice swallowed by the cavernous Met.

As his covert nemesis Iago, Lučić drew from a more stentorian reserve, though directorial fiat deprived him of passion. Calculating real-life villains can indeed maintain poise and reserve as they go about their evil deeds, but Verdi's score and Boito's libretto lay bare this evil character on such a profoundly emotional level that suppressing Iago's brazen conceit, arch self-loathing, and pure hatred under a veneer of strict control stood out as one of the evening's poorer artistic choices.

Only Yoncheva really seemed in her element, floating splendid notes and unmarred ascents as she moved through Desdemona's exquisite *portamento* passages to loud acclaim. The portrayal was not always as innocent as one would expect but registered a strong personal success in an otherwise fallow field. Günther Groissböck was luxuriantly cast in the lesser role of Lodovico, the Venetian emissary.

Nézet-Séguin's conducting favored a carefully cultivated subtlety over the score's driving rhythms. Nevertheless, the unintended effect was usually languid and listless. Such a failure to tap the Met Orchestra's prowess underserved memories of its rousing performances of Verdi's score in productions past.

Giuseppe Verdi, *Il Trovatore*
New York, Metropolitan Opera, September 25, 2015

Sir David McVicar's gritty production of Verdi's middle period masterpiece – often called "the last bel canto opera" – has commanded unusually tenacious traction and even some badly needed popularity for the Met as it aspires to greater relevance and appeal. This season's starry revival features two of the greatest singers before the public today. Superstar soprano Anna Netrebko only began singing Leonora last year, in a judicious move from the lighter lyric roles that made her famous to heavier dramatic parts now better suited to her maturing voice. The famous baritone Dmitri Hvorostovsky has had more practice in the role of the wicked Count di Luna. Last night he drew a prolonged ovation from a sympathetic house that knew he was appearing at the Met for just three performances between treatments for a brain tumor.[14] They were joined by the young Korean tenor Yonghoon Lee, whose energetic Manrico held its own in an evening of auditory delight.

Netrebko's facility with her newly adopted heavier parts delivered a captivating performance. It feels merely repetitive to praise it to the skies. Robust projection matched a voluptuous, full bodied sound to explore Leonora's wide-ranging emotions as the character grows from a bel canto teenager in heat to a quietly determined *spinto* convincingly

---

[14] The brain tumor claimed his life just over two years later, on November 22, 2017.

prepared to give her life for the man she loves. In a special feat of desperation in the "Miserere" scene, when the character registers her realization that all will end in the downbeat aria "D'amor sull'ali rosee," Netrebko scampered partway up the fence barring her way to Manrico's place of imprisonment.

Hvorostovsky's medical condition placed no limitations on his cool, authoritative delivery of the villainous Count di Luna's music, much of which communicates barely controlled rage. There were moments when the character's aristocratic reserve could have yielded to greater passion, but this paled in significance when he delivered the role's signature aria "Il balen del suo sorriso" with a standard of Verdi baritone singing to which all performers aspiring to that most challenging of vocal types should aspire.

Lee's Manrico contributed a high spirited, clarion sound that paired well with thrilling dramatic flair. The voice did not always bloom to equal his colleagues, but impetuosity of his caliber rarely finds its way to the stage these days. In the role of Manrico's mother Azucena, the gypsy whose mistaken burning of the wrong baby sets the whole plot in motion, veteran mezzo Dolora Zajick buzzed with the appealing low notes that have made her performances essential in any serious contemplation of the part. Štefan Kocán's Ferrando, the captain of the guard, was a stentorian addition to the cast.

McVicar's production is holding up, though the massive rotating wall that dominates every scene is becoming tiresome. This revival has spruced up the action with some muscular stage action – di Luna, for example, takes a serious beating when his plot to abduct Leonora from the convent is foiled. Marco Armiliato led a reasonably paced performance, though the singers, for all their marvelous appeal, did not always agree with his tempos.

Giacomo Puccini, *Turandot*
New York, Metropolitan Opera, September 26, 2015

After the Met's tepid opening night new production of Verdi's *Otello*, this revival of one of the company's warhorse productions offered an instructive comparison. Franco Zeffirelli's opulent production of Puccini's last opera, which premiered in 1987, is now approaching its third decade. Yet it remains as strong and crowd pleasing as ever. Judging by the enthusiastic nearly sold out audience at its second performance, under review here, its endurance should serve as a fine lesson in an era when so many of the Met's most memorable achievements – Zeffirelli's more than any others – are getting the axe in favor of disappointing concept productions that seem designed more for HDTV projection in cinemas than for the enjoyment of loyalists in the house. Opera is indeed about spectacle, and the New York audience thirsts for it.

The grand news of *Turandot's* return was the assignment of the title role to the rising star Christine Goerke, already well known for numerous triumphs as several Richard Strauss heroines and on tap to sing Brünnhilde in the next outing of the Met's "machine" production of Wagner's *Ring of the Nibelung* a few seasons hence.[15] Goerke took up the challenge with alacrity and never wavered in power or stamina. The interpretation registered a strong success, helped in no small way by truly a compelling dramatic interpretation that explored the character's icy front as well as her inner weakness. We should welcome as a great luxury the opportunity to compare Goerke's performance with the forthcoming ones later this season of Lise Lindstrom and Nina Stemme.

As her suitor Calàf, the talented dramatic tenor Marcelo Álvarez seized the role with uncommon energy. The high notes were not always beautiful, particularly at the climax of "Nessun dorma," but his passionate ardor ran high throughout the evening. Calàf's own admirer Liù was outstandingly sung by Hibla Gerzmava, an artist whose impressive growth imbued the role with a refined and sympathetic soubrette quality and ethereal pianos. James Morris, now having clocked in over forty seasons with the company in dozens of leading roles, found a respectable place as Calàf's father Timur, the blinded and exiled King of Tartary. Performers of this role must command pathos and resignation, and Morris's ample dramatic powers delivered an impressive success. Met roster singers capably filled out the comprimario parts. Maestro Paolo Carignani commanded a rousing performance from orchestra and chorus.

---

[15] Goerke sang three full Met *Ring* Cycles in 2019.

Richard Wagner, *Das Rheingold*
Tokyo, New National Theatre, October 14, 2015

Since Tokyo's New National Theatre opened in 1997, this thoroughly state of the art venue has risen to house what is arguably Asia's most important opera company, a joint venture of the theatre itself and the Tokyo Philharmonic, which supplies the orchestra. With a searching new production of Wagner's *Parsifal* last year, the New National's music director Iimori Taijiro completed his ambitious goal of presenting all ten of the composer's mature works in Japan, including a full *Ring* Cycle. With that very large feather securely in his cap, he has now moved on to a second interpretation of the four-opera tetralogy, which will be presented in annual installments beginning with this season-opening production of *Das Rheingold*. The production is billed here as "new," but ardent Wagnerians will recognize it as a revisited version of the "other" *Ring* by the late German director Götz Friedrich. Originally staged in Helsinki in 1996, it departs from the stark apocalyptic motifs of the director's earlier effort for Deutsche Oper Berlin (still in repertoire in that theater) to present a simpler and less idea-driven interpretation.

Alas, the effort remains less effective than Friedrich's first attempt, imparting a generic post-Cold War message of "greed is bad" rather than deep commentary on life, society, or the human condition. Set on a slick inclined stage with subdued pastel colored backdrops arranged in geometric patterns, Gottfried Pilz's designs and 1920s-vintage costumes suggest something closer to a comic book morality tale. This might work best in *Rheingold*, the Ring's "preliminary evening," in which the Nibelung dwarf Alberich renounces love to seize the magic gold of the Rhine, which he then fashions into an all-powerful ring that will allow him to rule the world. Of the four Ring operas, *Rheingold* is shortest on introspection and depends more on cunning sleights of hand and actions that are identifiably human than the three longer evenings that follow.

In a city where Western high fashions, luxury brands, and famous galleries dominate the shopping streets of the chic Ginza and Rappongi districts, it seems almost expected that notable Western soloists would populate Tokyo's opera productions. Finnish baritone Jukka Rasilainen led the cast as the chief god Wotan, though at times I wondered whether the voice might sit a touch too high for the part. Thomas Gazheli's Alberich won the prize for most dynamic performance. His menacing tones resonated with crystal clear diction throughout the evening, but I have never encountered a more emotive Alberich in the scene where he loses the ring – here brutally torn from him by Wotan after he uses his spear to sever his antagonist's whole right hand. He fully reminded us that Wagner's tetralogy is really named after his character.

Christa Mayer's Erda captured this quintessential mother earth part's purring low tones. Mezzo Simone Schröder was fair in voice but could have relayed more than the standard nagging wife to which the role of Fricka so often descends. Yet what a luxury it was to have Bayreuth's latest Tristan, the star American tenor Stephen Gould, sing the amusing part of Loge, god of fire and trickery. Exuding decadent mischief in a three-piece suit accessorized with red sunglasses and cape, this Gatsbyesque conman fuels his deceptive schemes with bumps of cocaine and mocking gestures, such as holding up Alberich's severed hand to see if he wants to take it with him as a lovely parting gift. Andreas Conrad's Mime and Christian Hübner's Fafner admirably rounded out the Western soloists.

A young group of talented Japanese singers capably staffed the other roles. Ando Fumiko's Freia captured the goddess of love and youth with charming innocence. As Donner, baritone Kuroda Hiroshi joined the lithe-voiced tenor Katayose Junya among the panoply of Norse gods. Tsumaya Hidekazu's Fasolt also deserves an honorable mention. Taijiro led a solid performance even if the orchestra sounded a bit too brassy for my taste.

Nearly as interesting as the performance was the experience of hearing Wagner in Japan. Like Wagner audiences everywhere, the production called forth a mix of steely-eyed businessmen, mauve-clad hipsterati, a smattering of devoted Westerners, and a few extremely elegant Japanese ladies who donned kimonos for the occasion. The subdued interior of the opera theater (capacity 1,804) lent itself well to what was perhaps the most reverential reception of Wagner's music I have ever witnessed outside Bayreuth. The curtain calls impressed with a polite restraint that became more and more excited as the soloists took their bows.

Richard Strauss, *Elektra*
New York, Boston Symphony at Carnegie Hall,
October 21, 2015

This season the Boston Symphony swept into Carnegie Hall with perhaps the season's most anticipated role debut: that of the rising dramatic soprano Christine Goerke in the title part of Richard Strauss's *Elektra*. There is no doubt that her performance was one for the ages. Round, blooming tones resounded over the orchestra without a second of failing. Piercing high notes delivered mercifully on pitch rose to the challenge of the character's emotional wild ride. And the concert performance format was well served by the singer's strident entrance in a blood-red dress.

A strong supporting cast contributed to this successful evening. For the most part, the remaining members of the House of Atreus held their own with Goerke's stupendous Elektra. Gun-Brit Barkmin won complete redemption in the more suitable role of Chrysothemis. The character's inescapable sweetness paired well with a steely determination to produce the perfect dramatic foil to her unstable sister. James Rutherford's Orest has less stage time and was not always in the fully macabre form that other singers have brought to the role, but served the role effectively. It was only Jane Henschel's underpowered Klytämnestra who seemed a bit out of place in the otherwise driven ensemble. The role of Elektra's mother demands more than a little grit, but too much can diminish its effect. Among the remaining cast, the excellent character tenor Gerhard Siegel delivered an ironically enthusiastic Aegisth – loud and buoyant on his way to inevitable death.

Andris Nelsons, the recently arrived but already renewed (until 2022)[16] music director of the Boston Symphony, fully affirmed his place as one of the most exciting young conductors working today. With deft gestures he drew the vast orchestra necessary for this densely scored work

---

[16] In October 2020, Nelsons's tenure was extended again, to 2025, with an automatic renewal clause.

into marvelous unison as it delivered perhaps the most coherent orchestral performance of *Elektra* I have ever heard.

Giuseppe Verdi, *Giovanna d'Arco*
Milan, La Scala, December 7, 2015

Since 1951, festive St. Ambrose's Day – December 7 – has marked Europe's most important annual cultural event: opening night at Milan's famed La Scala. With ticket prices topping 2,400 euros, the stupendous gala evening draws the rich and famous of Italy and the world, or at least those intrepid enough to brave the thickets of semi-automatic toting police and *carabinieri* guarding the event from evildoers.

This year's red flag-festooned leftist protest was a pale reflection of last December's Molotov cocktail-hurling crowd, but security was tightened in the wake of the recent attacks in Beirut, Paris, and California, with several intelligence sources (and an ominous U.S. embassy warning bulletin) naming the theater along with other Italian landmarks as a possible terrorist target. Law enforcement rigorously profiled everyone who approached, inspected tickets blocks away, and screened the entering audience with metal detecting wands to make sure no one was packing heat under all the furs and frocks. Italian Prime Minister Matteo Renzi attended undaunted, along with his culture minister Dario Franceschini, Milan's mayor Giuliano Pisapia, and a number of celebrities glampots. Even La Scala's notorious *loggionisti* were well behaved, perhaps heeding the new general director Alexander Pereira's warning that their traditional booing and hissing will no longer be tolerated. The only untoward incident came during curtain calls, when a protestor threw herself into the orchestra pit in an apparent but barely noticed attempt to call attention to wealth inequality.

Artistically, the evening marked the literal passing of the baton to Riccardo Chailly, who took over as La Scala's principal conductor from Daniel Barenboim earlier this year and will officially become music director effective January 1, 2017. For his first opening night, the program moved uncharacteristically outside the standard repertoire to present Verdi's rarely performed *Giovanna d'Arco*, which premiered at La Scala in 1845. Although the opera was an immediate hit for its already popular

31-year old composer, it quickly fell into obscurity. Even La Scala, the theater most closely identified with Verdi and his operas, has not staged it for the last 150 years.

Adapted from Friedrich Schiller's play *Die Jungfrau von Orléans* (*The Maid of Orleans*), this absurdly romanticized retelling of the Joan of Arc tale suffers from perhaps the weakest plot and thinnest characters in Verdi's *oeuvre*. In his version of the tale, Joan's (Giovanna's) divine inspiration to lead the French forces against English invaders quickly melts into a fictional romance with the hapless French king Charles VII (Carlo). Admonished by angels to remain innocent of earthly love, the unlikely heroine is simultaneously plagued by a chorus of disappointingly tame demons (introduced by a waltz, of all things) who covet the ruin of her soul. Her inner spiritual turmoil wrecks her romance with the amorous king, who turns out to be about as guileless as any character in opera. But nevertheless, Giovanna's apprehensive father, Jacques (Giacomo), decides that his daughter's visions are the work of the devil and, without much further reflection, betrays her to the English. In the final act he for no apparent reason changes his mind, realizes the truth of Giovanna's mission, and frees her to return to the battlefield. Victorious in an offstage attack, she is brought back mortally wounded (no burning at the stake here) and ascends to heaven mourned by both the besotted Carlo and the repentant Giacomo, who join her in a moving trio reminiscent of the one that ends Verdi's earlier opera *Ernani*.

The task of staging this underwhelming work fell to the creative partnership of Moshe Leiser and Patrice Caurier. Recognizing the obvious pitfalls of a straightforward staging, the duo has intriguingly probed Giovanna's fractured psyche to render the events of the opera as a vast hallucination seen entirely through the prism of her disturbed mind. Giovanna does not inhabit the historical figure's fifteenth-century martial surroundings, but rather a plain nineteenth-century drawing room dominated by her sick bed and an armchair for her fretting father. Tall transparent walls allow visions to appear to her – first the chorus that mourns France's fate, then impressive video projections of fierce combat and angelic illuminations of divine inspiration.

As Giovanna's psychosis deepens, her delusions become intensely interactive, with warriors, angels, and demons entering her space to inspire, entice, and threaten. Carlo enters in the guise of a living bronze statue to receive Giovanna's pity and pine for her love. In the third act, which conventionally features a coronation ceremony during which the king parades his adoration of Giovanna, her fantasy allows Rheims's Cathedral of St. Denis to rise for the festivities and then fall in flames when she insists on maintaining her purity. It also allows her to accept a literal cross to bear from an imagined Christ figure. Throughout the opera, no action happens without her and only Giacomo, whose main function is to comment on her state before betraying her, shares her real time and place. Yet even his dastardly betrayal and regretful rescue of her remain within the hallucination. In the finale, Giovanna's death results in the culmination of both her fantasy and her illness.

It has become virtually redundant to heap praise on superstar soprano Anna Netrebko, who remains without hyperbole the most exciting singer before the public today. The role of Giovanna has few truly memorable moments, but presents a high tessitura and dramatic demands that prefigure Violetta in *La Traviata*, Leonora in *Il Trovatore*, and other heroines of Verdi's more mature operas now solidly in Netrebko's repertoire. She reached these heights with cool confidence and absolute clarity of tone. The production's only drawback was that it caused her spellbinding dramatic skill to lose itself in the hallucination trope, which confined her to portraying a madwoman who is imagining rather than effecting the events around her.

Francesco Meli brought an inviting warmth and resounding brightness to the role of Carlo, though at times one might have wished for a regal richness in the voice. Baritone Devid Cecconi admirably served as a last-minute replacement for the ailing Carlos Alvarez. Appearing without much rehearsal time, he captured Giacomo's paternal concern and paternal frustration with an endearing warmth.

Chailly led a brisk and energetic performance, often finding elements of the score that have eluded other conductors of record. Pereira has offered this production as a challenge to traditionalists, who have objected to aspects of his management and nearly abbreviated its term before the conflict was resolved last year. By endowing a forgotten Verdi work with an insightful and well sung psychodrama, he may well have succeeded.

Johann Strauss, *Die Fledermaus*
New York, Metropolitan Opera, December 10, 2015

The demise of Otto Schenk's lavish production of Johann Strauss, Jr.'s famous operetta left many to wonder whether a new production would stand up. Jeremy Sams's effort, which premiered two seasons ago on New Year's Eve, veers more toward art deco elegance. The action is updated 25 years, from Strauss's setting in 1874 to December 31, 1899, but fills the bill nicely. Schenk's production went forward in German for the singing with adapted English dialogue comically attuned to the news of the day. Sams has dispensed with that to present the entire performance in English, leaving one to wonder why it should even still be called Fledermaus instead of *The Bat*.

In some ways Sams's production delivers a fine, festive atmosphere fit for the holiday season. The revival has been pared down a bit, with a number of extraneous details edited out. Among the more striking is the removal of the menorah that originally decorated the Eisensteins' drawing room. The Christmas tree remains, but the question of whether or not they are assimilated Jews neither helped nor hindered the plot, and someone obviously realized that. The English book remains the same, unfortunately, with too many dumb jokes, tedious malaprorisms, and cloying metaphors to serve the operetta's sophistication. Do we really need Alfred to test Rosalinde's wavering fidelity by asking, "Care to canoodle my strudel?" I hope not. Christopher Fitzgerald's painful comedy in the speaking role of the jailer Frosch marked an inauspicious Met debut.

Fine music saved the endeavor as the Met deployed some of its best talent, in many ways a cast more impressive than that of the original run. Music director James Levine appeared on the podium, conducting the work for the first time in his 45 years at the Met. His brisk and lively pace handily answered bumptious critics who called publicly for his departure after he dropped out of the recent new production of Alban Berg's *Lulu*.

Susan Graham added the trouser part of the bored Prince Orlofsky to her repertoire with customary vocal prowess and dramatic skill. Her performance was nothing less than a superb case of luxury casting. Tenor Toby Spence and soprano Susanna Phillips were in excellent form as the Eisensteins. Paulo Szot's Falke portends a fine career throughout the baritone repertoire. As Alfred, Dimitri Pittas hit the comic notes with a talent that only seems to grow. The chorus and dancers helped the performance rise to star levels. And it was a nice touch to move the *Thunder and Lightning Polka* to the curtain calls rather than integrate it into the already tune-laden score.

Giacomo Puccini, *Tosca*
New York City Opera, January 20, 2016

After a disastrous bankruptcy and prolonged court battle over the late company's remaining assets, New York City Opera – a cultural institution that had endured from the 1940s until just a few years ago – has returned to the scene. Having left its longtime home at Lincoln Center's New York State Theater (now the David H. Koch Theater), City Opera spent what many assumed to be its death throes in other venues around New York. Now it may have a new home – and a long-term strategic plan – to offer seasons at the Rose Theater, which was originally built to house Jazz at Lincoln Center. Substantial adjustment can clear the way for an orchestra pit and a credible theatrical stage on which 1,100 spectators can view what we should all hope will be new and invigorating programs. Just over one-fourth the size of the Met, the greater intimacy will surely allow for thoughtful productions of more intimate repertoire than the larger house can manage.

It was, then, a bit offbeat for the company to return with that reliable old powerhouse of melodrama, Puccini's *Tosca*. But judging by the sell-out crowd at the opening performance, the choice was at least commercially judicious. Additional interest blossomed from Lev Pugliese's production, which reproduced the sets and costumes of the opera's original world premiere, in 1900, by the Russian-born German artist Adolf Hohenstein (credited in the program). After years of disappointment following the Met's junking of its own highly realistic and dearly beloved Franco Zeffirelli production of *Tosca* in favor of the late Luc Bondy's spare, vulgarized, and widely despised new take, the visual elements were easier on New York eyes. The only unfortunate moment came in the second act, when the evil Baron Scarpia, Rome's ruthless and lustful police chief, closed the doors of his Palazzo Farnese apartment a bit too forcefully, causing the canvas backdrop to wobble too comically to preserve the scene's gravitas. But that aside, the sets and costumes were for the most part attractive and occasionally even beauties to behold.

The opening night cast did not draw on the opera world's greatest strengths. In the title role Kristin Sampson could hold her own, but not without some torturous ascents and wavering pitch problems. City Opera's stalwart tenor James Valenti certainly delivered an impassioned Cavaradossi, but his verve could not make up for a voice that sounded rather too baritonal in its stridency. As the evil Scarpia, baritone Michael Chioldi fared noticeably as the best of the three leads, with a strong stentorian voice that captured the part's vigorous evil. Kneeing Cavaradossi in the groin at the height of their second act confrontation may have been a bit gratuitous, but the point was clear.

Under Pacien Mazzagatti's baton the reconstituted City Opera orchestra played a reasonable rendition of the score, though at times there were rough edges and the occasional crack. On the whole, the experience was, well, like being at City Opera. And this is a good thing.

Pietro Mascagni, *Cavalleria Rusticana*/ Ruggero Leoncavallo, *Pagliacci* New York, Metropolitan Opera, January 21, 2016

Sir David McVicar continued his reign as the closest thing the Met has to a house director last season when his *Cav/Pag* replaced yet another storied Franco Zeffirelli production. The new effort has not settled in as one of the director's greater successes, however, and its revival last night displayed an odd unevenness.

The conceit here is that both operas happen in the same village a few decades apart, with *Cavalleria Rusticana* set in the late nineteenth century and *Pagliacci* following in the 1940s. The action thus unfolds before high reddish-beige walls that suggest a prison, factory, or some other kind of confining institution that condemns the characters to their pathetic fates. The cliché of the wall and its suggestion of entrapment is easily recognizable to anyone familiar with *soi-disant* "avant garde" European directors and their collective lack of imagination.

It is unclear how Sir David's reliance on phased temporality serves either work. In some ways it actually imposes limitations. If *Pagliacci* happens in the 1940s, then it must logically follow that the townspeople enjoy a more visually interesting life than their ancestors did in *Cavalleria*. Here this is suggested by a bellowing truck that carries around the company of itinerate actors, an improvised electrical tower, and brighter period costumes. Making *Cavalleria* more retrograde forces the direction to eliminate these elements, leaving a chorus dressed in severe black with nothing but rough tables over which to pour out their disappointments. The only hint of color arrives during the "Innegiamo" hymn aria and chorus, but here the iconographic religious statues offer little corrective relief. McVicar seems to have compensated with the use of the Met's rotating stage, but here, too, the temporal limitations were too great to save the concept. While its subtler use in *Pagliacci* allows for effectively subtle changes in angles and sightlines, in *Cavalleria* it simply spins the seated chorus around in a bewilderingly pointless whirl. One might be forgiven for concluding that the production's principal message was that the Southern Italian peasants were happier under Mussolini.

The vocal efforts paralleled the visual and dramatic unevenness. In *Cavalleria*, it was hard to take the wan voiced Violetta Urmana very seriously in the role of Santuzza, whom Turridu has impregnated and thrown over for the married Lola. The role requires more youth, naïveté, and susceptibility than a dramatic soprano past her prime can really muster. The overall effort was reduced to a pallid sulk that conveyed little pathos. Yonghoon Lee's more successful Turridu radiated some clarion high notes but seemed out of place in such a dull village. The solid baritone Ambrogio Maestri sang well as Alfio, Lola's wronged husband and Turridu's killer, but seemed a bit miscast from his more legendary comic characters.

Pagliacci soared with the immensely talented tenor Roberto Alagna as the cuckolded clown Canio and the fragile Barbara Frittoli as his faithless Nedda. George Gagnidze's stentorian baritone captured the treacherous Tonio, who maliciously reveals Nedda's love affair after she spurns him, with a baseness redolent of the nastiest stage villains. Fabio Luisi led a measured performance, though at times, particularly in the more soaring moments of *Cavalleria*, the orchestra sounded rather too restrained.

Chapter Seven

2016-2017

Richard Wagner, *Tristan und Isolde*
New York, Metropolitan Opera, September 26, 2016

As Peter Gelb ushers the Met into staid middle age, what could be more
fitting than for the "new" house to open its 50th anniversary season with
another of his signature overblown flops? Entrusted to Polish
director/filmmaker Mariusz Treliński, this was the first time *Tristan* has
opened a Met season since 1937. The hesitant applause and howling boos
of a varied audience of white-tied socialites, B-list celebrities, downtown
fashion victims, overmanicured Wall Street types, amiable gay couples,
and awkward hipsters united in a noisy consensus that a great historical
opportunity had been missed. Replacing Dieter Dorn's controversially
stylized but lithe and elegant production, in repertoire since 1999,
Treliński's dismal effort stripped the opera of most meaning, muddled its
psychological dimensions, and even succeeded in obscuring the music.

The Met's attempts to enliven opera for new audiences have relied
on visual effects of ever greater sophistication. *Tristan*'s famous prelude,
a work of immense intimacy and delicate sensuality, slammed the
audience with an electronic nautical compass projected over a giant black-
and-white video of a ship tossing in rough waters. The compass insipidly
reappears at the beginning of each subsequent act, but this distracting
homage to the *Victory at Sea* series vitiated the music long before the
screen yielded to a pantomime of a uniformed father embracing his son
(presumably the young Tristan) before the family home is shown bursting
into flames. Without any allusion to the prelude's powerfully sexual
suggestions of seduction, buildup, climax, and afterglow, we are dragged
into a crude psychological character analysis to which Wagner's
monumental piece is merely incidental. The fire image only reappears

during Tristan's Act III hallucination scene, when his younger self appears in the form of a small boy worryingly playing with a cigarette lighter. Did Tristan kill his parents in an accidental blaze? We are never told, but if he did there is no indication of why this is important to his affair with Isolde or really anything else in his life.

  The ship that conveys Isolde to Cornwall is a three-level cutaway of a grim modern vessel. Each deck is compartmented into square and rectangular rooms. This vast shadowbox allows individual spaces to be illuminated while others are blacked out. Treliński's likely intention is to bring each scene into greater relief by eliminating distraction, but the overall effect sacrifices the Met's enormous stage space for palpably claustrophobic confinement. The captive heroine laments her fate in a drab cabin on the middle tier while Tristan navigates the vessel from a starkly modern bridge above her. The decks are connected by a flight of functional steel fire stairs, up and down which the characters hurl insults and sometimes pursue each other. Tristan covertly monitors his captive on a closed-circuit surveillance system, pausing for the occasional wistful gaze upon her disappointed visage, which the Met appears to have chosen as the iconic visual for this season's promotional materials. The confrontation that leads to their consumption of the love potion takes place deep in the hold, alongside drums containing hazardous waste. Is this really the association we want for the emotion that Wagner composed the opera to monumentalize? One hopes Treliński is a happier man than that.

  Act II oddly continues on the ship, with the lovers' rapturous rendezvous and scandalous discovery consigned to its depths. The pair are only found out by King Marke's brave warriors wielding flashlights, which they insist on abrasively shining into the eyes of the audience during one of the most climatic scenes in all of opera.

  One would have to read the program notes carefully to grasp the conceptual point that the image of the ship is meant to represent Tristan's "internal journey" as well as his and Isolde's literal passage, but the effect was so numbing that no one seemed to understand or care. If anyone did, informed opinion would recall that Christoph Marthaler's recently replaced Bayreuth production already used the trope of sinking the action into the frowzy depths of a modern ship (to equally uninspiring effect), while the Russian director Dmitry Tcherniakov's Mariinsky Theater production boxed the first act into the confines of a submarine.

Inverting transcendence into neurotic internality is thus nothing new, original, or exciting. Scarcely a hint of true passion escapes characters reimagined – even in the most enchanted heights of bliss – as denizens of bourgeois tedium. Isolde delivers her narrative lament clutching an unlit cigarette like a petulant teenager afraid of going too far. Her memory of her betrothed Morold's death at Tristan's hands reveals it not to have been the luckless result of chivalrous combat but rather a coldblooded prison execution for which Tristan feels improbable remorse. When she and her conqueror swallow the love potion anticipating that it is in fact the death potion, they react more like people suffering through their stormy forties with acid reflux than larger than life heroes whose passionately shared death wish is transformed into breathtakingly boundless ecstasy. Their consequent raptures are reduced to PG-rated petting, culminating in Isolde resting her head on a passive Tristan's shoulder as the *Liebestod* resolves in the opera's finale. The cuckolded Marke is neither wrathful nor shattered but instead scolds Tristan, in life as well as in death, like an annoyed schoolmaster costumed to resemble the ill-fated Lord Louis Mountbatten. The only sense of doom, apart from the production's charmless and emotionally draining darkness, is the projected image of an astral body wrapped in mist, a rather pointless borrowing of the inescapable planetary collision in Lars von Trier's *über*depressing *Tristan*-saturated film *Melancholia*.

The production's only saving grace was its superb casting, anchored on the leading dramatic soprano Nina Stemme. After more than a decade of singing Isolde around Europe, this was her North American role debut. Happily, it did not come too late. With cold, steely tones she delivered the full range of Isolde's emotionality for the full five hours with utterly no sign of faltering. Her vocal presence alone carried the performance, even if her drama sometimes lacked the raw energy so captivatingly present in her European appearances. But surely this was the fault of the production's unfortunate conceit that Isolde is just an ordinary deceived woman in love and not a reflection on this stellar artist's well established stage potential.

Stuart Skelton paced himself reasonably through the first two acts before unleashing a torrent of pent-up, high-octane vocalism in the challenging Act III scenes. Some might quibble with the contention that he is a true Heldentenor (he certainly comes very close in my opinion), but his performance went above and beyond the usual plaudit that a tenor singing Wagner is good if he simply gets through the role.

René Pape stretched his superb legato over the wronged King Marke's somber lines. Ekaterina Gubanova contributed a fine low-ranged Brangäne, and Evgeny Nikitin gave a muscular Kurwenal.

Sir Simon Rattle conducted in one of his rare Met appearances. At times his slow tempi unfolded ponderously over a score that needs a less cerebral approach. But often he tapped into the legacy of James Levine, whose orchestra was trained to follow nuance in order to pollinate each note with deep meaning. A notable feature of the orchestral performance was a cut of about nine minutes of music before the Act II love duet. It is unclear whether this was Rattle's decision or a creative compromise with Skelton, whose character's vocal line presents major challenges in those moments. Purists will quail, but outside of Bayreuth and Levine's tenure at the Met, this cut has been quite common and does not take much away from the overall flow. Rattle's reading would bear a second listen, but preferably one without this burdensome production's distractions.

Richard Wagner, *Das Rheingold*
Lyric Opera of Chicago, October 1, 2016

"Forget calm," announces a marquee outside Chicago's Civic Opera House, "this is opera." With his exciting new production of *Das Rheingold*, British director David Pountney kicks off Lyric Opera of Chicago's sixty-second season with the first installment of an ambitious new *Ring of the Nibelung*, Richard Wagner's four-evening masterpiece recounting the creation and destruction of the world. This is the first time Lyric has ever opened its season with a Wagner opera, and Chicago's new *Ring*, to be delivered in complete cycles in 2020,[17] keeps the company in pace with America's other leading houses in New York, San Francisco,

---

[17] Alas, it was not to be. The full *Ring* Cycles planned of 2020, and the production's *Götterdämmerung* instalment, were cancelled by the pandemic.

Washington, and Houston, all of which have introduced elaborate new productions of Wagner's tetralogy in the past decade; Chicago's new production is shared with Madrid's Teatro Real.

In an age when it is de rigueur for directors to impose some sort of tendentious interpretive "concept" on opera productions, to say nothing of Wagner, audiences will find welcome relief in the Windy City. Pountney, who leads the Welsh National Opera as chief executive and artistic director, astutely avoids politicizing the *Ring*. Those who embrace his approach will dodge *soi-disant* ironic commentary on the corrupting pursuit of power, duck warnings of imminent environmental catastrophe, escape bludgeoning feminist critiques of male-dominated society, and go to sleep at night untroubled by somebody else's annoying quest to impute contemporary relevance to a work that is fundamentally about humanity at its most profound. At the same time Pountney's effort is lively and stimulating enough to keep clear of the witless caricature that so many lamented in Robert Lepage's disappointing Metropolitan Opera production, now scheduled to return in 2018-2019. It is all the more remarkable that Pountney accomplished this feat without resorting to hi-tech special effects of the type that mercilessly clutter the action and sideline so much of Wagner's music in other productions. Having seen Mariusz Treliński's muddled and over-engineered new *Tristan und Isolde* at the Met's opening night just five days before the Chicago premiere, the ascendant simplicity had a palpably reassuring effect.

Pountney's alternative to an obnoxious interpretative approach is an appealingly narrative one. The story of *Rheingold*, which sets off the tetralogy with the theft of the Rhine Maidens' magic treasure by Alberich, a base being who forswears love, unfolds in the guise of a late industrial era stage drama. Stagehands facilitate the action from wooden towers bracketing the performance space beneath a false proscenium arch. At opportune moments, they arrive to add or remove sets and props, brighten or darken the stage with old fashioned klieg lights, or provide elements of the action. The giants who built Valhalla, for example, are huge puppets with limbs that can be manipulated to menace and fight. We are clearly watching a performance of *Rheingold* being staged parallel to the action. But the "play within a play" concept is far from intrusive. Pountney admits that his idea might very well be naïve, but it nevertheless allows the work to proceed on its own original merits; it highlights rather than hijacks the opera's ability to be taken on its own narrative terms. In short, it goes a long way to restoring the "drama" so essential in Wagnerian "music drama."

Freed from unwieldy ideological constraints and obtuse directorial concepts, it was a revelation to see the characters stand for what they truly are, that is to say human. Pountney's *Rheingold* exposes the unrestrained folly of the psyche, the war between ego and superego. One readily gets a solid sense of Wagner's sarcasm and biting cynicism, as yet untouched by the Schopenhauerian doom and gloom that influenced him as his work on the *Ring* continued. Moments that gave a sense of black comedy emerged in ready relief. In about 25 performances of the work, I have never heard a *Rheingold* that got so many laughs. When Alberich makes his existential choice to gain power by forswearing love, he gives one of the gowned Rhine Maidens a solid shove off of her stage-managed lift so that he can take the gold. His whole persona, magnetically played by the excellent bass-baritone Samuel Youn in his American debut, snorts and sneers and snarls through the entire performance. It is entirely appropriate that access to his lair in Nibelheim comes through a trapdoor sewer cover marked "*Achtung!*"

Regal gods in attire suggesting medieval Habsburgs are wheeled on stage in vast contraptions hinting at their divine powers (Donner with a large hammer, Freia with an apple tree, Wotan with his ravens perched on the desiccated branches of the faded World Ash Tree). Eric Owens's much anticipated role debut as Wotan introduced a refreshingly unusual bout of skepticism to what can be a stolid part. He laughs mockingly through Alberich's disgrace at his hands, nursing a bright glass of rosé before sawing off his alter ego's entire left arm with a butcher knife to get the ring. Štefan Margita's Loge, in full-length red English riding coat, maintains his detached poise with aristocratic aplomb, delivering his final lines musing on burning up the gods in a vast fire (which he does at the end of the Ring) not from a discreet part of the stage but rather facing the audience from the conductor's podium. The Rhine Maidens send the gods on their way to Valhalla – suggested by a wall decorated in popular fin-de-siècle Oriental tropes – by crawling out from their watery depths to point with starlet vindictiveness at Wotan, who laughs them off. The moment was more brutally effective than the usual disembodied voices wailing off stage. The Norns, whom we do not normally meet until *Götterdämmerung*, shadow the action knitting what will become the Rope of Fate like a trio of obsessive Mesdames Defarge.

After his much applauded Alberich in Lepage's Met production and elsewhere, Owens's Wotan drew the most attention in the buildup to the premiere. Unhappily, it might not have been the wisest casting choice. The voice is stentorian and rests on a firm technique. But neither the high notes for this young incarnation of the god nor the stamina needed to support the role through nearly three hours of music were at the singer's command. The last thirty minutes or so, which feature some of Wotan's best music, sounded disappointingly undervoiced. Youn's visceral Alberich fared rather better, leading one to wonder whether he should have reprised his recent Berlin Wotans. Along with Margita's buoyant Loge, Tanja Ariane Baumgartner's supple Fricka (another American debut), Zachary Nelson's determined Donner, and Laura Wilde's lilting Freia made fine impressions among the supporting cast. Jesse Donner's (no relation to the god) Froh and Rodell Rosel's Mime seemed a bit overwhelmed and overacted. Okka von der Damerau had a fine stage presence in Erda's brief scene, even if her natural mezzo did not quite descend to the contralto depths with which Wagner endowed the earth goddess.

Lyric's music director Sir Andrew Davis led a fast-paced performance. Not everyone will appreciate his brisk tempos, but they moved the action forward in excellent time with the action on stage with scarcely a moment of drift or distraction. Hearing the future installments of this dynamic new production will keep Chicago on every Wagnerian's map.

Camille Saint-Saëns, *Samson et Dalila*
Paris Opera, October 4, 2016

Paris has settled into more familiar standard repertoire runs, now with the return of Camille Saint-Saëns's *Samson et Dalila* after a twenty-five year absence. Since its world premiere, in Weimar in 1877, the work has endured as a great operatic warhorse that combines a then-chic Biblical Orientalism with the sumptuous *femme fatale* trope that had just begun to migrate from the page to the stage. Adapted from the Old Testament Book of Judges, *Samson* retells the downfall of the ancient Hebrew hero whose strength, which flows from his voluminous hair, promises victory over cruel Philistine conquerors. Only his weakness for the wiles of the temptress Dalila compromises his fortitude and leads him to betrayal, captivity, and ruin. In one of opera's most striking finales, God mercifully responds to his prayer and restores his strength for one last go so that he can topple the supporting pillar of the Philistines' pagan temple, killing all within.

Traditional approaches to *Samson* usually wallow in Orientalist kitsch, filling out the opera's dramatic weaknesses and embellishing its relatively simple plot with over-the-top grandiosity. *Regietheater* reimaginings try with almost nauseating regularity to impute contemporary relevance to the work by unnecessarily updating the Hebrew-Philistine confrontation to some solemn reminder of the Arab-Israeli conflict. Both approaches tend to overwhelm the personal interactions and negate any opportunity for original characterization. Samson generally comes off as a hapless fool and Dalila is inevitably a ferocious bitch goddess. The end.

In a production shared with the Metropolitan Opera, the ambitious Venetian director Damiano Michieletto rises to the challenge with customary interpretive license. Having set Puccini's *La Bohème* on the gritty outskirts of contemporary Paris and Verdi's *Un Ballo in Maschera* in the milieu of a modern election campaign, he is no stranger to radical reimagination. Here he transforms the Biblical confrontation into modern-day settings but mercifully extracts the action from loaded Middle Eastern politics. The oppression strikes an anti-globalization chord by setting the conflict as a nondescript war between an unidentified group of the downtrodden and a well heeled (and well armed) but faceless elite. The oppressors occupy a vast elevated shadowbox, furnished in trendy minimalism, which dominates the victims' plain main stage. They only descend to inflict harm. The spatial contrast is stark, but the conflict's inspiration is ultimately only a background that eschews decorative coloring, Biblical or otherwise. Indeed, the opera's only unavoidable trace of Oriental ambiance, its Act III *bacchanale,* is cleverly dispatched as a celebratory masquerade party during which the victorious Philistines change into hastily delivered costumes of the ancient world and dance without spilling too much of their champagne. The walls come down not through a divine restoration of Samson's lost strength, but rather in a blinding blaze of gasoline tossed all over the set and then "ignited" via the medium of blinding yellow lights.

Michieletto's approach allows for probably the most dynamic characterizations in modern memory of the opera. Anita Rachvelishvili's sultry Dalila departs far from the usual cynical motif of seduction and betrayal. From her first interactions with Aleksandrs Antonenko's powerful Samson, we realize that Dalila's affection is genuine despite her ties to the other camp. Her Act II seduction scene, centered on the famous aria "Mon coeur s'ouvre à ta voix," reveals a woman sincerely in love. Delivering bone crushing low notes and a flair for depicting a woman's conflicted soul, Rachvelishvili endowed the part with exceptional emotional gravitas and intensely excited drama. As she awaits Samson's arrival, a pantomimed interaction with gun-toting Philistines followed by her scene with a groping High Priest of Dagon, menacingly sung by Latvian baritone Egils Silins, suggests that her betrayal is coerced by villains who abuse her as much as they abuse the Hebrews. Her summoning of the Philistines to apprehend Samson is achingly hesitant; she melts into real tears and helpless sobs as he is taken down. In Act III, when she addresses him blinded and imprisoned, the lines do not come out in the usual cruel mockery but instead register deep regret and profound loss. In the end it is she who douses the "temple" of the Philistines with gasoline and brings down the show in blazing fire, almost as much to spare herself and Samson more pain than to punish their tormentors for their vile debaucheries. Paris's music director Philippe Jordan led a powerful performance with his signature light touch.

Giacomo Puccini, *Madama Butterfly*
Milan, La Scala, December 7, 2016

La Scala has opened its 2016-2017 season with Puccini's greatest tearjerker – the sad love story of an American sailor who impulsively marries a Japanese geisha girl only to leave her behind, find himself a "real" American wife, and return three years later to discover that he and the abandoned geisha have a son. When he asks her to turn over the child, she embraces ritual suicide as the only way out.

Such melodrama is hardly out of place at a La Scala opening, arguably Europe's most important annual cultural event. This year was especially tense, for only a few days before Italian Prime Minister Matteo Renzi decisively lost a constitutional referendum that would have concentrated more power in the lower house of parliament and thus himself. Widely seen as a public vote of no-confidence in his leadership, the results led him to a tearful resignation announcement. Neither Renzi nor Italy's president Sergio Mattarella appeared in what used to be called the Royal Box, which was festooned for the premiere with imitation cherry blossoms (La Scala's general director Alexander Pereira read a platitudinous greeting from the president before the performance). Security was tight as always, with platoons of regular police and *carabinieri* carefully monitoring the area around the theater. The usual anti-globalization protest was a bit muted this year, with only a few dozen red flag-waving malcontents cordoned off across the piazza. Inside, the theater teemed with all manner of Italian and international celebrities, including ex-King Juan Carlos of Spain, who was, alas, relegated to an ordinary box and not seated in the former royal one. One of Italy's major television channels broadcast the performance to an audience that included an estimated one-fifth of all Italians.

When *Madama Butterfly* premiered here in February 1904, it was a catastrophic failure. Puccini described the experience as a "lynching" and never personally returned to work at La Scala. He withdrew his opera from performance after the failed premiere and reworked it in no fewer than four revisions before settling on what we know today as the opera's definitive version. La Scala's new production takes us back to the absolute original, which Milan's theater has not performed since that disastrous evening 112 years ago (even the opera's revised version was not performed at La Scala until 1925, the year after Puccini's death). It was a bold decision, which comes on the heels of the company's 2015 production of Puccini's unfinished final opera *Turandot* featuring the alternate ending of Luciano Berio. Puccini's descendants, especially his granddaughter Simonetta, vociferously criticized the decision to take on the original *Butterfly*, claiming that revisiting the initial version violated the composer's wishes. The Italian media has quoted her more diplomatic statement that she "appreciates" the opera's first edition but "prefers" the canonical one.

Butterfly's horrific initial reception was probably orchestrated by Puccini's detractors, who were out to ruin him and his music publisher. Nevertheless, it is easy to see why the original version could not stand. Composed in two acts rather than the better known three, it contains a distracting amount of extraneous material, both musical and dramatic. Three crucial scenes – Butterfly's wedding to Pinkerton, their love duet, and her suicide – unfold languorously, the first two with extended dialogues that vitiate the drama. Sometimes this is just a nuisance, including, for example, an annoying run around for the rambunctious child of one of Butterfly's relatives as the nuptials are performed. Elsewhere, more attention than necessary falls upon the minor characters. Butterfly's tippling uncle Yakusidé is drawn out in relief, with a castigating chorus that mocks his love of sake. Butterfly's religious uncle, the Bonze, who turns up in the opera's final version, makes his booming entrance to denounce her conversion to Christianity after earlier dialogue builds him up as wise and reasonable. Greater disappointment arrived with the interruption of the rapturous love duet by blander statements of Butterfly's doubts. It struck some in the audience as truer to life, but is that really why we go to the opera? The suicide scene was so drawn out that one almost wished she would just get it over with. Not all of the early material was useless – I liked the pronounced scoring of harps to highlight Butterfly's innocence and sincerity – but most of it was dross better left abandoned.

Puccini's later additions were sorely missed. The most glaring case, then as now, is the absence of the tenor aria "Addio, fiorito asil," in which Pinkerton, in his only solo piece, reclaims a shred of humanity in a tenderly regretful farewell to his life with Butterfly. While some believe that Puccini's inclusion of the aria seems forced and artificial, without it Pinkerton comes off as an almost unbelievably unsympathetic cad. The original first act dialogue, moreover, makes him sound rather racist, dismissing the Japanese as "silly" ("*sciocchi*") and characterizing the household servants as "*musi*" ("snouts," colloquially used in Italian in the same way gangsters in old movies refer to people they don't like as "mugs"). As a character, he is a bounder much more easily dismissed as a sex tourist than he would become in later versions, and even a bit of a bore. The role of Butterfly, whose original suicide scene already suffers from off putting *longueurs*, is disappointingly disserved by the absence of her life-ending high notes.

Latvian director Alvis Hermanis designed an invitingly picaresque production with some nods to recent fads in stagecraft. The decor and costumes derive from classic Japanese prints, with warm colors predominating. The chorus of Butterfly's family members moves largely in pantomime taken from Kabuki theater. Hermanis's sets yield the three-tiered shadow box effect that is quite current (think of the Metropolitan Opera's season opening production of *Tristan und Isolde*). Most action unfolds on the first level, with the upper tiers reserved for the intrusion of the Bonze in Act I and the brief appearance of Pinkerton's American wife in Act III. At other times the extra space allows for print-inspired projections of Nagasaki Bay or the flowers with which Butterfly calls upon her steadfast servant Suzuki to inundate her when Pinkerton's ship returns. Often it is simply a translucent area that focuses attention on the drama below. The props are mostly simple, with hints of Butterfly's Americanization – a sewing machine, a picture of Jesus, and so on – inhabiting the second act.

La Scala assembled a superb young cast. In the title role the voluptuous Uruguayan soprano Maria José Siri floated gorgeous piano notes with diaphanous elegance. The signature aria "Un bel dì" rested delicately on a seemingly effortless technique to deliver the character's fragility reinforced by true love. One could only wish that she had the chance to sing the final high notes, but the limitation is the original score's and not the artist's. Her Pinkerton, the American tenor Bryan Hymel, possesses a vast, buoyant voice that captured the role's seductive ardor with intoxicating energy. The steady baritone Carlos Álvarez took on the part of the American consul Sharpless with alluring resonance. Tenor Carlo Bosi skillfully voiced the part of the marriage broker Goro, and Annalisa Stroppa's Suzuki struck purring low notes that portend a great future. La Scala's new music director Riccardo Chailly, who arrived last year, led a studied performance that preserved as much of the passion as the flawed original score would allow. No nuance was wasted. Musical excellence alone justified the thirteen-minute final ovation, but it was worthwhile to see what will likely remain a curatorial exercise in exploring Puccini's *oeuvre*.

Giuseppe Verdi, *Nabucco*
New York, Metropolitan Opera, December 12, 2016

Nabucco was Giuseppe Verdi's first important success, but the work's musical oddities, dramatic flaws, and Biblical kitsch long kept it out of the standard repertoire. The Met only saw its first production in 1960 and has revisited it just once, with Elijah Moshinsky's production of 2001. Its revival this season was noteworthy as it featured the Met's music director emeritus James Levine on the podium, now long into the twilight of his career. On stage the title role fell to Plácido Domingo, the veteran tenor, conductor, arts administrator, and, more recently, baritone of sorts. Now well into their seventies, both men bring decades of experience and stardom.

The big question was whether these sunset deployments could really work in practice. The rousing ovations suggested hope, or at least support, from a large segment of the audience. Alas, the effort portended the end of an era. Levine's health problems have been in the news for years. His recovery was applauded and heralded. His occasional performances – a few stage productions a year and, until last season, reduced work with the Met Orchestra at Carnegie Hall – unfold with flashes of the lustrous direction well remembered from his prime. Last night the orchestra was in its customary good place. But Levine's direction lagged, often sounding mechanical rather than dynamic and pedantic rather than inspired. Domingo, too, was out of his best sorts. The obvious problem is one of a tenor singing a part that should properly go to a sturdy baritone. In the past if one could simply accept that it was Plácido Domingo singing, then the evening could still pass quite enjoyably. Here apparent physical limitations enforced an almost quaint "stand and sing" approach, even at Nabucco's nastier scenes as a conqueror. It should be said, however, that there were also beautiful moments. In the Act IV aria "Dio di Giuda," in which the insanity-stricken ruler pleads with the god of the Hebrews to restore his sound mind, the sonorous, cello-like voice we all remember emerged in excellent relief.

The remaining cast had only one real standout in mezzo Jamie Barton, who sang the often overlooked role of Fenena. Russell Thomas's Ismaele, her love interest, had some pleasant moments but tended to be overwhelmed by the orchestra. The central and extremely difficult role of Abigaille went to the Met's stand-by Verdian dramatic soprano Liudmyla Monastyrska. The voice is big and wide-ranging enough to accommodate the part's leaping high notes and grumbling lows. The middle range singing wafted with the occasionally majestic moment. Abigaille's Act II aria "Anch'io dischiuso un giorno," a plaintive memory of the kindness of which she has shorn herself, was well balanced and even touching. The more challenging elements, however, tended to lack focus. An overreliance on vibrato marred many of the choicest lines. The cadenzas betrayed distracting pitch problems.

Despite these tepid results, no one can fault the Met's superb chorus, which delivered the famous "Va, pensiero" in perfect harmony. Encored in this production, it was the evening's most vivid memory. Moshinsky's highly traditional production, based on tiered stone blocks that suggest sites of the ancient world, does well enough. But it might be time for an updated effort and a more current cast.

Giaochino Rossini, *Il Barbiere di Siviglia*
New York, Metropolitan Opera, January 9, 2017

Rossini's famous comedy stands as one of the few truly successful productions mounted at the Metropolitan Opera over the past decade. While most new productions have suffered from directors in other media coming to the opera for the first time, the celebrated Broadway director

Bartlett Sher scored a hit with his *Barbiere*, which is revived with relative frequency and has been adapted by the Met in an abbreviated English-language "family version." The full-length original Italian version has now returned for a healthy run of ten performances, the first of which is under review here. The use of space – with entrances from the audience and an extension of the stage around the orchestra pit – is still an effective vehicle for Rossini's comedy. But unhappily the production now looks less luminous and even a bit tired.

Fresh voices help. The dynamic young soprano Pretty Yende, barely over thirty, sang an enchanting Rosina. A creamy tone recalled a younger Kathleen Battle in the part and energized what can be overly familiar music with delightful melismas and expansively intricate coloratura runs. The character emerged playfully but without going over the top. Purists may take umbrage, as at least one towering bore did in my presence at intermission, but the thunderous ovations spoke for themselves. The role of Rosina's suitor Almaviva fell to the newly famous Mexican tenor Javier Camarena. Just two years off his unexpected and highly praised breakout Met performances, he, too, radiated an uncommon sweetness of tone that enraptured much of the audience. Command of the higher register was not always strong, however, and there were some strained notes in the early moments. But as he went on with the evening, his confidence grew and his sound bloomed with more effulgent harmonies.

Peter Mattei may be the most pleasing lyric baritone before the public today, and his Figaro was sublime. At times the pairing of his stentorian voice with hammy drama recalled why *Barbiere* can be a challenge, but it is hard to imagine a better singer in the role. Maurizio Muraro's Bartolo evoked but did not quite equal the comedic menace of the late John Del Carlo, who commanded the basso buffo repertoire at the Met in the decade or so before his untimely death last fall. Karolina Pilou made a charming company debut in the role of Bartolo's housekeeper Berta.

Maurizio Benini has been known to conduct more performances in one week than there are days of week. He led a steady but not exactly thrilling performance.

Luigi Cherubini, *Medea*
Lebanon, Al Bustan Festival, February 26, 2017

As the rest of the Middle East swirls in chaos, Lebanon remains a peaceful eye in the center of the storm,[18] peaceful enough to boast world renowned fashion designers, powerwalking yuppies, a slow food movement, and, of course, Uber. Among the trappings of modern cosmopolitanism, one even finds that bucolic refuge of so many Western urbanites, the out-of-town classical music festival. Mainly located in the hills above Beirut, scenic locations combining the country's storied past with its dramatic natural beauty draw convoys of SUVs – and even a few humble Ubers – to a variety of offerings. Operating since 1994, the stately Al Bustan Festival presents five weeks of music developed around a theme. This year it is "Queens and Empresses of the Orient," a mixture of historic and mythological women who inspired great works of (almost entirely) Western art. The festival program usually features one opera, sometimes chosen well outside the standard repertoire. This time Euterpe's favor daringly fell on Luigi Cherubini's stormy *Medea* (1797), given in the Italian version introduced at La Scala in 1909 and popularized as a vehicle for Maria Callas in the 1950s.

Lest any university-based pedants raise tired hackles of "Orientalism" to denounce the festival theme, the program's introduction expands on the very current point that while women played important roles in the Middle East's ancient past (there are evenings dedicated to Semiramis, Cleopatra, and Zenobia, among others), their current involvement is marginal. This is an acute concern of the festival's president Myrna Boustany, the first woman elected to the Lebanese parliament, a body that is at present barely three percent female. Among *le tout Beyrouth* who sponsor and attend (many of whom still sport French given names), however, there seemed to be little more concern than scrutinizing each other's outfits and silently estimating the authenticity of the various fur garments on display as Lebanon shakes off its mild winter.

---

[18] Lebanon's tranquility did not last. About two and a half years later, the country collapsed in a continuum of crises that remain unresolved and worsening as of this writing.

Medea is Cherubini's best known work, which is not saying much given his steep fall into obscurity. His lack of renown, however, belies his sweeping reputation during his lifetime. Beethoven called him the greatest musician of his era, presumably surpassing even himself. A couple of generations later Brahms described *Medea* as "the highest peak of dramatic music." Cherubini's storied career took him from promising and well supported Italian beginnings to an adulthood spent almost entirely in France, where he proved equally adept at weathering the storm of revolution, waiting out Napoleonic uncertainty, and settling back into official good graces during the Bourbon Restoration. Exceedingly famous, he ended his days as the director of the Paris Conservatoire and the stoic composer of a *Requiem* mass for his own funeral. His music departed from Italian and French convention by hewing more toward the dramatic. A precursor not only of Beethoven, but of Weber, Marschner, and ultimately Wagner and others who would react angrily against the *bel canto* tradition, Cherubini stood as a kind of godfather to the compositional school that developed tight harmonics and orchestral shade to explore the inner lives of characters and fundamental truth of unfolding drama. Only Cherubini's irascible temper seems to have doomed him to near oblivion. Hector Berlioz, who emerged as France's leading composer in the decades after Cherubini's death, clashed with him at the Conservatoire and described him in his influential memoirs as an outdated pedant with no relevance to the further development of music. The composer Adolphe Adam more wryly observed that Cherubini was in fact even-tempered – because he was always angry. When he died in 1842, he was a man many preferred to forget regardless of his artistic merits.

In the genealogy of opera, *Medea* anticipated not only the stylistic innovations of the nineteenth century's solidly Romantic composers, but even plot elements of more familiar works. Presenting a mythical subject taken from Euripides via the French classical dramatist Pierre Corneille, Cherubini's opera relates the demented tale of its eponymous character, who is betrayed by Jason (Giasone in the opera, he of the Golden Fleece) and takes her revenge by killing their two children after poisoning Giasone's new bride Glauce and torching the temple where they were to be married. Like Bellini's *Norma*, she is a wronged woman with two children by the man who abandoned her and badly wants to recover his fidelity. Her murder of Glauce looks forward to Cilea's Adriana Lecouvreur, who was also done in by poisonous gifts (flowers for Adriana; robe, crown, and jewels for Glauce). Looking forward to the malevolent Ortrud in Wagner's *Lohengrin*, Medea invokes pagan deities to steel her resolve and deliver her vengeance. Her sheer feminine villainy places her in the vanguard of an operatic tradition that would grow to include Venus, Dalila, Salome, Elektra, and Turandot, among others. In 1797, just a decade after the premiere of *Don Giovanni*, she was an altogether new type for stages more accustomed to diaphanous Mozart heroines and *opera seria* populated by antiquity's virtuous women.

The Al Bustan Festival can pull in impressive talent to bring the gift of opera to the Middle East. In Svetla Vassileva, the role of Medea received an excitingly sustained performance with soaring high notes and a level of emotional distress that suggested a serious study of Callas's famous recording of the opera. Lorenzo Decaro's Giasone resonated with a buoyant, clarion tone but at times seemed a bit forced. Rather more solid was the talented Georgian bass Goderdzi Janelidze's Creonte, the father of Glauce, whose authority drives much of the action but cannot prevent its terrible denouement. Ilona Domnich's Glauce seemed to lack balance, but this seemed appropriate for a woman in her awkward position. The role of Medea's slave Neride gave room for the impressive technique and eloquent delivery of the lovely Italian mezzo Daniela Pini. Maestro Gianluca Marcianò, Al Bustan's artistic director, did what he could with the Festival Orchestra, which brought only occasional flair to Cherubini's sophisticated score. Choruses performed by the well rehearsed choir of Serbia's National Theatre added powerfully to the drama.

Georges Bizet, *Carmen*
Lyric Opera of Chicago, March 16, 2017

As the storms of winter yield to mild springtime, Chicago has rounded out the main part of its season with this tried and true revival. At first glance, standard repertoire may not make for exciting criticism these days. But casts are everything and Lyric's talent for assembling impressive performance rosters has reached lofty heights.

Carmen has never been one of my favorites. I once even authored an article about people who do not like it and why. But Rob Ashford's new production, mounted jointly with Houston Grand Opera, neatly cuts out most of the overdone *espagnolerie* and delivers raw drama – the stuff opera is made of. Vaguely updated to the time of the Spanish Civil War (as so many *Carmens* now are) and yet refreshingly free of political baggage, the more modern stylings of David Rockwell's sets were serviceable without too much distraction. Ashford's own choreography added an unusually lithe expression to sequences that can become too bogged down in "atmosphere." Particularly original was the emergence of male dancers from under the long trains of their female counterparts during the opening music of Act IV.

A split cast yielded the title role at this performance to the stunning Lyric Opera debut of the Georgian mezzo-soprano Anita Rachvelishvili, for whom Carmen was a breakout part when she filled in for another artist to make her surprise debut at La Scala. Summoning smoky, sultry tones, she mastered Carmen's music so impeccably that she arguably stands as the most exciting dramatic mezzo-soprano singing before the public today. Rachvelishvili's vocal performance was no less impressive than her astonishingly original delivery of the part's dramatic demands. This is a Carmen in conflict – not the fickle tease or clichéd *femme fatale* we almost always see – but rather a vivid anti-heroine torn between her professed desire for freedom and her feelings for Don José, which are both real and deep. The character's cutting lines and vicious behavior are set in an alluring relief that masks a hidden vulnerability few performers ever really explore. When José's own forgotten amour Micaëla wrenches him out of his conflict with Carmen and her new lover, the toreador Escamillo, the gypsy seductress collapses in laughter at his temper but then bursts into revealing sobs after he departs.

Rachvelishvili was wisely partnered with the robust tenor Brandon Jovanovich, who likewise offered an unusual reading of the hapless Don José. Normally a proud man moved to the opera's signature crime of passion, here he cut a ridiculous figure – certainly the first Don José I have ever heard anyone laugh at. The vocal part's ardor does not always lend itself to this characterization, but close attention to his words and actions does reinforce the interpretation that Carmen's spurned lover is at heart a pathetic milksop whose puerile temperament, petty jealousy, and sheer neediness drive her away more reliably than anything capricious in her psyche. I wondered what would have happened if he had just ignored her. Jovanovich's French was not always convincing, but the clarion tones and muscular ascents compensated amply. Christian Van Horn's swaggering Escamillo tended toward caricature, but he was a real enough rival to keep the action moving.

It is usual to end reviews of *Carmen* with a perfunctory note on the part of Micaëla, the "good girl" no one really cares about, who seems forever condemned to inhabit the shadows of the stronger characters around her. In another stunning Lyric debut, however, the rising soprano Eleonora Buratto employed crystal clear tonalities to render this otherwise forgettable character something more than memorable. Indeed, she was the only Micaëla to whom I ever recall having paid much attention. The young Latvian conductor Ainars Rubikis led a well-paced performance that allowed his stars to shine.

Richard Wagner, *Parsifal*
Vienna State Opera, April 6, 2017

The Easter Season occasions performances of Wagner's final and most mystical opera, *Parsifal*. Long a challenge even to diehard Wagnerians who object to its static drama, musical *longueurs*, and deep symbolism, the opera's champions take it very seriously, often because they celebrate those very features. Vienna has launched a new production by the Latvian director Alvis Hermanis. Much of the Viennese audience still dresses in solemn black, and almost unanimously maintained silence after Act I, following a tradition that originated with the work's premiere in 1882, which holds that it is wrong to applaud after a scene of great religious solemnity. The few poor souls who did applaud were mercilessly shushed.

Suffused with Christian meaning but also borrowing heavily from Eastern religion via Wagner's reading of the philosopher Arthur Schopenhauer, who advocated renunciation of earthly desire to find the path to spiritual enlightenment, *Parsifal* is at heart a coming of age story. Its hero is foretold in a prophecy as a "pure fool" who will save the knights of the Holy Grail from ruin by achieving wisdom though compassion and healing their king Amfortas, who suffers from a wound that will not heal. Parsifal's innocence enables him to defeat the evil sorcerer Klingsor's magic, resist the diabolical Kundry's attempt to seduce and destroy him, and recover the Holy Spear, which Klingsor had used to inflict Amfortas's injury. After a long period of wandering, Parsifal returns to the knights a wise hero bearing healing and redemption.

Hermanis's concept provocatively embraces the city of Vienna itself in its long tradition as a center of psychiatry and neuroscience. This *Parsifal* unfolds in the neuropathology ward of a Catholic hospital. The sets identify it as the "Wagner Hospital," but it is visibly the Secessionist-style Steinhof hospital (designed by the architect Otto Wagner, who was not a relative of the composer), which was originally one of the city's leading psychiatric hospitals. Gurnemanz is a chief doctor presiding over "knights" who are delusional mental patients. The opera's prelude begins when Gurnemanz sets a needle on a record on his office phonograph. Rather than intone his long narrations about the knights' history and recent plight, he reads them to the patients from a story book. Its illustrated pages are projected on the rear wall. Kundry, here another of the patients, enters flailing wildly in a straightjacket and is confined to a hospital bed within a cage. Parsifal enters as another delusional patient, his armor and bow serving as props for his fantasy rather than accoutrements of reckless youth. The Grail rite that ends Act I is the ward's coffee hour, with the "Grail" presented as a crystaline model brain that rejuvenates the patients through what clinicians call "compassion energy."

Klingsor's evil machinations destroy the knights and seize the Grail unfold as the unethical doings of a rival doctor. If Gurnemanz's ward is about healing, Klingsor's is about control. As Act II opens on his "realm," he is busily performing the latest in a series of bloody lobotomies. We later see his Flower Maidens identically costumed as obedient automatons. He brings Kundry to consciousness with electric shocks. Their catty exchange is not the standard battle of wits, but an analysis session with Kundry sprawled on his office sofa. This is where we realize Hermanis's vision that she, rather than Parsifal, is the opera's central character. Her seduction scene is a carefully supervised experiment as she indulges in her own fantasies of salvation and redemption. Klingsor's confrontation with Parsifal plays to her neurosis. When Parsifal seizes the Holy Spear - presented here as a giant orbitoclast (the surgical probe used to lobotomize patients) - and pronounces doom for Klingsor's realm, the doctor merely nods as Kundry returns to the couch under his studied clinical gaze. It should be no surprise that the production's resolution has little to do with transcendent spirituality or the restoration of a damaged sacred order. When Parsifal returns in Act III, the Grail rite is playacted with solemnity, but its actual performance goes to Kundry, who is delivered from her madness and happily leaves the hospital as the others remain in their delusional states under a frustrated Gurnemanz.

   Hermanis's production could be derided as yet another "Eurotrash" Wagner production. Yet it asks profound questions about the nature of self and perception, the role of myth in our psyches, and other quintessentially Wagnerian concepts. I was never bored by what I was seeing, but what I was hearing thrilled me more. The production's most notable musical feature is the star soprano Nina Stemme's first run of performances as Kundry. Possessing a cool, full bodied Nordic tone, she deployed it here to encompass the part's essential lower range. With flawless delivery and perhaps the most expressive eyes in opera today, she brought the character vividly to life regardless of production constraints.

   Christopher Ventris took the title role with commanding vigor, though the pacing sometimes left him a bit underpowered. The role is long and demanding, and Ventris seemed to hold back in the Act II exchanges with Kundry to save his voice for the glorious music in the opera's final act. Kwangchul Youn sang Gurnemanz with dignified authority and low notes that never got lost in the muddy reverberations often heard in the role. Jochen Schmeckenbecher was a stentorian Klingsor who used his dark timbres to play up the psychopathic dimensions of the role as presented in this production. It was only Gerald Finley's Amfortas that seemed a bit out of place. The voice sat rather too high for the part and occasionally battled the orchestra to be heard. Semyon Bychkov favored slower tempos, but the Staatsoper's orchestra knows this music so well that every attenuated note shined with resplendent beauty.

Alban Berg, *Wozzeck*
Paris Opera, May 9, 2017

As a rather stale opera season approaches its end, few exciting new productions have swept Europe. But Paris is presenting a respectable run of one of the twentieth century's defining works, Alban Berg's *Wozzeck*. Having premiered in 1925, Berg's opera is an adaptation of the German playwright Georg Büchner's slightly differently named play *Woyzeck* (1837), which the author never completed in his short lifetime (he died of typhus at age 23) and was only pieced together from fragments. Büchner's early demise did not keep him out of the pantheon of German literary heroes. With a revival of his writings later in the nineteenth century, and the most important German literary prize named for him from 1923, he struck an enduring chord.

His legacy still does. Büchner, who closely followed the utopian socialists who preceded Karl Marx, made searing points about the neuroses that arise from the antagonisms inherent in skewed social relations. Wozzeck, Berg's pathetic protagonist, is a poor solider who must support his amour Marie and their out-of-wedlock child. His meager pay is insufficient, so he earns extra income by performing valet services for his captain and participating in the regimental doctor's medical experiments. His degradation, combined with Marie's insatiable sensuality, leads to her attraction to a handsome drum major, who bests Wozzeck in a bar fight and drives him to murder his faithless mistress in a fit of jealousy. His guilt leads him to a watery grave as he psychotically searches for the knife he used to kill Marie. At the end their uncomprehending child is left to the mockery of his peers.

The deranged plot is not difficult to imagine in the pages or on the screens of today's yellow press, which just loves to report on the failed lives of the sick and sad. Christoph Marthaler's production premiered in 2008, the year of the most recent world financial crisis, and the trappings are modern enough. Here the story is updated to a bleak present, with the action confined to a tent in the courtyard of a vast brick building that has no apparent exits. Rows of picnic tables suggest one of those indoor beer gardens visible anywhere between Metz and St. Petersburg. The military atmosphere emerges in the watered-down uniforms of contemporary Euroarmies, with Marie and the other dependent civilians attired a level or two above street people. Cheerless accoutrements like fading balloons, a rusting playground, and a slide that inclines through an oversized clown's mouth (into which Wozzeck later disposes of Marie's corpse) suggest ancillary family life. This *Wozzeck* is thus a thoroughly contemporary drama unfolding somewhere in the widening crevices of a decayed European welfare state.

The production comes most alive, however, not in the traditional Brechtian/Marxist reading – which holds that Wozzeck is the traumatized product of a corrupt and abusive society - but rather in the more holistic Romantic tradition that democratically extends neurotic victimization to all of society's members. Here the captain and doctor – voiced by the nervously pinched tenor of Stephan Rügamer and the still powerful bass of the veteran singer Kurt Rydl – are just as bonkers as their victim. Indeed, the alienation and atomization are so pervasive that one wonders whether they even realize or care that they are just as easily victimized by the same system that destroys Wozzeck's psyche.

The accomplished baritone Johannes Martin Kränzle left little doubt about the extent of the title character's problems. Its vocal line is one of the most formidable challenges in the repertoire, but Kränzle moved through it with stunning agility. As his Marie, the German soprano Gun-Brit Barkmin delivered a glittering performance. She was powerful without giving in to stridency, incisive without becoming shrill. The rising tenor Štefan Margita, rapidly becoming the reigning Loge in Wagner's *Das Rheingold*, rounded out the cast with a well voiced but suitably obnoxious Drum Major. Under the baton of the splendid conductor Michael Schønwandt, the Paris Opera Orchestra gave a precise and at times even hair-raising reading of the score.

Giuseppe Verdi, *Don Carlo*
London, Royal Opera House, May 12, 2017

More thrills were on display in London, where Giuseppe Verdi's monumental *Don Carlo* – conceived as a French grand opera in five acts and (at least originally) with a ballet – returned tonight in a revival of Sir Nicholas Hytner's production. Shared with the Metropolitan Opera, it opened to mixed reviews in London in 2008 and New York two years later. Rather than fall for Iberian sumptuousness, the sets are stylized to accommodate rapid scene changes. Sometimes this approach works – simple walls with rows of open windows suggest the characters' entrapment in an existence defined by strictures and expectations that they cannot escape. But just as often it is hard to take. The flexibility that Hytner may have thought an asset gives us tombs that almost comically slide in and out, garden barriers that evoke legos, and other visual absurdities that detract from the drama.

Happily, this revival eliminated the original production's weirdest feature - a completely invented speaking role for a Dominican priest who calls on the heretics in the *auto-da-fé* scene to repent before angrily condemning them to the flames. Originally, this intrusion blotted out the stirring orchestral music that instills sympathy for the Inquisition's victims, but now the character is refreshingly just a mute affectation. Gone, too, is the actual burning of the heretics, which used to happen behind a massive translucent image of Christ's face. Now the Jesus image remains opaque as the brutal act happens out of sight behind it. I was of two minds about the change. On the one hand, one does want to see the scene's bloody manifestation in all its horror, as the anticlerical Verdi intended. On the other hand, the mixture of religious imagery with a cruel act committed in Christ's name always did seem gratuitously preachy.

Casting rose to a high standard, but was, alas, not free of trouble. Both soprano Krassimira Stoyanova and baritone Ludovic Tézier, cast as Elizabeth and Rodrigo, respectively, dropped out of the revival as opening night approached. Fortunately, this was not the fate of the rising star tenor Bryan Hymel, arguably the finest *tenore di forza* singing today, who made his role debut as Don Carlo. Ardent in the title character's feeling and desperate in his struggle against cruel fate, Hymel's brilliant, ringing tone recalled the heartiest singing of the late Franco Corelli. His is a talent to watch and a voice to savor. Kristin Lewis replaced Stoyanova and did a credible job as Elizabeth, Don Carlo's betrothed who must then marry his old father, King Phillip II. The voice has a bloom recognizable from her singing in Italian theaters, but the top notes tended to waver in their full deployment. The same was true of German baritone Christoph Pohl, who sang the role of Carlo's best friend but ultimate betrayer Rodrigo – a noble middle register and solid low notes did not presage the exciting highs that a true Verdi baritone can produce.

The remaining cast is tasked with tormenting the heroes, and for the most part they reached monstrous heights of power and intimidation. The role of Phillip II went to the still rather young Russian bass-baritone Ildar Abdrazakov. Anyone singing the part today will fall under the inevitable shadow of comparisons to the great Ferruccio Furlanetto and, before him, Cesare Siepi. Abdrazakov could not, alas, equal them in scare power. His real strength lay in the character's unexpected vulnerability. Availing himself of a truly baritonal vocal line, he delivered the seminal aria of masculine despair, "Ella giammai m'amò" – Phillip's recognition that his wife never loved him, with affecting pathos. Paired with the much scarier bass of the veteran Georgian singer Paata Burchuladze's Grand Inquisitor, the subsequent and deeply meaningful confrontation between throne and altar resounded as well as any in the opera's recorded performance history. Mezzo Ekaterina Semenchuk put striking power into the role of the king's mistress Princess Eboli, who, to make the opera even more complicated, also loves Don Carlo and moves the plot along by revealing his love for Elizabeth when he spurns her. Semenchuk has been around for a while, but her warm, burnished voice only seems to become more powerful as time goes on.

Covent Garden's orchestra is not among the best for Verdi's challenging scores, but Bertrand de Billy led it credibly enough to support the mostly superior talent he commanded on stage.

Giuseppe Verdi, *Otello*
London, Royal Opera House, July 2, 2017

"Well, if he doesn't cancel...," snapped the sour quip of opera cognoscenti all over the world. "He," of course, is the renowned German tenor Jonas Kaufmann, whose propensity to cancel performances over the past few years has disappointed many audiences and done some damage to his reputation and career. New York has not seen him for years, and will not see him as originally planned next season. But here in London, despite all the catty doubts, Kaufmann kept his commitment and made a stunning role debut in the title part of Verdi's *Otello*. The composer had wanted to call the opera *Iago*, since it is the great Shakespearean villain who really drives the action, but the tragic anti-hero is so compelling that there was no sensible alternative. And what a role it is – its high tessitura mixes with a thrillingly desperate need for baritonal authority. The vocal challenge and extreme dramatic requirements make performing the part the highest aspiration for any dramatic tenor. Since the opera's premiere in 1887, very few have mastered it.

It is no exaggeration to say that Jonas Kaufmann falls into the category of performer – probably not exceeding the single digits over the past century – who can rightly claim to be in the gold star category of Otellos. With bracing tonalities well suited to his Wagner roles, Kaufmann drew on a smoky, mahogany sound to deliver the role with a charge not heard since the heady days of Plácido Domingo's triumphs of more than two decades ago. From his one-line entrance, "Esultate!" ("Rejoice!"), it was immediately clear that Kaufmann follows firmly in the tradition not only of Domingo but also of Jon Vickers, Ramon Vinay, Mario del Monaco, and Giovanni Martinelli, arguably the only other superb exponents of the role available on audible record.

Dramatically, Kaufmann offered a studied performance with tremendous poise that avoided the all too common tendency to degenerate into soapy melodrama. Indeed, in Verdi as in Shakespeare, one of the work's most harped upon weaknesses is that Otello morphs from noble hero to homicidal maniac in the course of a few hours. Kaufmann's inherent dignity allows for an intriguingly cerebral processing of his predicament. Murdering Desdemona seems almost a necessity. When he pounds on the floor after "Dio mi potevi scagliar," the character's great aria of regret and deluded realization, it is less out of uncontrollable pain than a careful focus on duty.

London audiences will long remember Kaufmann's debut, but his fellow principals were exceptionally well chosen. Maria Agresta is moving on from the bel canto roles for which she has been best known to more sophisticated dramatic parts. Her Desdemona was an entrancing mélange of soft, creamy tones delivered on what could only have been perfect pitch. The Willow Song and "Ave Maria" preceding her death were mesmerizing. Marco Vratgona took on the role of Iago after Ludovic Tézier dropped out. The performance was solid and affecting. Just as Kaufmann did not overdramatize his damaged character, so, too, did Vratogna avoid the temptation to turn Iago into a snarling villain. Supported by thrilling ascents, this Iago was a practiced psychopath, remaining alluringly controlled and even courtly up until the moment of his exposure. Normally called upon to flee the scene in a pathetic attempt to escape justice, here he slashes his wife Emilia's throat and stabs Montano and other courtiers before being apprehended.

Keith Warner's production seems to be yet another of those stage efforts better designed for the movie theater broadcast than for those willing to pay the price to attend live. Almost monochromatic, it features sleek walls with oblong apertures that rarely serve any purpose. A statue of the iconic Venetian lion appears in various stages of destruction to shadow Otello's descent into wrath. The effect is almost comically obvious. But for the most part it was a relief not to have too much distraction from the performance's excellent singing, enhanced as it was by the brilliant choral leadership of the newly arrived (from Deutsche Oper Berlin) William Spaulding. Antonio Pappano led a measured performance, though the Royal Opera's orchestra rarely rises to truly Italianate levels of passion.

Modest Mussorgsky, *Boris Godunov*
Deutsche Oper Berlin, July 7, 2017

Modest Mussorgsky died of alcoholism at the youthful age of 42, leaving his magnum opus subject to reinterpretation. *Boris Godunov*, an adaptation of an 1826 play by Alexander Pushkin that for political reasons remained banned from the stage for the next forty years, has come to be regarded as the quintessential Russian opera.

A trusted lieutenant of Ivan the Terrible (reigned 1533-1584), Godunov hailed from a line of Tatars who had come into Muscovite service as the Mongol legacy collapsed into warring successor states that their former Russian vassals eventually gobbled up. Anticipating the reign of Ivan's feeble son and successor Fedor I (1584-1598), Godunov positioned himself even closer to the throne by marrying off his sister to the new ruler and enjoyed broad powers of government. The suspicious death of Prince Dmitrii, Ivan the Terrible's younger surviving son (he had killed the eldest of three in a fit of rage), set the stage for an even greater power grab. When Fedor died childless in 1598, Godunov had himself proclaimed Tsar and reigned until he died a natural but stressed-out death seven years later.

Ever since, the curious circumstances of Dmitrii's demise gave rise to the conspiracy theory that his death was a cynical contract killing ordered by Godunov to clear his path to the throne. Further rumor held that Dmitrii had escaped and would return to save Russia. As Godunov sat uneasily on his throne, a runaway monk called Grigorii Otrepiev fled to neighboring Poland, claimed that he was the murdered Prince Dmitrii, and marched back supported by a Polish army. Godunov died as the False Dmitrii approached Moscow, leaving him to seize power. He lasted for about a year before he was overthrown and killed by restive Muscovites, but the story remained a powerful one, and at least two other false Dmitriis emerged. Only a national struggle against the residual Polish occupation force united Russia sufficiently to restore order under the new Romanov dynasty, ironically chosen because its leader at the time was considered the weakest available candidate.

Like so many aspects of Russia's culture and history – including the reign of the historical Boris Godunov himself – there is no definitive version of the opera. The Imperial Theaters found Mussorgsky's original seven-scene pastiche too somber and ordered him to produce additional material to furnish a romantic love story between Dmitrii and the Polish princess Marina Mniszek, whom the pretender in history did actually marry. Ever since, discoveries of new manuscript material, re-orchestrations of the music, and re-sequencing of scenes have intrigued musicologists interested in realizing the most accurate possible version of the composer's true intentions.

Richard Jones's production follows the visceral original score of 1869, which did not see the light of day until it was discovered in a Soviet archive in 1928. The basic story unfolds in essentially the same way, with only a few noticeable changes in the libretto. The major difference from other editions of the seven-scene version is the omission of the final

Kromy Forest scene, in which a rebellious crowd – often interpreted as "revolutionary" – hails the arriving Prince Dmitrii. The 1869 version ends starkly with Boris's death, a scene of pitiable contrition expressed as he tries to warn his ill-fated son Fedor about the evils of the world and burdens of the crown.

Jones's production is not especially inventive. Stylized walls featuring images of bells dominate all the scenes. The obvious reference is to the death knells that emerge from the orchestra during Boris's death scene, which are foreshadowed as early as the equally magnificent coronation scene that opens the opera. Costumes are not temporally specific, but relatively simple garments that could easily have been worn anywhere from the actual time of the opera through the nineteenth-century era of the opera's provenance. A pantomime of Dmitrii's murder, which occurs no fewer than four times during Boris's vicissitudes, is acted above the stage, with masked men who look vaguely like ISIS fighters slashing the throat of a large child puppet spinning an oversized top. At the finale, the pantomime is repeated again, only instead of the puppet representing Dmitrii, the murder victim is the boy soprano who sings Boris's son. The historical young Fedor Godunov was in fact murdered by the False Dmitrii's henchmen, so the moment was a poignant reminder of the fickle nature of power. As the knife is drawn across the boy's throat, the assembled courtiers forget all loyalty to Boris and bow to the new leader.

The Estonian bass Ain Anger took the leading role with a brutishness that could intersect with familial tenderness and what looked like the humble contrition required in the death scene. Stentorian though Anger was, he was nearly overshadowed by the monk Pimen, sung by his Croatian colleague Ante Jerkunica, a fellow bass who vocally duels with Boris from afar by relating the back story that inspires the False Dmitrii's plot and confronts Boris with divine judgment for his bloody deed. It would be hard to imagine that performances of the title role do not lie near on Jerkunica's horizon. Among the remaining cast, the Deutsche Oper's excellent roster contributed the skilled character tenor Burkhard Ulrich in the role of Prince Shuisky, a schemer who exposes Boris's madness (and who historically reigned as Tsar after the False Dmitrii). The young tenor Robert Watson sang a convincing Dmitrii. Matthew Newlin was moving as the Holy Fool, another archetypically Russian character who observes Boris's failings. Ievgen Orlov and Jörg Schörner were comically effective as the wayward monks Varlaam and Missail, whose antics help Dmitrii escape Russia. The choruses carry several scenes in *Boris Godunov*. Deutsche Oper's chorus master William Spaulding left for Covent Garden last year, but his legacy remains strong in masterful ensemble singing. The young Ukrainian conductor Kirill Karabits's intensity brought a penetrating and impassioned reading of the score.

Gaetano Donizetti, *L'Assedio di Calais*
Glimmerglass Festival, July 16, 2017

Zambello brought this year's Glimmerglass Festival, held in bucolic upstate New York, to the forefront in her much discussed production of Donizetti's rarely performed *L'Assedio di Calais*. Featured here in its American premiere, the opera recounts the heroic Hundred Years' War story of the Burghers of Calais, six leading citizens of the French port who in 1347 offered their lives to the invading English King Edward III in exchange for clemency for their besieged town's starving population. Moved by their selfless sacrifice, Edward's queen, Philippa, successfully urged him to spare their lives while taking the city under English rule, where it remained until 1558. The tale's themes of conflict, sacrifice, and magnanimity suggest the makings of a great opera. But the absence of any serious romantic passion is probably the best explanation for the work's obscurity compared to the composer's much better known *Lucia di Lammermoor*, which had premiered a year earlier. Here the only intimate conflict rests between Eustachio – history's Eustache de Saint-Pierre, one of Calais's self-sacrificial burghers – and his son Aurelio, who out of filial loyalty wishes to share his father's sacrifice. Aurelio's wife Eleonora adds some elegantly scored bickering – what will happen to her and the couple's young son if Aurelio surrenders his life to King Edward?, – but to today's sensibilities this bourgeois family drama would need something more to inspire a director.

Enter Francesca Zambello. Known for occasionally provocative stagings of standard repertoire works, chic contemporary politics and aspirations to social relevance drove both her choice of Donizetti's forgotten opera and her approach. Modern Calais recently housed a refugee encampment called "the jungle." After many difficult months, French police finally cleared the area in October 2016. Zambello would like to convince us that the events of 1347 bear comparison to the charged issue of the flood of migrants into Europe now, and that we should be appalled by humanity's seemingly undiminished capacity for cruelty. The opera's Calais, therefore, is plucked out of the fourteenth century and recreated as "the jungle," with the name of the French town spray painted across a corrugated iron gate to remind us where we really are. The encampment within evokes images of Syria with its hopeless urban destruction. Eustachio and his fellow burghers are not leading citizens but deracinated community elders trying to hold together some kind of order among a distressed refugee populace. The English invaders of lore are black-vested Eurocops led by an Edward who looks more like an overdressed Brussels functionary than a bloodthirsty tyrant.

One can credit Zambello with indubitable humanitarian instincts. The "jungle" of the refugee crisis suffered alleged human rights violations, police brutality, and occasionally violent resistance to government directives that the migrants resettle in state-operated facilities. The issues involved are contentious and controversial, but does a sovereign state trying to manage a migrant population living in unsanitary conditions really compare to an epic medieval war in which one country spent more than a century brutally trying to take over another? To get to the story's heart, how often do contemporary Eurocrats offer leniency in exchange for human sacrifice? Dare one suggest that the "jungle" residents, however lamentable their fate, look like something other than patriots defending their homes against foreign invaders? Indeed, the only way Zambello can force that comparison is to eliminate all references to France, Christianity, and being either French or Christian from the translated libretto projected onto supertitles. As American alt-right toughs take to the streets to complain about being "erased" from history, Donizetti's characters – created by a composer whose own country languished under a foreign domination that many Italian creative intellectuals metaphorically denounced – suffer exactly that fate in the comfortably bourgeois confines of the Glimmerglass campus. The only apparent reason for this is

Zambello's overweening political conscience, generously supported by the National Endowment for the Arts.

Like most political art, this production is unlikely to last much beyond the headlines of today. Its contortions are too obvious to withstand trenchant analysis. Its moralizations are too shrill to convince anyone who does not already share them (the large number of Upper West Siders trekking upstate probably do, at least when they are not complaining about the area's lousy cell phone reception between gruesome bites of avocado toast). Its political message – hands off a refugee encampment that no longer exists – will be irrelevant by the time the production is revived, if ever it is.

Happily, qualitative performance is untouched by ideology, and some impressive talent was on display. The musical buzz was around the rising soprano Leah Crocetto, who sang Eleonora. The role, a housewife whose only rival is her husband Aurelio's determination to sacrifice his life alongside his father, is not the stuff of which bel canto fireworks are usually made. But there were sublime moments, and after a few rough patches early on Crocetto handled them with the lithe, buoyant sound for which she has become celebrated. She was paired with the talented mezzo Aleks Romano, who took on Aurelio, a trouser part. Trouser heroes are rare in Donizetti's works – the story here is that the composer could not engage the leading Neapolitan tenor of the day and improvised when he found the other tenor options inadequate, – but the role sounded strangely devoid of the delicate balance of animus and anima that the affectation requires. Romanian baritone Adrian Timpau emerged from Glimmerglass's Young Artists Program to sing a solid Eustachio. We should hope to hear more of him. Joseph Colaneri led the performance with a sophisticated reading of the score.

Richard Wagner, *The Ring of the Nibelung*
Bayreuth Festival, August 23-28, 2017

Controversy cannot diminish the appeal of the world's most elite cultural event, the annual festival devoted to Richard Wagner. Founded by the composer himself in 1876, it still takes place under family leadership in the Bavarian town of Bayreuth, deliberately chosen for its remoteness from the urban modernity Wagner despised. Little has changed. The Festspielhaus retains its covered orchestra pit, lacks serious air conditioning, offers no supertitles in any language, and still imposes low-backed wooden seats on spectators. Since 2015, Wagner's great-granddaughter Katharina has run the festival, amid rumors that her half-sister Eva was forced out in a tense test of wills. Wagnerians around the world still slavishly line up to attend. Ticket demand rests at around ten times availability. Despite calls to democratize access, most tickets remain available to aspirants who must wait up to a decade before being granted entry.

This year's Bayreuth Festival saw the final outing of Frank Castorf's *Ring* Cycle, which premiered in honor of Wagner's bicentennial in 2013. A much reviled effort, its unpopularity is so enduring that tickets to the performances I attended were reportedly still available at the box office up to curtain time, an unthinkable happenstance for anyone familiar with the art of attending Bayreuth for the last generation. It is easy to see why. Castorf styles himself as an arch provocateur, but in a world flooded with *Regietheater* productions – and *Ring* Cycles that are almost invariably set in some dystopian industrial universe, – virtually nothing about his *Ring* rises even to provocation.

Drenched in empty banality and dull incoherence, Castorf consigns Wagner's four-part tetralogy of power, destruction, and redemption to a tacky twentieth-century universe that crawls with bland cliché, intrusive distractions, and impositions upon both music and drama that one can describe as little more than "busy." Very often the pointless visuals detracted from both the story and the music in a way that ranks this *Ring* on par with Robert Lepage's witless Metropolitan Opera production as the least enriching one I have ever seen. High on the long list of useless clutter were a Soviet propaganda film playing as Wotan puts Brünnhilde to sleep at the end of *Die Walküre*; copulating crocodiles that lurk about during the love scene that concludes *Siegfried*; a communist version of Mount Rushmore that replaces the honored American presidents with Marx, Lenin, Stalin, and Mao; and a simian mute character who needlessly pops up in all of the operas as an abused servant.

Tarantino-esque sex and violence bordered on gratuitous but rarely deserved even that adjective. Siegfried, for example, shags Gutrune upon their first meeting and beats up a homeless man during his confrontation with the Rhine Maidens. Wotan's silencing of Erda ends with her performing oral sex on him, giving a whole new meaning to the chief god's parting admonition for her to go "*hinab*." Hagen kills Siegfried and Gunther by bludgeoning them with a baseball bat. "So what?," I asked myself every time. The most telling anecdote of the Cycle's sheer blandness arrived by accident. In an incident that may well have made operatic history, the production's Brünnhilde, Catherine Foster, injured herself during the violent confrontation with Siegfried that concludes Act I of *Götterdämmerung* and sang from the side of the stage for the rest of the performance. Her part was then mimed by a male assistant director fully costumed in a glittering gold gown. If this "trans-friendly" expedient had not been announced before the curtain rose on Act II, I would probably have assumed it was just another trite feature of Castorf's insipid production.

The only intelligible theme that percolated through the four evenings was the specter of oil politics in the last century's defining power struggle – the geopolitical contest between the United States and the Soviet Union. The first installment, *Das Rheingold*, is set entirely at a Confederate flag-bedecked modern gas station/motel run on Route 66 in Texas. Wotan is its proprietor, with his archenemy Alberich a motel guest tormented by prostitute-like Rhine Maidens around an above-ground pool that stands in for the Rhine. The next evening's *Walküre* moves us to early Soviet Azerbaijan, where Wotan has gone back in time to become a state oil well manager. A red star blazes atop the well, and he reads *Pravda* before launching into his vicissitudes. *Siegfried* uses Bayreuth's rotating stage to split the action between the communist Mount Rushmore and a seedy depiction of East Berlin's Alexanderplatz. Cue the copulating crocodiles. By the time we reach *Götterdämmerung*, we are torn between a dönerkebab stand in cold war Berlin and the almost refreshing (by this point) neoclassical façade of the New York Stock Exchange.

Like the other sets, however, no comment on the action emerges from whatever symbols Castorf favors at a given moment. Indeed,

Götterdämmerung reveals his frail concept at its weakest, for the cold war turned out to be cold precisely because there was no apocalyptic catastrophe that destroyed the world. His *Ring* ends with Brünnhilde lamely handing the cursed ring over to the Rhine Maidens, who then drop it into a flaming barrel as the covetous Hagen impotently looks on. Nothing is destroyed, so nothing can be redeemed. And if the work's essential themes are discarded or ignored, then why should anyone bother to see it? Indeed, why did Castorf bother to stage it?

The only saving grace was the production's glorious music. No singer in the entire cast seemed overwhelmed or out of place. Foster's Brünnhilde stood out as its greatest star, with ascents swelling in great clouds of sound and beaming B's and G's radiating at the expressive moments. Her study of the role may well be at its apogee after several years of this production and stands as a marked improvement over her earlier essays in lesser European theaters.

The purist in me prefers consistent casting, but alas our Brünnhilde had three different Wotans. Iain Paterson handled the god's *Rheingold* incarnation with a solid baritone that may have been slightly too high for the later, more mature incarnations of the role. John Lundgren's *Walküre* Wotan added a deeper resonance and benefited from an excellent legato. Thomas J. Mayer was more muted in the role's *Siegfried* moments but did a credible job.

The part of Siegfried is arguably the most difficult Wagner *Heldentenor* role, and even just getting through it is often lauded as an accomplishment. Like his Brünnhilde, Stefan Vinke has never sounded better, particularly in the fresher *Siegfried* version. He had fine moments in *Götterdämmerung*, but the voice carried less well overall that evening. As his parents Siegmund and Sieglinde, Christopher Ventris and Camilla Nylund gave moving performances. Georg Zeppenfeld's Hunding deftly destroyed fateful love with real menace. Stephen Milling's Hagen was as brutal as any I have heard. Albert Dohmen, a Wotan of great distinction in his time, admirably continued his engagement with the *Ring* as a snarling Alberich. Andreas Conrad's Mime, Markus Eiche's Gunther, and Günther Groissböck's Fasolt stood out among the supporting cast. Marek Janowski, now 78, made his Bayreuth debut with this production last year and recently recorded the whole work. He favored an even pace but judiciously reached into the score to draw out many of the most moving elements with deliberative intensity. The only pity was that such a worthwhile musical effort seemed so tragically underserved by what was happening on stage. It is anyone's guess how long Bayreuth can sustain nonsensical *Regie* productions, but for the first time in my life I saw empty seats in the Festspielhaus.

Richard Wagner, *Die Meistersinger von Nürnberg*
Bayreuth Festival, August 27, 2017

Bayreuth's only new production this year is the Australian director Barrie Kosky's new production of the only comedy among Wagner's mature works, *Die Meistersinger von Nürnberg*. Much has been made of the fact that Kosky, a self-described "gay Jewish kangaroo," is the first Jewish director to stage an opera in Bayreuth. He introduces Wagner's paean to the sanctity of German art amusingly enough. The first act is set in the spacious library of Wagner's Villa Wahnfried, the Bayreuth residence gifted to him by the mad King Ludwig II of Bavaria. Instead of the opera's literal characters, we see a home reading of the opera performed by a mature Wagner as the noble cobbler and mastersinger Hans Sachs. Wagner's devoted wife Cosima plays the role of Eva, whose hand in marriage is the prize of the opera's grand song contest. The composer Franz Liszt, Cosima's father and frequent Wahnfried visitor, performs as Eva's operatic father Veit Pogner, with household servants and others filling the smaller parts of Sachs's apprentice David, Eva's maid Magdalena, and the corps of Mastersingers. A younger version of Wagner himself performs as the knight Walther von Stolzing, who, with Sachs's selfless help, will transcend the stale pedantry of artistic convention and devise a winning song to claim Eva as his bride.

Notably for our age of relentless identity politics, the role of Walther's rival Beckmesser, often interpreted as an anti-Semitic stereotype, is given to the conductor Hermann Levi, a Jew who famously resisted baptism when engaged to conduct Wagner's final opera, *Parsifal*. As the first act unfolds in an atmosphere of saccharine bourgeois *Gemütlichkeit*, we realize that just as Beckmesser's designs on Eva are problematic in the opera, so, too is Levi's faith in the production's nineteenth-century milieu. Wagner-as-Sachs, voiced throughout the evening with unflagging stamina by the excellent baritone Michael Volle, captured all of the composer's frenetic narcissism by forcing Levi-as-Beckmesser into an uneasy prayer during the hymn that grows out of the opera's prelude. As the first act ends, a moving *coup-de-théâtre* retracts the Wahnfried library set to reveal a very different impression of Nuremberg, the courtroom where the post-World War II war crimes trials were held. Left alone to contemplate Walther's innate talent, Wagner-as-Sachs enters the witness stand as the curtain falls.

Back in Wahnfried's bucolic environs, Kosky's interpretation darkens as Beckmesser's advances toward Eva become bolder. Act II centers around his attempt to serenade her, which Sachs deliberately interrupts as Walther tries to pull off his own assignation. In Wagner's comedy, the noise ignites a melee among the townspeople that ends with Sachs sheltering Walther so that he can help him perfect his talent. Kosky recasts the brawl as a pogrom against Beckmesser. Now fitted with a mask that makes him resemble a Nazi anti-Semitic caricature, he is roundly pummeled and – symbolically important – beaten with the same cobbler's hammer that Sachs used to disrupt his serenade. In case anyone missed the point, the injured Beckmesser is subsumed within a vast inflatable puppet version of the caricature, which deflates only slightly to leave the palpably discomforted audience contemplating a stage-dominating Star of David atop the puppet's yarmulke.

Spirited intermission discussion speculated that Kosky was advancing a grinding condemnation of Germany's past and insisting that Nazism and the Holocaust were natural outgrowths of a violently anti-Semitic culture and society. But upon returning for the opera's long third act, his message suggested that bygones can indeed be bygones. The pageantry of the song contest occurs within the same Nuremberg courtroom, but all of its elements except for the witness stand are removed to make way for Sachs's final monologue, in which he advocates the sanctity of German art and the need for its preservation. Alone on stage, he takes the stand to plead his case directly to the audience before turning to conduct the noble strains of the opera's finale at the head of a faux orchestra. It is for the spectator to decide whether the Germans can be forgiven, but the question is obviously Kosky's and not Wagner's. Although one missed the opera's deeply human element, we can at least forgive the director for leaving the message open for interpretation instead of imposing his own.

However one reacts to the production, the musical evening was marvelous. In addition to Volle's strong and stentorian Sachs, Klaus Florian Vogt's Walther resounded with a mellifluous, velvety quality that made the character irresistible in any guise. Over the years the voice has become more grounded in a way that may allow for deeper Wagner roles than Vogt's iconic Lohengrin. The bass Günther Groissböck sang an elegant Pogner, and Johannes Martin Kränzle's dramatic talents tackled the difficult challenge of Kosky's interpretation of Levi-as-Beckmesser. The normally solid soprano Anne Schwanewilms seemed to have an off night, without much verve in Eva's most exciting music, but performed well enough. Philippe Jordan led a brisk performance with more gravitas than I have ever heard him bring to Wagner. The chorus, selected from the finest ensembles for the special experience of Bayreuth, resounded with a perfection that almost makes one forget that Wagner aesthetically opposed choral music in opera.

Chapter Eight

2017-2018

Pietro Mascagni, *Cavalleria Rusticana*/ Ruggero Leoncavallo, *Pagliacci*
Royal Opera House, December 2, 2017

As long ago as 1928, a British critic called the inseparable operatic double bill of Pietro Mascagni's *Cavalleria Rusticana* and Ruggero Leoncavallo's *Pagliacci* "the ham and eggs of opera." The unique phenomenon of this pairing of two works that have long been overly familiar from film and parody took a bit longer than that to be irrevocably entrenched, but it has been a commonplace of the operatic world for at several decades and, in London, since 1959 (though there was a standalone production of *Pagliacci* staged as a vehicle for Plácido Domingo in 2003). After a long absence from the stage of the Royal Opera House, the Venetian director Damiano Michieletto brought the conventional program to life in 2015 with a new production that won the Olivier Award.

Arguably opera's most promising director working today, Michieletto has a profound talent for reading between the lines and rooting his productions firmly yet very creatively in the text. Here he looks into what else *Cav* and *Pag* have in common besides their alluring tales of murderous solutions to insolvable problems. His creative innovation is to thread their stories together. Their respective Sicilian and Calabrian settings are combined to have the drama of both works unfold simultaneously in the same atmospherically decrepit village in the Italian south. Hence *Cavalleria* hints at the plot of *Pagliacci*, with posters proclaiming the arrival of the latter opera's performing troupe and tender glimpses of the budding affair of Nedda and Silvio, which ends in their double homicide at the vengeful hands of Nedda's husband Canio. In *Pagliacci*, we see the aftermath of the previous opera's death by duel of the ne'er-do-well seducer Turridu. To the music of *Pagliacci*'s stirring intermezzo, his abandoned girlfriend Santuzza wins his mother's affection by revealing her pregnancy. The effect is clever without being intrusive and reminds us that the petty dramas of life can and do overlap in even the humblest communities.

Cav/Pag is such a reliable standard repertoire program that a revival of even an award-winning production might easily be overlooked. But this year's revival cast, headed by the rising superstar tenor Bryan Hymel, was hard to ignore. Originally cast only as Turridu in *Cavalleria*, a colleague's indisposition also yielded the starring role of Canio in *Pagliacci*. Both of these difficult parts were Hymel's role debuts. His virtuoso performance only strengthened as the December 2 premiere evening continued. His Turridu – violent, despicable, and savage – yielded to Canio's aching vulnerability and murderous rage with a pronounced rise in pathos and dramatic power. The voice rang out with clarion tonalities recalling Franco Corelli's impassioned singing. After a long evening, Canio's "Vesti la giubba," – an aria that explores the need to suppress unbearable emotional pain – stood out as the production's greatest solo moment.

It is hard to call the remaining cast "supporting." Elīna Garanča's cool, affecting mezzo delivered a mellifluous, velvety Santuzza that combined suffering with ethereal love. Carmen Giannattasio's Nedda lost no coquetry in its exploration of forbidden passion. Veteran baritone Mark Doss sang a malevolent Alfio with a pride that easily matched Turridu's bravado. In the role of Tonio, the villain of *Pagliacci* who exposes Nedda's affair after his own rejection, Simon Keenlyside captured his scheming ways but seemed a bit wooden in delivery. Perhaps for that reason only the daring Prologue scene captured much admiration. Daniel Oren led a steady performance.

Gioachino Rossini, *Semiramide*
Royal Opera House, December 4, 2017

Semiramide falls into the serious part of Gioachino Rossini's *oeuvre*, which we rather seldom hear in an endless stream of *Barbers of Seville* and *Cenerentole*. Premiering at the Royal Opera this season, none of

Covent Garden's operatic enterprises has presented it since 1887. Based on Voltaire's play *Sémiramis*, Rossini's opera could easily have turned out to be an Enlightenment work exploring virtue as its own reward and the inevitability of punishment for existential misdeeds. Instead its lurid plot – which inspired at least 65 other composers – propels it to the frontier between lyrically expository baroque opera, of which it is held to be the last example, and the more psychologically demanding Romantic works that dominated the rest of the nineteenth century.

The opera's title character, the Queen of Babylon (she of the wondrous Hanging Gardens), is mired in her own murderous corruption. Tortured by bad omens and guilt for having murdered her husband Nino with the help of the army commander Assur years earlier, she must now square off against her ambitious collaborator to secure the throne for her newest love object Arsace, who inconveniently turns out to be her son and has now returned from exile after growing to manhood. By way of convoluted intersecting love plots, fate forces Arsace to deal Semiramide, whose identity as his mother eludes him until nearly the end, an "accidental" death blow that clears his path to a virtuous new reign over a realm cleansed of her sin.

Dating from 1823, Rossini's opera still has enough of the composer's signature up-tempo music to recall his earlier comic works and enough coloratura to recall the great eighteenth-century scores. Yet in other ways it follows the path from Cherubini's *Medea* to the more insightful scores of Bellini and Verdi, with melodic devices suggesting theme and character and a captivating dramatic focus on a tormented hero and anti-heroine. Plunging into vicissitudes and anticipating her *femme fatale* descendants, Semiramide is much more Lady Macbeth than Donna Elvira, Arsace more Arturo than any displaced Handelian heir of mistaken identity. Sometimes the results verge on comic. The assembled Babylonians sound quite cheerful as they prepare sacrifices to Baal, their Rossinian choral music looking forward to the sing-song devils who would less than convincingly torment Joan of Arc in Verdi's *Giovanna d'Arco* two decades later. Murderous passion arrives in cadenzas that sounds irrepressibly joyful. And at four hours in length with only one intermission, one wonders whether the old practice of cutting *longueurs* might be a wiser approach than upholding the curatorial ethos that now dominates an opera world thirsting for authenticity.

The Royal Opera's Music Director Antonio Pappano showed some sympathy to his audience, and perhaps solicitude of union concerns, by maintaining a brisk pace. But this did not diminish the shining star of Joyce DiDonato, arguably opera's leading lyric mezzo-soprano, who embodied the title role with magnetic presence. Though announced as recovering from a throat infection, she admirably radiated tones that were by turn charming and chilling. Some faintness could be detected in the cadenzas, which could have stood more embellishment, but this was hardly a flaw in the overall impression. As Arsace, the superb Italian mezzo-soprano Daniela Barcellona met all challenges in the role's higher register and delivered a stunning reading of this conflicted trouser part. Michele Pertusi, more familiar from his comic roles, dispatched the gruff role of Assur with the oaken resonance of a born conspirator. Lawrence Brownlee blossomed in the supporting part of Idreno, an Indian prince who courts Semiramide.

David Alden's colorful production gives us a modern setting in an anonymous country in the Middle East, where numerous leaders have recently met unpleasant ends. But in a world where opera gasps for relevance, and in which virtually all operas set in the Middle East therefore demand a modern staging, one wonders whether this might be a new Orientalism in which no other idiom is possible. Here the Temple of Baal is a vast chamber dominated by a Stalinesque statue of a beloved dear leader – the deceased Nino. It could easily stand in the courtyard of an antiseptic presidential palace anywhere between Ankara and Pyongyang. The walls are dominated by imperious family portraits foregrounding him, immaculately tailored and sporting chic sunglasses, before vast natural vistas, ironically alongside his murderous wife and lost son. Assur and the other military characters wear over-decorated uniforms that strike an authoritative imitation of the gaudiest Soviet command-rank outfits, still rather in fashion around that part of the world. Semiramide's seductive powers are captured in the couture that draws third-world princesses and their corrupt fathers' credit cards from their grimy national capitals to the welcoming shops of Regent Street. If the message is that people and politics never change, it is well received, if not completely original.[19]

Umberto Giordano, *Andrea Chénier*
Milan, La Scala, December 7, 2017

Two years after her dazzling performance in the title role of Verdi's rarely performed early opera *Giovanna d'Arco*, the opera world's reigning superstar has returned to Milan for her second opening night at that musical city's venerable La Scala. This time the usual assembly of the great, the good, and the not-so-good gathered to hear her role debut as the ill fated Maddalena in Umberto Giordano's *Andrea Chénier*. Over the past few years Netrebko's voice has darkened and thickened, leading her, via a highly intelligent progression of roles, from her early career bel canto and Mozartian parts to the earthier repertoire of the late Italian Romantic. Along with her recent and for the most part successful forays into Verdi and Puccini, tackling Giordano's demanding heroine is a logical next step.

And what a night it was! The rounded, full bodied tones for which Netrebko is justly celebrated emerged in stunning relief in this tale of a young French noblewomen who finds solace amid revolutionary chaos by embracing the love of a soulful but subversive poet and joining him in his unjust death by guillotine. Maddalena's signature aria "La mamma morta," in which she recounts the death of her mother at the hands of revolutionaries and proclaims her own inspiration to live at the command of life itself, emerged with a vivacious, smoldering passion that recalled the steadiest of Zinka Milanov's performances on record. It is difficult to imagine any other soprano performing today who could deliver the part with such aching sympathy.

Stardom has its benefits, and one of them may have manifested in the decision to cast Netrebko's husband, tenor Yusif Eyvazov, in the role of Maddalena's devoted love, the poet Chénier. It is completely fair to say that Eyvazov brought fine companionship onstage, even if the voice might not rate equally alongside his wife's Golden Age sonorities (but then

---

[19] It was extraordinarily well received – Alden's production won the Olivier Award for Best New Opera Production, while DiDonato and Barcellona both won individual Olivier Awards for their performances.

again, whose does?) He started the evening cautiously, with the entrance aria "Un di all'azzurro spazio" sounding rather restrained. But as the evening went on, he displayed more and more prowess. The Act II duet, in which the characters embrace the inevitability of their deaths, unfolded gracefully, yet it was really in the second part of the evening that showed Eyvazov at his best. The defiant aria "Sì, fui soldato," delivered to a courtroom filled with violent rebels commanded by a ruthless prosecutor, resounded in bold clarion voice. The finale duet "Vicino a te" combined the spousal voices in what will long be remembered as a solid onstage partnership.

A strong supporting cast complemented their success. Stalwart Italian baritone Luca Salsi was a menacing Gérard, a household servant of Maddalena's family whose sense of oppression and frustrated love for Maddalena drive him to the heights of revolutionary leadership. Annalisa Stroppa did more than we usually see with the role of Maddalena's friend Bersi. Judit Kutasi contributed an affecting Madelon, a sympathetic but horrifically misguided character who surrenders her younger grandson for the same revolutionary military duties that killed her other male offspring. Mariana Pentcheva offered a moving portrayal of Maddalena's mother, the Countess de Coigny, who sadly does not survive into the second act. La Scala's music director Riccardo Chailly ran a brisk performance that lingered on the most sentimental moments while leaving little room for applause after the arias and duets. The effect made the work more appealingly cinematic.

Andrea Chénier is a work of irony. Its hero is a rebel poet who is nevertheless condemned by revolutionary "justice." Its villain is a revolutionary rabble rouser whose changing convictions lead him to a failed attempt to save his rival, Chénier, whom he has denounced to the tribunal. The glamorous atmosphere of Europe's most important annual cultural event made the irony even more palpable. With Italy's prime minister and other leading politicians, socialites, and business leaders in attendance, La Scala's traditional December 7 opening night performance is a perennial target for Italian adherents of today's revolutionaries of the anti-globalist left. As usual, the protestors were out in force, unfurling a banner calling for "Rights for Everyone" as an opera about the French

Revolution – an event that held such rights to be universal (at least for all men) – was about to go on across the square. It was all the more daring in the centenary year of the even more tragic Bolshevik Revolution, which plunged the star soprano's homeland into unparalleled horror.

Inside the well guarded theater, however, the Euro-elite confidently embraced Mario Martone's inventively traditional production and seemed to have no problem dining at the gala that followed on a dish that included *"crostini alla Robespierre."* In a continent dominated by much loathed *Regietheater*, in which contemporary ideas external to the work are often inscribed upon it, it was perhaps a radical innovation to create a highly realistic set that captured the era of the French Revolution in all its doomed aristocratic glamour as well as its gritty revolutionary affectations. The Coigny manse boasts a vast wall of mirrors that evokes the Palace of Versailles. Ursula Patzak's meticulous period costumes recalled the stunning ball scene in Visconti's *The Leopard*. In sartorial elegance they easily outdid the flamboyant couture of many of the fashion victims in the audience. Their well choreographed gavotte was divine. Martone's revolutionaries push around a tumbril that carries off the condemned to a completely realistic guillotine, and it was fitting, if ahistorical, to have the procession of revolutionary leaders in Act II cross the stage carrying severed heads.

Richard Strauss, *Salome*
Royal Opera House, January 30, 2018

With no fewer than three productions by Sir David McVicar running in the Metropolitan Opera's repertoire this January alone, one might think of travelling to escape the Scottish opera director. Nevertheless, he is so ubiquitous in the opera world today that his production of Richard Strauss's quintessential expressionist opera has returned to London in the same gritty, gray tones to which New York audiences are wintering.

Salome has a storied history in London, and really everywhere else since the time of its premiere in 1905. In just one act, its perverse plot offers up lust, murder, incest, and necrophilia. The story dresses up a Biblical anecdote about a Judean princess who tempted her lascivious stepfather Herod into giving her the head of John the Baptist (Jokanaan in the opera and the Oscar Wilde play on which it is based) in return for the seductive Dance of the Seven Veils. After she passionately kisses it, the horrified Herod orders her murder to repeated percussive strains that suggest retributive rape. Strauss adapted the German translation of Wilde's play as his libretto, but made carefully selected cuts to eliminate any suggestion of Salome's innocence and to magnify her malevolence. The resulting opera proved so incendiary that after only one performance in 1907 the Metropolitan did not present it again for twenty-seven seasons. Britain's theatrical censorship kept it off London's operatic stage until 1910, when it was allowed to appear with limitations, and banned Wilde's play until the 1930s.

McVicar's production, which is featured in a video installation on the work in the Victoria and Albert Museum's ambitious and contemporaneously running exhibition "Opera: Passion, Power, and Politics," hark back to a decadent 1930s, the approximate time when both play and opera entered general acceptability. Jokanaan is kept in the subterranean chamber of a gray concrete basement illuminated by crude electric lights. Herod's party of guests eat, drink, and argue around a table shadowboxed at the extreme upper reaches of the proscenium. They descend to watch Salome's lustful antics and Jokanaan's somber pronouncements as a kind of morbid *après-dîner* entertainment. After the Dance of the Seven Veils, which in this production looks like a faux seduction followed by sexual assault, Herod takes her off into a side room to have his brief (and perhaps unsatisfying) way with her. Salome echoes the original Wildean hints of purity in a white gown, which matches the cold, deathly surface of the moon to which she is compared. By the end of the opera, it becomes a blood splattered mess after she rolls around kissing Jokanaan's severed head. Perhaps only François Girard's production of Wagner's *Parsifal*, which returns to the Met this season, boasts more sanguinary effusion.

The title role falls in this revival to the Swedish soprano Malin Byström. She follows in a fine tradition of Swedish Salomes, including Birgit Nilsson and, though she has performed the role less often, Nina Stemme. Byström's cool, Nordic tones serve the character's amoral narcissism as well as anyone's. She is strident without losing cohesion, pleading without sounding desperate, triumphant without melting into shrillness. Byström's command of the range and its dissonant leaps is impressive and benefits from gleaming, rounded top notes. But it does not quite plum the purring depths of the part's ominous lower range. When her Salome observes that the mystery of love is greater than the mystery of death, the sepulchral low G on the second syllable in the word "*Todes*" ("of death") remains elusive.

Strauss declared that Salome should be a sixteen-year old girl with the voice of an Isolde. Byström came close in vocal terms, but the performance's stock rose on a Jokanaan with the voice of a Wotan. Michael Volle has by this point in his career captured much of the late German Romantic baritone repertoire – from Wotan and Hans Sachs to the lighter Strauss parts – and excelled in this challenging role. He adorned it the usual solemnity, which Strauss did not really intend: the avowedly atheist composer thought of Jokanaan as a comic figure. But the sheer stentorian glory was riveting. John Daszak brought fresh insights to the role of the lecherous Herod, a part often foisted on declining Heldentenors. Here he was brash and insistent, and finally horrified, but deftly avoided clichéd sleaze. Michaela Schuster sang a sophisticated Herodias. Usually she is only there to pluck at Herod's nerves and egg on her murderous daughter, but in the scarier moments Schuster indulged in enough pathos to radiate horror. She never quite touched on regret, if one could expect such a sentiment from the woman who gave birth to Salome, but her conflicted feelings were something to relish. The superb Hungarian conductor Henrik Nánási, general music director of Berlin's cutting-edge Komische Oper, led a searing performance that chilled one to the bones.

Richard Wagner, *Parsifal*
New York, Metropolitan Opera, February 28, 2018

When François Girard's production of Wagner's mystical final opera premiered at the Met in 2013, it was heralded as one of the few successes of the Peter Gelb era. With ticket sales now sagging well below 70 percent capacity and long-time music director James Levine (arguably the Met's greatest *Parsifal* conductor on record) fired and suing the company amid sexual harassment allegations, Met acolytes have held onto Girard's staging like the opera's proverbial Holy Grail.

Alas, the Girard production never was quite as good as the critical acclaim made it out to be. Its revival this season – the first since its premiere five years ago – remained a visually gloomy affair. Its only noteworthy optical asset is the vast pool of blood that inundates Klingsor's realm in Act II. One never learns why it is there or what it is meant to suggest, but the sight of Flower Maidens splashing around in it adds a horrific idiom to the evil sorcerer's machinations. When Kundry attempts to seduce Parsifal, however, the scene turns unintentionally comic as they try not to splatter each other too much and disport on the generously proportioned bed that magically rises onto the stage for the non-consummation of their prospective "*Stunde.*" From the orchestra level, even the garish blood pool is practically invisible; those who really want to look upon it will have to sit upstairs or buy the DVD.

There is a sliver of philosophical interpretation on hand. The realm of the Grail is not a holy place defended by fervent warrior-knights, but rather a fragmented society of mortals in which the genders (in 2013 we still had only two) are alienated from each other, with the women in black dresses and the men in white button-down shirts. In Act I they are physically separated by a narrow, dried up river bed. Their respective groupings morosely loiter about or loll on folding chairs while making stylized, biomechanic movements that vaguely keep time with Wagner's score. When Parsifal returns with the Holy Spear and restores the divine order in Act III, the stream again starts to flow, allowing the estranged sexes to intermix in a gathering that culminates in what looks like a unisex yoga class. Parsifal joins them, donning a white shirt as one of the females slowly approaches him for what may be a more wholesome but probably less enjoyable experience than he might have hoped for with Kundry. We have no idea what comes next, but this may be both the most banal depiction of salvation I have ever seen and a black-and-white party I would rather avoid. Like much *Regietheater*, the overall effort fails even to rise to provocation.

Girard fans swooned over the cast, headed by the clarion German tenor Klaus Florian Vogt. A Lohengrin of great repute, his purity of tone and lithe timbres captured Parsifal's innocence with a truly ethereal quality. Alas, the voice's otherworldliness underserved the character's progression into maturity. As the evening went on, it rested too high and resounded too brightly to match the deepened orchestral strains that depict Parsifal's attainment of wisdom through pity.

Evelyn Herlitzius's long overdue company debut as Kundry was a happier casting choice. The role of this eternal seductress demands an actress of considerable skill, and Herlitzius offered one of the most compelling portrayals on the scene today. Vocally, she followed the part's treacherous scale with incisive modulation and full bodied notes at all levels of the range. The talented Peter Mattei reprised the role of the long suffering Amfortas, who suffers from a wound that will not heal, with insight still readily memorable from his performance in the premiere run. Evgeny Nikitin also returned to sing a rough and tumble Klingsor, full of spite and menace. René Pape, a third veteran from the premiere cast, contributed a sturdy bass that has owned the role of Gurnemanz for the last decade and a half, but the voice shows signs of decline. Disappointingly, he held back in the Act I narrations, sometimes descending to near inaudibility. But in Act III he boomed out the challenging Good Friday scene with the force and authority one remembers from his best days.

The Met's music director-designate Yannick Nézet-Séguin will enter the position full time this fall – two years early – due to the Levine scandal. Originally assigned to lead this *Parsifal*, he entered the forefront of superb Wagner conductors. He shares Levine's deliciously slow approach, pollinating every note with careful attention to the score's exquisite sonorities. His mastery of the orchestra rose to stunning heights of musicianship that were well worth the long wait.

Giuseppe Verdi, *Don Carlo*
Washington National Opera, March 3, 2018

For a center of power and intrigue, it is perhaps surprising that the nation's capital has not seen Verdi's most political opera for seventeen years. But this season it has returned in a short, two-week run in a new Washington National Opera production. Now recovering after a period of financial trouble, the company has steadily benefited from artistic director

Francesca Zambello's leadership to present a spate of admirable achievements. With this *Don Carlo*, however, the WNO has brought to life a truly transformative effort arguably unequalled in the company's last fifteen years.

Tim Albery's staging of the opera's four-act version, shared with Opera Philadelphia and Minnesota Opera, is a stark geometric grid, with rust-colored walls punctured by rectangular cells rising on either side of the stage. A giant, sideways octagonal dome provides the backdrop for the first two acts. In the final two acts the dome is torn off to reveal grim skies over the Spanish court, here updated to a nineteenth-century anyplace where the hapless title character shares a love with his stepmother Elisabetta (originally his own fiancée in a politically arranged match) and a passionate combination of friendship and political idealism with his best friend Rodrigo, who is also his royal father's favorite. Driven to an act of open rebellion complicated by his romantic feelings, which are then betrayed a woman he does not love, the prince is condemned to death by no less an authority than the head of the Spanish Inquisition. Parting with his beloved stepmother, Carlo meets the end of his earthly existence, in this production dying by suicide rather than the standard rescue by a monk identified as the abdicated Holy Roman Emperor Charles V.

The stark optics allow the interlocking human and political dramas to unfold in full relief. Verdi's opera rises and falls on the strength of its ensemble cast, a demanding necessity as the composer moved away from his earlier bel canto style of set piece arias into more psychologically compelling progressions of scenes. The cast was headed by the young tenor Russell Thomas, whose brash ardor flashed across the stage with an incisive passion that no one could doubt. Thomas avoided some of the role's riskier high notes – the lack of one at the end of the Act I duet was one of the evening's few disappointments – but delivered a moving reading.

As Carlo's father, the tormented King Phillip II, Eric Owens added another triumph at what is arguably the apogee of his career. He played Phillip more as a bemused father who might have been a bit too indulgent of his headstrong son, but developed this paternal vexation into moments of real pain. The famous third act aria "Ella giammai m'amò," in which Phillip ends a sleepless night with the realization that his wife never loved him, resounded with a pathos in the great tradition of the Italian bassos Cesare Siepi and Ferruccio Furlanetto. Paired with the stentorian, if a bit rough sounding, Grand Inquisitor of the bass Andrea Silvestrelli, the characters' confrontation of state and religious power chilled the audience to the bones. Quinn Kelsey's steady baritone conquered the part of Carlo's friend Rodrigo in a continuing *tour de force* that has taken this exciting young singer from triumph to triumph in the Verdi baritone repertoire. His double aria in the third act was nuanced with silvery tones that evoked the fading of an autumn day as the character's life ebbed from him.

In Leah Crocetto's Elisabetta, Washington heard a magnificent *spinto* voice equally adept in solo parts and in the opera's challenging ensemble singing. An excellent legato delivered steady streams of passion while effortless ascents captured the role's heavenly aspirations. The arduous six-part final act aria "Tu che le vanità" was a recital-worthy model of musicianship. No less impressive was mezzo-soprano Jamie Barton's coolly collected Eboli, the court damsel whom Carlo spurns. She captured the part's emotional conflict with purring tones that were by turns vicious and repentant. The role's signature aria "O don fatale," a cursing of her beauty, figured among the evening's highlights.

Under outgoing Maestro Philippe Auguin, the Washington National Opera Orchestra sounded better than it has in many years. He will be missed. The orchestra's vitality in narrating the story on stage grew from precision of virtuoso quality into a formidable psychological challenge to Washington's movers and shakers.

Charles Gounod, *Faust*
Lyric Opera of Chicago, March 12, 2018

Johann Wolfgang von Goethe's *Faust* stands as one of humanity's grandest morality tales – at what price can we regain youth as we reach the end of our time on earth? In the depths of despair, Goethe's disillusioned scholar is willing to sell his soul to the devil, who promises in return all the pleasures of restored yesteryear, especially the passion and romance that inevitably fade with time and experience. The story, which dates in various forms from a Renaissance legend, recommends itself to the eccentricities of opera. French composer Charles Gounod carried the idea on his creative conscience for nearly twenty years before an impresario commissioned him to compose such a work for Paris's Théâtre Lyrique. Of all the composers who tried (Hector Berlioz, Arrigo Boito, and Ferruccio Busoni, among others, all wrote Faust operas; Beethoven, Schubert, Schumann, Mendelssohn, Liszt, Wagner, and Mussorgsky composed music on the Faust theme in other genres), Gounod came closest to realizing Goethe's inspiration in musical theater. Indeed, his *Faust* was the first opera staged by the Metropolitan Opera, and from the time of its Parisian premiere in 1859 the work has remained firmly in the standard repertoire all over the world. But even Gounod's superlative version, staged in a new production by the Lyric Opera of Chicago this season, never quite succeeded in capturing the literary work's philosophical profundities.

As in most *Faust* adaptations, Gounod's opera delivers selected scenes dramatized for maximum effect over five sprawling acts. The 40-year old director Kevin Newbury notes that he is not quite at an age to mourn his youth, but he assembled a clever production team to enliven the work with an imaginative approach. Its major inspiration is the roughhewn wooden sculptures of the Californian artist John Frame, which seek to capture the human form in an expressionist idiom. Here Faust is not the stale academician of tradition or the disaffected scientist we increasingly see, but rather an artist, whose exhaustion results from the futile musings of his creative mind. He summons Méphistophélès in a last gasp of artistic purpose by carving his figure from a block of wood. The powerful suggestion is that the devil and his temptations might be products of our own minds rather than malevolent entities prowling the earth to tempt and seduce.

Frame's sculptures tend to look appositely dour, but Newbury's team imbues his set designs with flashes of color and movement. Sometimes the effect is a bit garish. Costume designer Vita Tzykun might have thought better than to dress both Méphistophélès and the rejuvenated Faust in pastel plaids. But David Adam Moore's projection designs make inspired use of film, photography, and stop motion animation to engage the audience in the action. A baritone by musical training (with two Lyric Opera stage credits on his resume), he synthesizes stage action with tremendously engaging optics. Most effectively, the Act III seduction scene opens with projected flowers blooming and ends with Faust and Marguerite swirling in multidimensional hell fire as they reach their tender embraces. Likewise, when the infernal flame returns to consume the defeated Faust in the opera's finale, he does not descend into the abyss, but is rather compelled to join Méphistophélès's band of masked servants, who have done his evil bidding throughout the opera and dutifully march off to help him despoil new victims

Strong casts can help any production concept come alive, and Lyric assembled a fine ensemble of exciting young singers. French tenor Benjamin Bernheim lived up to the vaunted lyrical tradition of sensitive, effective Fausts most recently remembered in Roberto Alagna's performances of what is arguably his best role. Visceral ardor accompanied an almost gymnastically elegant delivery of the combination of despair and sensitivity that has turned Faust's name into an English-language adjective. The ascents had an occasional pinched quality, but this young singer's North American debut production marks a career to watch.

Likewise, bass-baritone Christian Van Horn reached back into the finest traditions of Méphistophélès to summon an arch and beguiling devil, one whose power and presence showed no sign of faltering even as his victims collapsed in ruin. Rollicking *basso cantante* sonorities delivered the opera's best lines with diabolical turns of wit, charm, and irony.

The innocent Marguerite coalesced in the limpid, lithe tones of the young soprano Ailyn Pérez, in her first staged production with Lyric. Delicate warmth characterized the portrayal, which was helped by costuming her not merely as a simple maiden, but as disabled one, moving about the stage on a crutch. The metaphor of vulnerability handily matched raw innocence and balanced well with the character's refined simplicity. Edward Parks's Valentin was rather forgettable. Jill Grove's Martha and Annie Rosen's Siébel were fine studies in character performance.

Emmanuel Villaume conducted a stirring performance, losing none of the work's emotive lyricism. There were moments, particularly in the Act III seduction scene, when he lingered a bit ponderously over the orchestral passages, but he sped things along alluringly when the deed was done. Productions like this one certainly mark Chicago's vaunted company as a leader in twenty-first century opera. Ambitious programming will continue, as will updates to its storied theater, which in 2017 was appropriately renamed the Lyric Opera House. Among its delights are the Pedersen Room, an elegant dining venue that fits seamlessly with the building's art deco milieu. Open exclusively to Lyric ticket holders, it boasts a superb menu and wine list for pre-performance and/or intermission dining. For *Faust*, one could even find a veal selection to honor Méphistophélès's expository aria "Le veau d'or," a self-referential meditation on the Biblical Golden Calf.

Giuseppe Verdi, *Macbeth*
Royal Opera House, March 25, 2018

Macbeth was Giuseppe Verdi's first foray in turning to the timeless *oeuvre* of Shakespeare, his favorite dramatist, as a source for opera. After long contemplating a setting of *King Lear*, which he never realized, the composer's engagement with the bard culminated at the end of his career in his last two operas, *Otello* and *Falstaff* (the latter based on *The Merry Wives of Windsor* with material from *Henry IV*). This season the Royal Opera revives Phyllida Lloyd's 2002 production of Verdi's first encounter with Shakespeare, featuring superstar Anna Netrebko as the troubled Scottish warlord's scheming spouse. *Falstaff* will follow in the summer season.

Premiering in 1847, *Macbeth* sits awkwardly toward the end of Verdi's early period. The musical forms he favored in his younger years is still audible, but much of the characterization anticipates the fuller development of his dramatic sensibilities in later works. Verdi would likely agree that one might expect no less from Shakespeare. Indeed, the composer wanted the singers who created *Macbeth*'s leading roles to be so real-to-life that he praised their ugly looks as a decisive factor in casting. Eighteen years after the premiere, Verdi revisited the opera to insert more "advanced" musical forms, including Lady Macbeth's seductive aria of guilt ("La luce langue") and the expressive Act III vengeance duet ("Ora di morte"), which in this production ends with Macbeth slashing the throats of Macduff's doomed children.

Lloyd's production imbues the work with a *film-noir* effect. The sets are based on walls of black blocks that can slide open in a variety of directions to accommodate entrances and exits and changes of scene. Their main feature, however, is to serve as a background for judicious light projections that allow for shadow, close-ups, and contrasts pregnant with dramatic insight. As the Macbeths contemplate their acts of malice or reflect on what's done, we can observe their moods highlighted in permutations that evoke *The Maltese Falcon* or *Double Indemnity*. Occasionally characters are showcased in a gilded cage, both highlighting vital scenes and suggesting their imprisonment by fate and prophecy.

Anna Netrebko is certainly the most compelling singer before the pubic today, and her practiced Lady Macbeth offered few causes for disappointment. Already in her repertoire for a number of years now as her first Verdi role, the interpretation has only benefited from further exploration of the composer's repertoire (including now Aida and Leonara in *Il Trovatore*). The voice has become darker and thicker since Netrebko's bel canto years, with a burnished quality that allows for the most satisfying exploration of Lady Macbeth's essential lower range than I have ever heard. Netrebko's expression of the part's intense sensuality was subtle without lapsing into somnolence, seductive but not cheaply sexual. One might have liked a more attenuated line on the ethereally high D-flat that ends the sleepwalking scene, but the overall effect was stunning.

It is fashionable to deride Neterbko's husband Yusif Eyvazov as a hanger-on, but such snipes hardly do justice to this fine singer's true talent. He sang a vivid, compelling Macduff and never lacked for stage presence or vocal ardor. The Serbian baritone Željko Lučić continues to triumph in the title role. The study only gets stronger as time goes on, and his comfort with the subtleties of the Verdi baritone range has culminated in remarkable growth. His portrayal is frightening yet insecure, menacing yet sympathetic. The final arias "Pietà, rispetto, amore" and "Mal per me" were models of pathos. Ildebrando d'Arcanegelo sang a steady Banco (Banquo), a noble yet helpless victim of the witches' prophecy. Over the past two seasons, the Royal Opera has benefited from the engagement of William Spaulding as its chorus master. After an impressive career at Deutsche Oper Berlin, he brings an extraordinary talent to the London stage. *Macbeth*'s choruses do not enjoy the intensity of those in later Verdi works, but in this performance they were terrifyingly lethal. In the pit, Covent Garden's music director Antonio Pappano brought more energy to the score than he has to any other Italian opera I have ever heard him conduct.

Richard Wagner, *Lohengrin*
Royal Opera House, June 17, 2018

Covent Garden has produced a new *Lohengrin* for the first time in more than forty years. David Alden's austere production nods in unison with many other directors who grasp at making opera "relevant" to our times.

Wagner's medieval romance of an enchanted knight who saves a damsel falsely accused of murder only to lose her when she asks the forbidden question of his name and origins, and the eternal psychological tropes juxtaposing faith and taboo, no longer seem to do for some, though to me approaches such as these only highlight their timelessness. But another crowd of refugees who look like they have fled in penury from any European locale in the 1940s? Creative appetites can never be quenched. Our particular crowd of the downtrodden are intended to be the nobles and freemen of Brabant, but they seem to have emerged from a disastrous war that has shattered their society, traumatized their rulers as well as them, and left them at the mercy of resurgent fascism, here suggested by third act black-white-and-red banners of Wagner's iconic swan rather than the iconic swastika of one of Wagner's later admirers.

In a populist era, we may well be vulnerable to leaders who appear magical, but there was a coarseness to this production's *reductio ad Hitlerum* that did not quite allow the magic of the opera to work. Two acts of sets enclosed by a shattered, multistory brick building drew closely from Claus Guth's La Scala production, which has made the rounds. But I was more taken with the unique Act III set, a basic white paneled wall beneath one of the *Lohengrin*-inspired paintings from the Wagnermaniacal King Ludwig II of Bavaria's Neuschwanstein Castle. Does mythology literally hang over our heads as we try to make sense of our lives and deeds? Alden may not share my point of view, but I hope it does, for it is, after all, what resides inside us.

Whether reminding us of the power of myth or sourly commenting on the harsh realities of the world that shaped us, a superb cast brought Wagner's early masterpiece to life. Klaus Florian Vogt simply owns the title role worldwide. A light, lyric timbre in the voice responds with preternatural perfection to Wagner's score – it is in fact so well matched to the part of Lohengrin that Vogt sounds unjustly out of place in heavier Wagner parts, even when singing extraordinarily well. Matched with a muscular form and gestures of heroic sweep, he could easily bestow hope on anyone.

The production's Elsa is the young and relatively untested Irish soprano Jennifer Davis. Having appeared only in smaller parts and as Adina in Donizetti's very different *L'Elisir d'Amore*, she filled in for the announced Kristine Opolais, who withdrew from the production. Davis sang with a gorgeous, full bodied voice that captured Elsa's innocence while still preserving its essential dramatic power. The heavenly couple's nasty foils, the faithless backstabbing Ortrud and proud and defiant Telramund fell to the superb talents of equally gifted performers. Christine Goerke's delicious smirks and sneers dominated the stage, even in those first act moments when the character has few words to sing. In her Act II revenge sequences, she was all charm when necessary and vicious harridan when invoking the vengeance of her pagan gods and denouncing Elsa's champion. Thomas J. Mayer's Telramund was appropriately snarling, though he was announced as allergy-afflicted in a performance that caught him sneaking coughs. Georg Zeppenfeld's wounded King Henry, the historic tenth-century German ruler, gave us an idea of what a European ruler a thousand years later might have been like had there been no Marshall Plan.

Andris Nelsons is second only to Vogt in personal identification with the opera today. Observing the deft precision of his gestures in the pit readily reminded one of his mastery of the score. William Spaulding's choral work was on brilliant display, making Wagner's choruses an extraordinary highlight of the performance.

Modest Mussorgsky, *Boris Godunov*
Paris Opera, July 9, 2018

The Paris Opera's new production of Mussorgsky's tale of a ruthless leader haunted by guilt over his bloody path to power boasts a universality of Shakespearean dimensions. Almost from the beginning, this psychological mastery secured *Boris Godunov* its unchallenged place as the quintessential Russian opera. Testifying to the potency of its story, the play upon which it was based, by Russia's deified national poet Alexander Pushkin, was banned from performance for 35 years after its publication in 1831 and then only approved with cuts. Mussorgsky's opera, which premiered in 1869 (three years after the performance ban on Pushkin's play ended but at a time when the depiction of tsars on stage remained technically forbidden) emerged in the wake of an acrimonious generation-long debate about what a "Russian" opera should both represent on stage and sound like. The answer was an eerie and uncannily prophetic psychodrama of insecure power drawn from the primordial depths of the nation's quasi-mythical past, balanced against the untamed instincts of the enraged masses, and told musically through a mélange of Slavic folk rhythms, Orthodox Christian ecclesiastical sonorities, and adaptations of the Russian language's distinctive prosody.

Throughout almost all of *Boris Godunov*'s performance history, there has been an axis of tension in determining the opera's protagonist. Is it the brooding title character – the guilt-ridden usurper of the ruling dynasty that preceded the Romanovs, an intriguer *par excellence* who rose to the top of the tree by arranging the murder of a small, innocent boy who was the rightful heir? Or is it the rebellious Russian populace, which mocks his failings and groans under his vices as a runaway monk who impersonates the murdered heir arrives to seize power for himself? In Soviet times, the angry choruses had appealing revolutionary credentials that resounded even on the other side of what became the iron curtain. When *Boris Godunov* opened the Metropolitan Opera's 1943-1944 season, at the height of World War II, an American critic admiringly compared the opera's angry chorus to the current generation of Russians, who by that post-Stalingrad point in the war were driving the Nazi invaders out of their land. On the other hand, Boris's compelling

Shakespearean dimensions made the tortured "great man" title role by far the most celebrated in the Russian operatic tradition – an aspiration for generations of Russian bassos who wished to emulate their avatar, the great Fyodor Chaliapin, and a tragic character offered up for the delectation of modern publics intrigued by the fantastically outsized fates of male anti-heroes from Macbeth to Frank Underwood.

Just as the opera anticipated a political divide, it also engendered differences of musical opinion. Mussorgsky's original version of 1869 unrolled in seven scenes uninterrupted by intermissions. Plumbing the story's turbulent psychological depths, this version proved too stark for the administrators of Russia's Imperial Theaters, who ordered up a revision featuring a prominent female role, introduced in a power-fueled love story for the young imposter and the Polish princess he historically wed. The revision, which appeared in 1872, principally gave the rebellious Russian peasantry a bloody day of rage in which they violently rebel against Boris's tyranny in the depths of the Kromy Forest, where they hail the new leader and lynch a stand-in boyar and Latin-spewing Jesuit priests for nationalist good measure.

In recent decades, an adapted form of the original version – which eliminates the love story but maintains the rebellious *jacquerie* in the seven-scene format – has gained ground, though both versions are still staged. Thanks to the opera world's curatorial bent, the latest trend is to go even further toward authenticity by embracing the unrevised original version of 1869 with no quarter for any later material. The effect renders the aggrieved choruses, who no longer have any explosive outlet, subdued and inured to their suffering. Boris, with lines adhering more closely to Pushkin's original, Shakespeare-inspired blank verse, emerges as less grandiose and more vulnerable, sensitive to an increased array of grinding insecurities. In an age of creeping authoritarianism, in 2012 the British director Graham Vick daringly used this version to stage the opera in an ultra-modern Russian setting at St. Petersburg's Mariinsky Theater just as Vladimir Putin reprised his presidency following an anomalous four-year term as prime minister. Protests had rocked the country at the time of the transition, but their lack of effect mirrored the experience of the original *Boris*'s downtrodden masses. Richard Jones's recent production for the

Royal Opera and Deutsche Oper Berlin took a more stylized traditional approach, but still struck a chord in a world dubiously shared with Erdogan, Chávez, and the monsters who put an end to the Arab Spring.

Director Ivo van Hove's Paris production advances this adaptation in an attempt to inscribe the work with hyper-contemporary relevance. Shearing both its "exotic" idiom (ironically its chief source of appeal both in and outside of Russia since the beginning) and the revolutionary spin emphasized by the Soviets, van Hove reflects on selected results of the most recent rounds of populist agitation. Just as the choruses of Mussorgsky's original *Boris* have no productive outlet for their rage, so has much recent populism dissolved into the sullen resignation of Parkland high school graduates heading off to college with zero prospect of meaningful gun control. In his darker moments, van Hove shows the masses dully compliant with authoritarian expectations while harboring backbiting animosity. In Boris's iconic coronation scene, they collectively stick up their middle fingers just after dutifully delivering their predetermined votes under police prodding into an electoral urn. At the end of the opera, which concludes with Boris's pathetic death, they stand at the front of the stage concealing their new hero, the imposter, who has just slain Boris's son and pensively contemplates his predecessor's lifeless corpse in a jarring premonition of his own fate (historically, the pretender had Boris's son killed and was himself later killed by enraged Muscovites). Van Hove attempts a depressing comparative message in staging the original version now, but it really was not worth sacrificing the more exciting elements of the opera's later compositional history.

There is a temptation to set *Boris Godunov* in modern settings, regardless of the version produced. In this, van Hove's staging loses much pretense to originality. Numerous earlier productions cast Boris as a suited president-for-life, attended and undermined by a bevy of equally well tailored oligarchs. Now we have another one. The set's only notable feature gives him a regal, red carpeted staircase that he can ascend to stand out from the crowd. The incorporation of video adds a dimension of insight. At high ceremonial moments, we are drawn into telling close-ups of pageantry that might have been worthy of the recent royal wedding. Other projections give us by turns the seedy surroundings of the opera's others scenes, searing colors to indicate savage moods, and, best of all, a montage of the "true" circumstances of Boris's accession to power – his ahistorical but dramatically compelling personal murder of the rightful heir by stabbing, immediately followed by an intense and larger than life show of immense remorse.

The new production split the casting of Boris between the internationally celebrated Ildar Abdrazakov and the noteworthy Ukrainian bass under review here, Aleksandr Tsymbalyuk. Both are in their early forties, perhaps a bit too early to comprehend the role's gravitas. Tsymbalyuk started cautiously, betraying a hint of restraint in the coronation scene, but moving on to a truly moving performance in Boris's later moments – his laments of having achieved great power and his bitter yet crushingly repentant death.

The Estonian bass Ain Anger has already tackled Boris, but seemed rather better suited the potent role of the wise monk Pimen, a dramatic foil who confronts Boris with the magnitude of his crimes. A simplicity in the delivery made him sound better than he did as a deranged monarch. The fine tenor Dmitry Golovnin sang the role of the pretender with special impudence. Maxim Mikhailov, yet another one-time Boris, added a stentorian cameo as one of the guards sent to arrest him. Evgeny Nikitin, who has also essayed the title role, gave a rousing and violent rendering of the monk Varlaam's tavern song about Ivan the Terrible's bloody conquest of Kazan. Damian Iorio led a hair-raising performance from the Paris Opera's orchestra and chorus.

Chapter Nine

2018-2019

Giacomo Puccini, *Tosca*
New York, Metropolitan Opera, November 9, 2018

As it does in most seasons, Puccini's *Tosca* has returned to the Met for a hefty performance run. Sir David McVicar's production has given the work a new lease on life in this house, premiering last New Years' Eve after an eight-year interregnum dominated by a cheap, bland, and universally despised flop designed by the late Swiss director Luc Bondy. McVicar's major virtue was that his approach gestured toward recreating the long beloved Franco Zeffirelli production, which had been discarded in what the Met's general manager Peter Gelb publicly acknowledged as a mistake. The visuals are a bit different, with the stunningly realistic recreations of the Church of Sant'Andrea della Valle, the Palazzo Farnese, and the Castel Sant'Angelo turned roughly on a 45-degree angle, but the public and critics alike were pleased. The new production's start was nevertheless inauspicious – the announced conductor and all three principal leads dropped out before the curtain went up, and the initial replacement conductor turned out to be the Met's former music director James Levine, who was removed after he was suspended due to sexual harassment allegations.

This season the drama was safely confined to the stage, with a respectable cast going forward relatively intact. Once infamously derided as a "shabby little shocker," *Tosca* is the tale of a predictably tragic love affair. Set in Rome at a time when Italy was in contention between revolutionary France, then technically still a republic but already ruled by Napoleon, and conservative Europe, the singer Floria Tosca falls under the gaze of Rome's lustful and corrupt police chief Baron Scarpia. Taking advantage of her love for the politically radical painter Cavaradossi and his help for an escaped political prisoner, Scarpia detains both of them and offers to free Cavaradossi in exchange for Tosca's favors. She pretends to give in, but savagely stabs her tormentor to death just after he appears to arrange to keep his word by way of a mock execution. Sadly, Scarpia had already planned a double cross, and Cavaradossi's firing squad turns out to be a real one after all. Devastated by loss and trapped by her own murder of Scarpia, Tosca jumps to her death to tortured strains of the romantic music recalling the unhappy couple's most tender moments.

All of the opera's principle roles demand tenacity, and it was on full display from this cast. Sondra Radvanovsky has experimented with bel canto singing in recent seasons, but her intensity and strong chest voice were deployed to better effect here. The voice has a metallic quality that not everyone likes, but she portrayed a vivid, passionate woman, plumbing the depths of Tosca's jealousy as well as her earnestness. The part's signature second act aria "Vissi d'arte" shimmered with modulations that drew well deserved attention and sympathy.

Joseph Calleja turned in a solid performance as Cavaradossi, but relied too heavily on his customary vibrato to pull off the high notes. The character's resounding cry of "Vittoria," uttered when Scarpia gets bad news from the military front, sounded more like a curiosity than an achievement. Calleja performed much better, however, in the third act aria "E lucevan le stelle," a quieter but powerful end-of-life reminiscence of a true love about to die. The young baritone Claudio Sgura made his Met debut as Scarpia this season, replacing the more familiar Željko Lučić, who withdrew from the revival after the first performance. With imposing height and a strong sense of the role's courtly qualities, Sgura left a powerful impression and backed it up with solid vocal technique. He did not always shine through in the ensembles, and sometimes his acting, possibly through fault of the direction, compromised the emotional coolness that makes a truly memorable Scarpia. But this is certainly a voice to hear and follow. The supporting cast seemed to go through the motions more than usual. Patrick Carfizzi's Sacristan was a campy distraction the performance could have done without.

Carlo Rizzi led a noble performance from the Met's orchestra and chorus. His tempos were balanced, and one appreciated the effort.

Charles Gounod, *Sapho*
Washington Concert Opera, November 18, 2018

A lion of the French Romantic tradition, Charles Gounod's popularity rests almost totally on his sprawling operatic exploration of the Faust legend, once a nearly perennial favorite, which still holds a respectable place in the standard repertoire. Apart from *Faust*, the composer's weaker and less popular *Roméo et Juliette* is about all that remains known of his work, even to cognoscenti. But Gounod wrote ten other operas, and the first of them, *Sapho*, has received an exceptionally rare performance by the intrepid Washington Concert Opera, a company dedicated to performing two works per season in concert at Lisner Auditorium on the campus of George Washington University. After a couple of decades of presenting operas that are relatively well known but far from popular, WCO's more recent repertoire has veered toward the obscure. If one's operatic appetite is piqued by Richard Strauss's pseudo-Wagnerian *Guntram*, Verdi rarities *I Masnadieri* and *Il Corsaro*, or (later this season) Rossini's forgotten *Zelmira*, this is the company to look to. The effort seems determinedly contrarian in its presentation of works of which even specialists have rarely if ever heard, and the danger of falling into a stale curatorial custodianship is ever present.

Nevertheless, WCO enjoys a devoted following in the nation's capital and occupies a lauded place in its musical life. Still, one of the unavoidable questions even its staunchest supporters pose to its artistic director Antony Walker is how he chooses the obscure works that appear before them. Whim appears to play a significant role. Gounod's debut opera saw the light of day thanks entirely, as he explained at a post-performance reception, to his long-time admiration for the title character's seminal aria "Ô ma lyre immortelle," a piece written for contralto voice that occasionally makes it into recital programs. Otherwise, *Sapho* is a hard choice to defend. It failed at its 1851 premiere, disappearing after just nine performances despite a cast headed by the famous Pauline Viardot, a theatrical legend who used her behind-the-scenes influence to bring it to life. Revivals came and went, but the opera never found much traction.

It is not hard to detect why. Dramatizing the eponymous poetess of ancient Greece, whose life story is barely known and almost all of whose poetry is lost, the opera places her in a conventional (and entirely heterosexual) bourgeois love triangle with the devoted but callow Phaon, who is in turn coveted by his discarded ex Glycère, a woman so mean that one wonders why Phaon feels any regret.

Undoubtedly influenced by Meyerbeerian extravagance, Gounod and his school friend, librettist Émile Augier, invented a political conspiracy as a device for Glycère to break up the happy couple. We never learn what motivates the conspirators or what they hope to achieve, nor do we ever meet or hear much about the despotic ruler against whom they are conspiring. In a classic case of an effect without a cause, to paraphrase Wagner's dismissive quip about Meyerbeer, the murky conspiracy exists simply to allow Glycère to get her way. After selling her favors to Phaon's besotted friend Pythéas to gather evidence against the conspirators, she blackmails Sapho into forsaking Phaon so that he will flee without her. Phaon heroically comforts himself by taking Glycère along. As they sail away together, Sapho delivers her aria at what oddly turns out to be the very end of the opera because she then jumps off a cliff in inconsolable despair. With the exception of Sapho's suicide aria, the music moves slowly, with ponderous meditations on subjects that are poorly drawn out, shallow conversations that go nowhere, and choruses about murder and upheaval that sound much jauntier than they should.

Serving as a vehicle for the exciting young mezzo-soprano Kate Lindsey, who has already appeared twice with WCO, this unbalanced work came alive despite its dramatic deficiencies. Lindsey is not the contralto Gounod had in mind, and the approach differs considerably from the extant old recordings one might hear from Louise Homer or Félia Litvinne. But she did adapt her smoky mezzo to deliver an astoundingly well modulated interpretation of the aria and carried off the rest of the part's music in a clear success that captured the high notes that might have eluded a darker voice. As Phaon, the tenor Addison Marlor displayed a gentleness of voice for a role that obviously lacks much dramatic strength. He pulled it off with extraordinarily well practiced French diction that one rarely hears even from European singers today. The young Egyptian soprano Amina Edris was a catty and menacing Glycère. Pythéas less than noble foibles fell to the capable talents of the Musa Ngqungwana. Maestro Walker led a lively performance from the WCO's orchestra and chorus.

Giuseppe Verdi, *Simon Boccanegra*
Royal Opera, December 1, 2018

For those old enough to remember the momentous geopolitical changes of 1991, it may seem shocking that they happened 27 years ago. It has been just as long since the Royal Opera introduced Elijah Moshinsky's production of Verdi's most conspiratorial drama, the tale of a Genoese corsair who becomes doge on the on the same day his paramour dies giving birth to a daughter that the late mother's father wants to raise. Fast-forward 25 years to Act I, and the daughter is rediscovered under a new name after a long disappearance. The corsair's enemies abduct her as part of a plot against him, and he ends up poisoned but reconciled with his fiercest enemies, who also love his daughter, all while defeating the less appealing conspirators. Moshinsky's effort is waning in vibrancy, though the blues and purples suggesting Genoa's seafaring empire are still rather beguiling. Nevertheless, the spartan Renaissance-style décor in Michael Yeargan's sets lacks much interest. The revival direction seems a bit facile as plot twists are turned, and the only really dynamic movement is in the sword play directed by the regally named Philip d'Orléans.

It is clearly time for a new production (the opera's earlier version, of 1857, was introduced in a production here in 1997 but has mercifully been abandoned – after all, it lacks the exciting Council Chamber scene), but a solid cast saved the evening. Carlos Álvarez has steadily climbed the heights of the Verdi baritone, with a solid, martial quality that endowed the role with more gravitas than one is used to in repeated performances by the operatic superstar and not-quite baritone Plácido Domingo. This was a pirate to be reckoned with on every level. Daughter Amelia fell to the young Armenian soprano Hrachuhi Bassenz. The voice is not quite the spinto soprano that the part needs, but Bassenz was lithe and pleasant in the more endearing scenes. Francesco Meli took the role of the amorous conspirator Gabriele Adorno, delivering a particularly impassioned late evening aria, "Sento avvampar nell'anima," which mixes anger and regret in a delicious recapitulation of his love for Amelia and hatred of the doge, who turns out to be her father. Who could ever despair of the great basso Ferruccio Furlanetto? He is getting on in years, and there can be an occasional dryness in the voice, but he was a strong, paternal Fiesco and held his own in his exchanges with the younger Simon. Mark Rucker sang a stalwart Paolo, a doomed conspirator who steals the show when forced to curse himself.

Henrik Nánási, fresh from a triumphant *Salome* last season, led a bristling and lively reading of the score. William Spaulding's choral direction was vivid and indefatigable.

Giuseppe Verdi, *Attila*
Milan, La Scala, December 7, 2018

Arguably Europe's most important cultural event, opening night at Milan's La Scala always falls on December 7 – the feast day of the city's patron saint, St. Ambrose. The usual gathering of Italian politicians, second-tier celebrities, and addled Eurocrats gathered among a glittering audience of the great and the good (and, these days, the not-so-good) for a performance of Verdi's *Attila*, reimagined by director Davide Livermore as a World War II-era struggle between Nazi German invaders (the Huns) and Italian patriots (Romans) who resist them. Nobody seemed to wonder whether the production offered a political statement about Italy's latest government, a coalition of two right-wing populist parties that maintain hard stances on immigration and the European Union, which Europopulists widely castigate as a German-controlled project designed to keep them down. Italy's centrist president Sergio Mattarella, who has pledged to restrain their excesses, received a stunning standing ovation that went on for several minutes, however, and the usual gathering of communists and anti-globalization types on the piazza outside was tiny and more pathetic than usual this year.

The opera on hand still suffers from the younger Verdi's unfinished approach to drama and adherence to musical conventions that were becoming outdated in his own time. Ostensibly a romantic tale of lovers united by a confused but ultimately successful plot to save what was left of the Roman Empire by assassinating the ferocious Attila the Hun, *Attila* serves as a strong metaphor of nineteenth-century Italy's liberation from Germanic domination under the Habsburgs. A real brute, the opera's warlord and his savage hordes have terrorized Italy and its people for no apparent reason other than the enjoyment of it. A cast of Italian underdogs resists them with varying degrees of chivalry. The opera's most notable chorus marks the founding of Venice by noble refugees of devastated Aquilea, who have fled to the inaccessible wastelands of the Adriatic littoral. The less than noble Roman general Ezio tries to make a deal, offering Attila, in the opera's most politically poignant line, to "have the whole universe, but leave Italy to me." Outraged by the offer's inherent disloyalty, Attila spurns it and pursues his campaign. At the same time, he becomes besotted with Odabella, the tenacious daughter of a local Roman ruler he had personally killed. Even after being captured, she has the temerity to threaten his life. Intrigued, he decides to make her his bride instead of his slave and frees her. Odabella plays the part well enough to stay close despite the protestations of her beloved Foresto, perhaps opera's most feckless Roman warrior, who is at the center of another anti-Attila conspiracy. In the end, their efforts overlap, and Odabella gets the honor of avenging her father by stabbing the horrible Hun to death.

Updating the action from antiquity to World War II, the opera world's current idiom of choice for almost any opera involving nasty warlords and oppressed people, makes some sense if one knows the history of Italy's turnabout as Germany began to lose the war – German forces occupied Italy and carried out brutal reprisals when they encountered resistance. The sets are dominated by war torn urban ruins, and Ezio gets an attractive *coup de théâtre* in igniting a charge that causes a bridge to separate (the original idea of a collapsing bridge was abandoned following the recent real-life collapsing bridge tragedy in Genoa). Onstage executions by firing squad and a vast video projection of the murder of Odabella's father by Attila endow the flimsy plot with some gravitas. Gianluca Falaschi's costumes omit controversial insignia and only hint at respective allegiances through contrasting colors – the severe black of the SS for the Huns and Mediterranean tan for the Italians – and with some distinctive sartorial elements, including an Italian campaign cape for Ezio and fur lining for Attila's overcoat. In case anyone missed the point, Attila rides in on a black horse while the Italians' moral leader, revealed to be

Pope Leo I, mounts a white stead. In a final touch, Odabella waves a small Italian flag over Attila's lifeless corpse.

The Russian bass-baritone Ildar Abdrazakov led the cast. The voice was soaring in the title role's grand pronouncements, but suffered in the lower range. In Attila's Act II dream sequence, the sober depths of his reflections sounded muddied as he dwelled on foreboding premonitions of Italian victory. George Petean's Ezio brought the strong legato of a true Verdi baritone to a role that is neither heroic nor dashingly villainous, but still related noteworthy music and attractive arching lines. The *ingénue* Spanish soprano Saioa Hernández made her La Scala debut as Odabella in this performance. She was reasonably well received but was too edgy in her delivery to score a real success. Foresto is a weak character who accomplishes little, and Fabio Sartori's strained delivery, which relied too heavily on vibrato for my taste, unhappily matched these demerits. La Scala's music director Riccardo Chailly conducted well, giving special emphasis to the strings, which do the most to endow Italian resistance with true heroism.

Ensconced in his post at La Scala since 2015, Chailly has moved in bold directions, reviving a number of works that had all but disappeared, programming virtually unperformed original versions of better known operas, and, more particularly, exploring Verdi's early works. The final category poses the problematic question: how to engage the early-career creations of an artist who had yet to master the signature technique and expressive idiom for which he would become known. There is a great risk of engaging in a purely academic or curatorial exercise, one that does not always resonate with stylish opening night audiences. In 2015, La Scala's opening night production of Verdi's *Giovanna d'Arco*, a work the house had not touched since 1865, would have been a case in point had it not served as a vehicle for the superstar soprano Anna Netrebko. But Verdi's early works hints of what was to come in his more operas, and *Attila*, Verdi's ninth opera, is not quite as obscure. La Scala has staged three productions since 1975 (most recently in 2011), while both New York and San Francisco have seen new productions in recent times.

Jules Massenet, *Cendrillon*
Lyric Opera of Chicago, January 17, 2019

Fairy tales have been with us for a long time. The field of proto-linguistics has revealed that they may be thousands of years old, incorporating the hopes, dreams, and moral lessons our primordial ancestors cherished before they settled down into what we call civilization. The Cinderella tale – of an oppressed daughter who escapes her trials by matching the right footwear and graduates to a regal existence – is drenched in a universal symbolism of fate triumphing over adversity.

Rendered in French as *Cendrillon*, the story evolved in Greek, Arabian, Chinese, and other cultures' mythologies long before Charles Perrault wrote down France's version in his collection of Mother Goose Tales. A son of France's glorious seventeenth century, Perrault turned to writing only late in life, after pursuing a career as a manager of royal properties for the "Sun King" Louis XIV. Enduring favorites ever since, his Tales have delighted and informed generations of readers, up to the present day, with and without their simplified (if no longer always politically correct) refraction through the animated lens of Disney. Indeed, director Laurent Pelly's production of Massenet's version of the tale, which has been seen around the world and reached Chicago this season, was inspired by his grandmother's antique leather bound volume. Barbara de Limburg's sets are enclosed within walls inscribed by Perrault's lucid text, the simplicity of which belies the tale's more serious psychological probing.

Pelly's production preserves a heartening *Alice in Wonderland* quality, with Cinderella's rivals traipsing about in oddly shaped red dresses recalling the Queen of Hearts (Pelly also designed the costumes) and bare sparse rooms, which were augmented by fairy tale props and some reminders that the myth retains relevance in modern times. The enchanted forest, that universal symbol of the subconscious, is rendered here as the chimney pipes mushrooming over the rooftops of Paris. The Fairy Godmother issues her final benediction from atop a vast stack of books. The spirits she commands are simulacra of the real Cinderella, female in form and easily adapted to the tasks necessary to take the real girl, called "Lucette," to the Ball. The Lyric Opera of Chicago wasted no effort capitalizing on the production's magical qualities to advertise it to young people, large numbers of whom were seen braving the town's frosty January weather to attend and, among other things, have their photos taken with dazzlingly tiaraed princesses in the Lyric Opera House's elegant art deco foyer. There was no shortage of enchantment displayed in the house's Pedersen Room, a unique dining venue open only to ticketholders, which offered a pleasant range of wines, exquisitely prepared lamb and swordfish dishes, and its signature coffee-flavored Opera Cake dessert.

Massenet's version of the Cinderella tale, which premiered in 1899, enriches it with some *fin-de-siècle* sensibilities. Gripped by an ecstatic Wagnerism in the decades after the titanic German composer's death, his younger French counterparts tried hard either to mimic his success or escape from his overpowering influence. Dismissed by detractors as "Mademoiselle Wagner" for his early imitative proclivities, Massenet tried to bridge the gap by engaging with Wagnerian color to illuminate his opera's ravishing duets while answering critics with a return to the traditional operatic forms of aria and recitative that Wagner had abandoned in favor of continuous melody and organic scenes. The effect endows the characters with developmental arcs that are usually absent from more standard retellings of the Cinderella tale, reminding us that myths endure because they tell us so very much about ourselves.

In the right circumstances this fractured approach can overcome the potential pitfalls of a mixed style. Pelly's tight direction and a splendid cast made this effort a success. The young Australian soprano Siobhan Stagg captured the title role with an effecting *douceur* that nevertheless rose to near-Wagnerian levels of dramatic power. Her Prince Charming, a trouser part in Massenet, went to the talented mezzo Alice Coote, who pulled off the role's androgyny so convincingly that one could have believed her to be a promising new countertenor. With looks recalling the suave French film star Louis Jourdan, her portrayal captured the Prince's transformation from a spoiled and shallow youth to an ardent romancer tempered into maturity by his quest for true love. Her arching tones combined extraordinary control and a solid technique in an extraordinary capacity for ardor that would bewitch any woman.

Derek Walton's stentorian Pandolfe, the appellation of Cinderalla's father herein, explored the nuances of a character who is more perceptive than the standard treatments of the tale allow. As the awful stepmother – the noble and obnoxious Madame de la Haltière, veteran singer Elizabeth Bishop could not be ignored. Her transition from soprano to mezzo has proved a full success, with contralto-range low notes blustering out the character's pushy posturing. Emily Pogorelc and Kayleigh Decker made noteworthy impressions as the horrid stepsisters, here Noémie and Dorothée. Soprano Marie-Eve Munger's Fairy Godmother had a wiry tone but hinted at some talented contralto singing. It was a bit unfortunate that only the more experienced Coote and Bishop, and the Québecoise Munger, fielded solid French diction among the principals. Sir Andrew Davis drew a masterful performance from the Lyric Orchestra.

Giuseppe Verdi, *La Traviata*
London, Royal Opera, January 26, 2019

Like everywhere, *La Traviata* is firmly rooted in the repertoire of the Royal Opera House. Sir Richard Eyre's sparkling production dates back to 1994 and, now in its twenty-fifth year, has been revived in at least every other season. The opera famously touches on fairy tale motifs to deliver a heartrending tragedy. Violetta, a dissolute courtesan who has lived only for pleasure, somewhat miraculously settles on the devoted Alfredo and devotes her life to true love, if only for a season. Her scandalous past haunts her, however, and Alfredo's father covertly visits to tell her that their relationship threatens his daughter's prospective marriage. Tenderly but cruelly, he convinces Violetta to give up Alfredo, an ironic sacrifice for true love. The uncomprehending Alfredo takes the breakup badly, publicly calls Violetta as a prostitute, and wounds her returning rival amour in a duel before fleeing the country. As Violetta succumbs to consumption, he learns the truth from his embarrassed father and returns to her, just as she is about to expire, with time only to renew their love with words.

Missed chances are an unavoidable part of life, and a successful *Traviata* must speak to them fully. The role of Violetta is one of opera's most challenging for the soprano voice. It is, in effect, three roles in one. The first act calls for a florid coloratura part to capture Violetta's playfulness. In Act II this must be followed by a resolute and sacrificial dramatic soprano. The dying heroine of Act III requires a light soubrette with the life going out of her. The rising star Angel Blue, who makes her Covent Garden debut in this production, did not quiet rise to the first and third of these challenges – the coloratura runs in the famous cabaletta "Sempre libera" betrayed some hesitancy, while the death scene was a bit throatier than one might prefer. Her second act singing, however, blossomed to foreshadow a brilliant career in the heavier Verdi parts, and maybe one day in Wagner.

Blue's Alfredo, French tenor Benjamin Bernheim, brought a sweet, rosy sound to the part. Not all chances were taken – the end of his Act II cabaletta "O mio rimorso" ended rather flatly – but he, too, has much to offer on the stage. As the awful father, known always by his family name, "Germont," Russian baritone Igor Golovatenko, also in his Covent Garden debut, showed signs of succeeding the late great Dmitri Hvorostovsky, who gave towering performances in the role. At times the voice sounded less burnished and more rough-edged than one might like. Germont is a stern, stiff character, but he can be livened up by a more nuanced approach.

Eyre's production has held up well. The party scenes still offer flair balanced by charm. The rundown country house in Act II looked a bit drab, but its unprepossessing character only helped to highlight the principals as they emerged in their fullest relief. Paul Wayne Griffiths led a measured performance. William Spaulding's chorus delivered the opera's crowd scenes with style and splendor.

Richard Strauss, *Elektra*
Lyric Opera of Chicago, February 18, 2019

The heroine of Richard Strauss's opera arose from the mists of antiquity but personifies an archetype that only the bravest few would dare mention in the current climate: the hysterical woman. Sophocles's original play tells the tragic tale of the House of Atreus as a great lesson in the power of fate. Agamemnon, a hero of the Trojan War, returns from great martial triumph only to be murdered in his bath by his wife and her new consort. The royal children range in their reactions, with the dispossessed heir Orestes disappearing to plot vengeance, his sister Chrysothemis seeking to put it all beyond her, and the title character dwelling on her murdered father's memory and looking forward to her own revenge plan.

Strauss's operatic version came on the heels of his searing and provocatively transformative pseudo-Biblical opera *Salome* (1905), about the deranged Judean princess who met her own vicious end after tempting her stepfather Herod into giving her the head of John the Baptist. He adapted *Elektra* less from Sophocles than he did from a modern dramatization of the ancient tale by the Austrian playwright Hugo von Hofmannsthal, who would become his longtime, if not exactly happy, librettist. Suffused in psychological studies of what used to be called "hysteria," Hofmannsthal's vision of Elektra has suffered in recent times from that term's politically incorrect connotations, even if they did lend a name to the famous Jungian psychological complex associated with obsessive daughters. Many productions try to make her "relatable" because of her immense suffering, and at the same time powerful because she at least holds out for the vengeance that Orest delivers while refusing to succumb to Chrysothemis's codependent fixation with getting on with domestic life in an unspeakably bad situation. Other productions have indulged in the insufferably bourgeois trope of the dysfunctional family, of which the scions of Atreus, from that limited point of view, merely form a more extreme iteration.

Sir David McVicar's more traditional production, with sets by John Macfarlane, is dominated by gray tones that scream "urban decay," but serves the work far better. Elements of it may strike some observers as garish – Elektra's nasty mother Klytämnestra looks like a *Mad Max* villainess, with a rotund, misshapen torso stuffed into a disturbingly revealing outfit. She has a penchant for human sacrifice, with a likely victim brought out for death only to be abandoned when Elektra joyfully tells her that *she* is the sacrifice everyone is waiting for. At the end, a trick of the stage allows her and her slain lover Aegisth's blood to flow down the steps of the decrepit palace. Elektra's wading in it is true to a vision she stridently voices earlier in the opera, but the literalism may go a touch too far.

Chicago spared no effort to bring together an excellent ensemble to support the long overdue company debut of the splendid Swedish soprano Nina Stemme. Well practiced in high dramatic roles on stages the world over, she has at last brought her cool, collected tones to the Windy City. With gripping control, she modulated through the title part's obsessive narrations, creepy observations, and perverse confrontations with natural talent and faultless technique. The movements of her large, expressive eyes alone were enough to capture Elektra's tortured personality – here darting about to detect persecutors, there silencing the other characters with a glance. Elza van den Heever gave a splendid Chrysothemis. In her confrontation with Elektra about the merits of revenge versus family, she was a worthy sparring partner. Michaela Martens sang menacingly as their mother Klytämnestra. The outlandish costume got in the way of the best articulation of the character's inner torment – a weird mixture of guilt and self-justification – but the voice did not. Iain Paterson was a righteous and stentorian Orest, a smaller but decisive part in resolving the action. Robert Brubaker sang Aegisth as obnoxiously as necessary to preclude any sympathy for the louche character's miserable death.

Donald Runnicles, also in his company debut, infused the performance with intriguing subtlety, and admirably resisted the score's natural temptation to push the orchestra – one of the biggest in opera – so hard that it drowns out the singers. His approach is not universally successful, a judgment I feel qualified to make after sitting through two rather pedestrian Ring Cycles led by him with different companies, but here it was perfectly well suited to the waving dynamics of Strauss's focus on Elektra as the opera's omniscient narrator. "Do I hear the music – it comes from me!," she exclaims in a line that ostensibly answers Chrysothemis's question about whether she hears celebratory strains heralding the double homicide but is often understood to be a fourth-wall breaking admission that her fractured mind and murderous thoughts have produced the dissonant score.

George Frideric Handel, *Ariodante*
Lyric Opera of Chicago, March 11, 2019

Chicago's main opera theater has a solid track record presenting the long-neglected works of George Frideric Handel. Mostly forgotten after Handel's own times, they began to enjoy a discreet trickle of new productions in the 1970s. Over the past twenty years, they have burst forth in a veritable flood of baroque torrents. Chicago has presented eight of Handel's 42 operas, mostly with success, and now turns to *Ariodante*, one of his later works in the genre. It premiered in 1735, a decade after the seminal *Julius Caesar* (*Giulio Cesare in Egitto*), and only a few years before Handel abandoned opera for oratorio. But it did arrive during a frenetic period of composing that also delivered *Alcina* and *Orlando*, operas that have again become reasonably well known to audiences.

The plot, adapted from an episode in the Renaissance poet Ludovico Ariosto's epic *Orlando furioso*, is a typically convoluted Handelian romance. Ginevra, the King of Scotland's daughter, is in love with the noble Ariodante, but is in turn coveted by the wicked Polinesso. Polinesso, meanwhile, is adored by Dalinda, whose affection (and, in this production, body) he abuses to convince Ariodante that Ginevra was unfaithful to him on their wedding night. Ariodante's brother Lurcanio hopes to spur the title character to take vengeance, but the devastated man instead throws himself off a cliff into the sea – and survives. Lesser characters of varying affections flit in and out of the action to reveal the truth. Polinesso is killed in a duel over Ginevra's disputed honor, and the happy couple is united in eternal bliss. Or not. In Richard Jones's reimagining of the opera, the happy end is abandoned in favor of Ginevra's neurotic flight from the situation. In a moment of depressing self-realization, she decides cannot stomach Ariodante's doubts about her fidelity, packs a bag, and hitchhikes out of the situation while the rest of the cast sing for joy.

How can a Renaissance damsel in distress become a hitchhiker who wants to do it all on her own? Jones seems to have thought it a swell idea to update the opera's setting to a bleak lower class 1970s island community in Scotland full of dowdy tartan sweaters and dresses (sets and costumes by a British designer known only as "ULTZ;" it is unclear whether this is a name spelled in capital letters or an acronym for something equally insipid). His apparent purpose is to convince us that Ginevra is trapped in a patriarchal society, in which the male characters control her actions and reactions to the point of emotional paralysis and withdrawal for self-preservation. Ariodante's honorable intentions are hard to sully in this idiom, but Polinesso's villainy is expressed by presenting him as a charlatan minister who alternates between clerical garb and the scrappy denim of an urban lowlife.

There is no room for the true love or sincere forgiveness expressed so artfully by the music, and the tender Handelian emotions effuse musically from characters who seem to be woefully out of place in the midst of stark Bible-thumping Presbyterians. Another director might use an update to try to tell us that the lofty sentiments of Renaissance heroes can be shared by quite ordinary people, but the unintentional message that comes across is that our society is so fractured that the margin for resolving misunderstanding has become razor thin, if it exists at all. Even the opera's sublime dances, a feature of what is supposed to be a royal court, are foregone in favor of puppet shows in which the local populace portrays the likely fates of the characters, most of which are dismal. The ultimate outcome of Ginevra's flight, for example, is foreshadowed as a descent into life as a pole-dancing stripper in a red-light district. There is, unfortunately, no reflective pause to consider whether marriage to the repentant Ariodante would really be so bad after all.

Fortunately, the music took us out of this dramatic dead end. Harry Bicket, artistic director of the sublime English Concert, is arguably the most talented conductor of Handel on the podium today. He led a majestic performance, with arching strings stirring real feeling through four hours of music that just flew by.

The British mezzo-soprano Alice Coote returned in the title role, just after triumphing here a few weeks ago as Prince Charming in Massenet's *Cendrillon*. She missed the opening night due to illness, but as the run continued her Ariodante was another triumph. Gorgeous arpeggiated singing resounded through the part's unusually affecting arias, which radiated a much wider range of emotion than one usually encounters in Handel. The seminal twelve-minute "Scherza infida," a virtuoso meditation on sexual betrayal, unfolded gloriously. In her Lyric Opera debut, the rising American soprano Brenda Rae delivered a light and innocent Ginevra, whose arias nearly match Ariodante's in expressive power. Kyle Ketelsen's King of Scotland was stentorian and authoritative. Everyone loves a villain, and Polinesso came to life in the alluringly clarion tones of the extraordinarily talented countertenor Iestyn Davies, who has made a specialty of Handel parts. In technical execution he easily rivaled Coote's quality of performance. Heidi Stober performed well as his victim Dalinda. This immensely talented ensemble deserved a better production.

Dmitrii Shostakovich, *Lady Macbeth of Mtsensk* Paris Opera, April 13, 2019

As an unseasonably chilly Paris was energized only by the blaze that devastated its iconic Notre Dame Cathedral, passions ran hot on the City of Light's main operatic stage. The last weeks of the season feature Krzysztof Warlikowski's stunning new production of Dmitrii Shostakovich's brutal second, and final, opera *Lady Macbeth of Mtsensk*.

Lady Macbeth has suffered a long and tortured history. Premiering in Leningrad in 1934, just as High Stalinism started to take hold, its setting of Nikolai Leskov's eponymous novella of 1865 spoofs provincial Russian life within the horrific story of the dysfunctional Ismailov family. Katya, the bored young wife of the loathsomely inadequate Zinovy, is crudely seduced by the farmhand Sergei. When Zinovy's father Boris uncovers her passion, she kills him with a dish of mushrooms laced with rat poison. Upon Zinovy's return, she and Sergei strangle and bludgeon him to death and then hide the body in the cellar. The town drunk finds Zinovy's corpse while pilfering booze and denounces the murderous couple the police, who arrest them at their wedding. On their way to Siberian exile, Sergei wearies of Katya but uses her devotion to procure her valuable stockings for his new crush Sonyetka. Devastated by his faithlessness, Katya spitefully throws Sonyetka and herself into an icy river, where they both perish as the column of convicts morosely moves on to the strains of an old convict's song.

Composed to an atonal score derived from folk tunes, circus music, and other nontraditional idioms, *Lady Macbeth* could not survive under stolid Stalinism. When the opera premiered in Moscow in 1936, an unsigned review in *Pravda* that may have been written by Stalin himself denounced it as "muddle instead of music." It disappeared from performance, and Shostakovich spent the rest of the Stalin era living in fear of arrest and suffering varying degrees of official disgrace. The opera was only allowed to resurface some twenty-five years after the Moscow debacle, and then only in a renamed and watered-down version. Shostakovich never composed another opera, and the original version did not see the light of day until the émigré conductor Mstislav Rostropovich produced a recording of it in 1979. Paris did not mount its first production until 1992, and even Russia did not see the uncensored version again until 2000.

Warlikowski's production opens a new chapter in the opera's chaotic tradition. All affects aside, the performance immediately before the one under review had to be stopped midway through when a stage accident reportedly severed part of the toe of the lead Lithuanian soprano Aušrinė Stundytė. It was reattached, however, and just four days later she remarkably returned to continue the scheduled run of performances, albeit outfitted with what looked like therapeutic boots.

This mishap notwithstanding, Warlikowski's staging is unapologetically raw and brutally realistic, easily reimagining the opera within the subdued authoritarianism of Putin's Russia. Few liberties are taken, and little is left to the imagination. The opera's climatic moment – Sergei's forceful seduction of Katya – is not relegated to an offstage encounter or stylized concept. Here he simply shags her with her active acceptance. There is no hint of the rape or even ravishment that the relentlessly percussive music suggests. Likewise, in another great moment – Katya's realization of her betrayal by Sergei, – which usually unfolds in a silent scream while the orchestra expresses her plight and horror, Warlikowski merely has her sob into the wall of the prison vehicle transporting her and the other convicts. Filmic projections capture other crucial moments. The opera's opening strains show two female figures plunging lifelessly into watery depths, an image that recurs at the end, when Katya indulges her anger and grief in murder-suicide. During the wedding scene, a projected curtain runs red with blood, an utterly unsubtle suggestion of her and Sergei's guilt.

Despite her injury, Stundytė delivered a stunning vocal performance, easily matching Shostakovich's searing score, which Ingo Metzmacher conducted rather less forcefully than other conductors in my experience. Her Sergei, the brassy tenor Pavel Černoch, has a lyric sound that lent itself ironically well to his character's seedy persona; anything more robust would have vitiated Sergei's hissable corruption. Dmitry Ulyanov sang a stentorian Boris, cruel throughout and yet pathetic in his death-by-poisoned-mushrooms. Among the supporting cast, Oksana Volkova stood out as a mercilessly tormenting Sonyetka. Alexander Tsymbalyuk's profound bass, which starred in the grand title role of Mussorgsky's *Boris Godunov* here last season, made for a menacing police chief.

Richard Wagner, *Der Ring des Nibelungen*
New York, Metropolitan Opera, April 29-May 4, 2019

It's back! For the second time the Metropolitan Opera has revived Robert Lepage's much loathed production of Wagner's epic tetralogy, which is famously dominated by a vast mechanical contraption known as "the machine," featuring twenty-four moving planks that are meant to deliver sets with plasticity. Alas, after nearly a decade in the Met's repertoire, this massive effort, which cost tens of millions of dollars to create and millions more to accommodate on the Met stage, is unlikely ever to escape its alliterative condemnation as "witless and wasteful." Indeed, it is entirely possible that we, like Hamlet, may not look upon its like again. Rumors fueled by open-ended statements from the Met's management suggest that the next time the company presents a full Ring Cycle, it will be in a new production. This may well underscore the sheer folly of the house's infatuation with Lepage's *Ring*, which the Met's administration assiduously declared "visionary" despite almost unanimous critical and popular comment to the contrary. Still more rumors, widely welcomed in many corners, hold that the sets of the beloved old Otto Schenk production are still tucked away somewhere, like a sleeping Brünnhilde waiting to save our aesthetic sensibilities.

The investment was huge and the hopes were high, but it may well be time for the Met to cut its losses. Bayreuth, after all, stages a new *Ring* every six or seven years regardless of how the previous production was received (poorly, the last four times). The Paris Opera just announced a new production to replace Günter Krämer's dismal effort, which is roughly the same age as the Met's. Many of the defects in Lepage's production persist. The machine's creaks and cracks are less intrusive than they were when the individual operas premiered, but they remain too audible to be excused. Mechanical problems are still in evidence. In Cycle II's *Das Rheingold*, the music stopped for nearly a minute when a stage elevator failed to deliver Erda on time for her dramatically vital admonition of Wotan to give up the ring.

Apart from a couple of showy transformations – the descent into Nibelheim and Brünnhilde's fading into her magic sleep come to mind, – the machine's best uses arrived when it was perfectly stationary and delivered reasonable background scenery via projection. Act I of *Die Walküre* and most of *Siegfried* went forward successfully for this reason, but if this can be counted as a success, it was only because this was when the machine moved the least. Stage direction has also improved. Characters emerged in greater relief, and the human conflicts that drive the work were less cartoonish than I recall from the individual premieres in 2010-2012. Sometimes, however, the direction was simplified to address safety concerns, which visibly marred the production in previous outings. Brünnhilde's entrance in Act II of *Walküre*, which literally tripped up Deborah Voigt at the installment's premiere in 2011, is now a much safer but far less dramatic walk along the machine's flat top. The changes in dramaturgy are welcome and generally improved the experience, but nothing can mask the production's lack of an interpretive theme. Even Schenk's production, which was criticized for being too picturesque in its traditionalism, concluded with a slow fade out of the gods' divine light as the mortals contemplated the beginning of their new age. In Lepage's production, the Rhine overflows its banks, with its waters undulating at the surface like nothing had happened and nothing had mattered. Nearly ten years on, it remains what the Germans derisively call "*ideelos*" – "idea-less," or "free of ideas."

The Cycle's vocal event was the emergence of Christine Goerke as the leading Wagnerian dramatic soprano before the public today. This was her first Met Brünnhilde, and the first time she performed all three Brünnhilde roles in a composite cycle (her earlier performances in Canada and Houston unrolled incrementally over successive seasons without culminating in full cycle performances. Her Chicago Brünnhildes have also unfolded season-by-season). Traditionally, we have judged Brünnhildes by their ability to reach the glorious high notes – the C's, of course, but also the B's and G's that the right throat can cast gleamingly alongside Wotan's vicissitudes and Siegfried's raptures. Goerke floated these notes in fine form atop the superstructure of a superb technique, but her real uniqueness came in her insightful exploration of the role's earthy qualities. As Brünnhilde matures, she must experience the darker and more complex side of human feelings and develop empathy for frailty both human and divine. Her low notes, especially in *Götterdämmerung*, were extraordinarily paired with the exuberant upper register, which vaulted above the orchestra.

Cycle II subscribers had the good fortune of hearing the German *Heldentenor* Andreas Schager's Sicgfried. After a long career in operetta, Schager has catapulted into leading Wagnerian roles in Europe over the past few years. With a ringing clarion tone and effortlessly expansive top voice, he has already mastered Parsifal and Tristan. His Met Siegfried performances (which included his house debut in the matinee Cycle's *Götterdämmerung*) proved a stunning success, arguably the best the house has heard since the days of Lauritz Melchior. Some observers objected to his puerile and insouciant stage antics, but that is who Siegfried really is and, for better or worse, the person Wagner wrote that he wanted his hero to become.

Michael Volle, now a Met stalwart in the Wagnerian repertoire, was a tower of vocal and dramatic force as Wotan. He brought a deeply human interpretation of the role that reminded one of James Morris's best nights. There were a few moments in *Siegfried* when Volle seemed to have to rely on the prompter to get his lines right, but the performance never faltered in either musical or dramatic power.

Most of the rest of the casting was equally luxurious. Stuart Skelton and Eva-Maria Westbroek delivered a gorgeously sung Act I of *Walküre*, though Skelton is far from the most compelling actor in the operatic firmament. Günther Groissböck matched them with a malevolent Hagen and also contributed a suitably menacing Fafner. Tomasz Konieczny's Alberich resounded with stentorian force and the astute diction that this moving role greatly needs to be the focal point of evil ill will. Jamie Barton's Fricka was lighter than Stephanie Blythe's had been in the first installments, but carried the day in another triumph for her promising career. It was a bit to odd to see Eric Owens cast as Alberich's evil son Hagen. After enjoying a solid success as Alberich in earlier years and mixed reviews as Chicago's Wotan, he seemed a bit too glib for the role of a master conspirator. At times he was a bit too charming, even to the point of getting a few laughs with comic gestures that accompany the character's more deceptive moves. Master conspirators can be deceptively endearing, but Hagen is written to be purely malevolent, his only pretense to humor expressed in a biting sarcasm. Owens's portrayal here did not ring quite true.

The Met Orchestra has sounded better in Wagner, not the least in the horns, which squalled out of turn at some point in each of the four performances in Cycle II. Philippe Jordan approached the sprawling score with an economy of style that recalled Pierre Boulez's fast but famously engrossing Bayreuth *Parsifal* performances, and he seems to have risen above the glacially slow and dramatically ponderous renderings he gave in Paris's *Ring* a few years ago. *Rheingold* dragged a bit listlessly, but Jordan's interpretations improved considerably over the subsequent evenings. *Siegfried* ranked among the best performances of the opera I have ever heard, while *Götterdämmerung* ended the Cycle in a truly spellbinding fashion.

Francis Poulenc, *Dialogues des Carmélites*
New York, Metropolitan Opera, May 3, 2019

Francis Poulenc's opera of faith doubted and reaffirmed through suffering occupies a curious place in the repertoire of the Metropolitan Opera. John Dexter's haunting production premiered way back in 1977, twenty years after the work itself premiered (in Italian) at Milan's La Scala, and seems unlikely ever to be replaced. Recently, and in this season, its revivals have coincided with full cycles of Wagner's much longer but equally spiritually probing *Ring of the Nibelung*, generally filling spots in the off days between the tetralogy's longer operas. There are usually three performances, which either sell out or come close. One wonders whether this is the limit of this idiosyncratic work's demand, or whether the programming has something to do with the Holy Trinity. There is no doubt, however, that the work's audience is unique – a pensive and contemplative gathering remarkable for its mildness of manner and aura of spiritual curiosity mixed with stray Wagnerians looking for extra diversion and members of the Met's dwindling subscriber base, who may or may not have realized what they were getting into when they accepted a subscription package that included a less well known opera tucked in at the end of a season.

Dexter's production, one of his few remaining in the Met's repertoire, is revered for its economy of place, with all scenes transpiring atop a huge crucifix-shaped base before a dark black backdrop. The action is set during the French Revolution. It tells the story of Blanche, a young noblewoman who feels a calling to take holy orders at a violent time in her country's history, when Roman Catholic clergymen were butchered *en masse* for refusing to accept the controlling dictates of the revolutionary regime. Despite her father's misgivings, Blanche duly joins an order of Carmelite nuns known to history as the Martyrs of Compiègne in tribute to their mass execution by guillotine in 1794, just weeks before the Revolution's worst excesses came to an end. Exasperated by the struggles of her sisters, Blanche falls into a *crise de conscience*, flees the order as it is about to be disbanded, and returns home. Recovering her faith when confronted with their impending martyrdom – a dictate of God rather than a matter of personal choice – she is restored in her calling and rejoins them.

To the strains of a brilliant "Salve regina" chorus, they are led one by one to the guillotine (mercifully off stage in this production), which reduces their chorus one voice at a time to the sound of its falling blade. Blanche and her closest friend among the nuns, Sister Constance, are the last to go.

Poulenc wrote his own libretto, adopted from a film script by the great French Catholic writer Georges Bernanos, which was itself based on a German novella derived from the memoirs of a surviving nun. Additional material imagined by Poulenc fleshed out Blanche's backstory, with some nods to then still fresh memories of the moral compromises France faced during the Second World War. In a stunning performance that must figure among the best of her career to date, the magnificent mezzo-soprano Isabel Leonard delivered every scene with searing emotional power. The young soprano Erin Morley sang beautifully as Sister Constance. The older nuns have less stage time, but veteran Karita Mattila movingly delivered the moral messages of the convent's dying prioress, Madame de Croissy. Her successor Madame Lidoine luxuriated in the splendid singing of Adrianne Pieczonka, and Karen Cargill gave a fine low tone to Mother Marie. Baritone Jean-François Lapointe made a noteworthy company debut as Blanche's father, the Marquis de la Force, and tenor David Portillo complemented him well as his less experienced son, the Chevalier.

Met music director Yannick Nézet-Séguin led a colorful and insightful performance from an ensemble that has become impressively responsive during his short time in the post. No intricacy in Poulenc's sonic balance between the tonality of the nuns' music, for which he *faux* apologized in a relentlessly avant-garde mid-twentieth century musical world, went unexplored, and the jarring atonality that characterizes the madness gripping the rest of the work emerged powerfully.

Richard Wagner, *Tristan und Isolde*
Berlin State Opera, June 15, 2019

Thirty years after the Wall fell, Berlin's historic center remains a hodgepodge of renovation and rebuilding. The famed Unter den Linden, the central avenue that leads eastward from Brandenburg Gate, remains dotted with cranes and shudders with the vibrations of jackhammers in a city that does not quite seem to know what to do with the legacy of its imperial downtown.

The Berlin Staatsoper, once the theater of Prussia's royal court, has been a focal point of this uneasy legacy. The smallest of Berlin's three opera houses despite its grander history, which dates back to its opening on a commission from Frederick the Great in 1742, it was rebuilt at the spartan mercy of East Germany's communist regime after bombs gutted the original theater in February 1945. A recent renovation, which lasted seven years and came in dramatically overbudget at some 400 million euros, has restored the building's gleaming Baroque legacy, enhanced its superb acoustics, and preserved the intimacy of its performance space. With a reduced 1,356 seats, its capacity is less than one-third that of the Metropolitan Opera. Where better to hear Wagner, at least outside the composer's custom designed theater in the Bavarian town of Bayreuth?

The Staatsoper's interior may be small, but its ambitions are large. Led since 1992 by the famed conductor Daniel Barenboim, whose contract was recently renewed despite allegations of professional misconduct, it is taking advantage of Berlin's warm summer days to feature free televised broadcasts of its performances outdoors, in a BMW-sponsored event called "Staatsoper für Alle," or "the State Opera for All." The outside crowd for this five-and-a-half hour performance of *Tristan und Isolde*, Richard Wagner's masterpiece of impossible love that can only find resolution in death, was far from overwhelming, but the intentions were good, and the performance inside the theater even better.

Barenboim can be hit or miss in performance. *Tristan* was his long overdue Met debut over a decade ago, and his direction then was rather uneven. But in his home theater, he brought uncommon focus and delivered a slow but deeply contemplative reading of the score from the company's resident orchestra, Berlin's superb Staatskapelle. It was one of those Wagner performances where time seems to stop, with hours of music seeming like mere minutes spent in the presence of greatness.

Austrian tenor Andreas Schager is rapidly becoming the *Heldentenor* of our time. Having just thrilled New York with his Met debut as Siegfried in Wagner's *Ring of the Nibelung*, he has returned triumphantly to his home turf, where he has also performed Parsifal to great critical acclaim. Schager started in operetta. Ten years in the genre has bestowed incredible breath control, a technique of near-perfect precision and refinement, and a bright, clarion sound that resists the rougher baritonal timbres that other singers can bring to the heftier Wagner parts. The tortuous demands of the role of Tristan rolled effortlessly along with only a warble on a couple of syllables in one of the character's intense Act III monologues.

Schager was brilliantly paired with the soprano Anja Kampe, who has risen from lighter Wagner parts to the summit of leading roles in the composer's oeuvre. Her approach is sensible, with surging highs reserved for just the right moment, while intelligently deployed middle and lower register tones matched the part's dramatic demands. She ended the famed *Liebestod*, the opera's concluding resignation of love in death, with a well practiced *pianissimo*.

The lesser roles were staffed by a dream team of luxury casting. Bass René Pape's King Marke, Tristan's uncle and Isolde's intended husband, only seems to grow more sensitive over time, focusing more on the cuckolded old man's pain than on his anger. Violetta Urmana once had a formidable international presence as Isolde and, after some audible decline, has wisely downgraded to the role of her servant Brangäne. The volume is still there, however, and brought the role to greater life than usual. The Israeli baritone Daniel Boaz was a stentorian Kurwenal, Tristan's trusted retainer.

Russian director Dmitry Tcherniakov used to have a reputation as an *enfant terrible*, staging productions that were often too far over the edge to be taken seriously. So it was with his first stab at *Tristan*, which premiered at St. Petersburg's Mariinsky Theater in 2005 and marked the opera's return to the Russian stage for the first time since before World War I. In that staging, the "ship" that carries the captive Isolde from Ireland to Cornwall was a claustrophobic submarine. Her assignation with Tristan took place in a sleek modern hotel room. Tristan's exile and death transpire in a country house bedroom, with specters of his dead parents materializing to haunt the action.

Tcherniakov's sensibilities have changed somewhat in this newer production, which the Staatsoper mounted only last year. The ship is now a luxurious drawing room aboard a modern yacht, perhaps one of those enviably monstrous ones that Russian oligarchs float all over the Mediterranean these days. Tristan and his chorus of retainers are sharply dressed associates of King Marke, Tristan's uncle and Isolde's intended husband. Elena Zaytseva has costumed them in that 1990s-vintage Brioni look that now looks dated anywhere west of the Rhine. Tristan and Isolde's assignation no longer happens in a perfunctory hotel room encounter but rather more elegantly, in a series of stolen moments behind the scenes at a villa shooting party. Their physical contact is a bit restrained, but recognition of their joyful predicament emerges in liberating laughter rather than the usual maudlin gestures and grimaces. Oddly, given the heavy presence of firearms, Tristan's death blow comes in an awkward wrestle with his traitorous friend Melot rather than from any obvious wound that would allow his lifeblood to flow. And curiously, Tcherniakov chose to retain the final act almost exactly as I recall it from his St. Petersburg production in the early years of this century. Perhaps he ran out of ideas, time, or energy, as many of his colleagues now seem to do when reaching the final acts of grand operas. Or maybe he thought no one would notice. Greater directors, including the recently deceased Franco Zeffirelli, left bigger marks by revisiting works altogether at different times in their careers. Tcherniakov, who is not without talent, could have striven for more.

John Corigliano, *The Ghosts of Versailles*
Glimmerglass Festival, July 25, 2019

John Corigliano's most important work occupies a unique position in modern American opera: it is successful. While other composers' works are rarely ever more than a flash in the pan – and often flop altogether – *The Ghosts of Versailles* has enjoyed numerous productions and revivals since its 1991 premiere as a work commissioned by the Metropolitan Opera. What makes it different? Corigliano, who worked on the opera with librettist William M. Hoffman for eleven years, intended it to be a satire or spoof of operatic traditions. He famously described it as a "grand opera buffa," an oxymoronic term since no grand opera could ever have a "buffa" quality to it.

Two hundred years after the French Revolution, the bored ghosts of Louis XVI and Marie Antoinette and their court continue to inhabit the grand palace at Versailles. The ghost of the playwright Beaumarchais, who authored the trilogy of plays that gave us the "Figaro" operas of Rossini and Mozart, seeks to win the dead queen's affection by inventing a new opera around his neglected third play, *La Mère Coupable*, which sets the familiar cast of Spanish characters in Paris – along with a young couple who are products of respective extramarital liaisons – at the height of the French Revolution. Corigliano labored to include traditional arias, duets, trios, quartets, ensembles, leitmotifs, voguish Orientalism, a wicked villain, a damning judgment scene, comical servants, dramatic plot twists, and even a Wagnerian soprano who, with spear and hat-with-horns, declares at the end of the first act, "This is not opera! Wagner is opera!"

But if the point was to satirize those operatic conventions, *The Ghosts of Versailles* merely affirmed them. "Sophisticated" composers deny it, but we still live in a fundamentally Romantic age. Memorable and moving music appeals to audiences. Corigliano may not have intended it that way, but "Come now, my darling," a flashback duet for Cherubino and Rosina that evolves with Mozartean precision into a quartet including Beaumarchais and Marie Antoinette, stands as the most ravishing love scene in American opera. The comedic antics have not gone stale. Marie Antoinette's finale reconciliation with her fate remains immensely moving. Thirty years on, it is more than fair to say that *Ghosts* has not only held the stage but may even be considered a modern classic.

It was certainly helped by James Lesenger's colorful production, which moved easily between the monochrome realm of the ghosts and the flashy but guardedly traditional trappings of the opera within the opera. It lacked some of the spectacular qualities of the Met's production (last heard there in 1995), but it was picturesque and made for a congenial evening. Later this year it will be presented at the court theater of the Palace of Versailles itself, an event that should be anticipated with great enthusiasm.

Apart from the lithe Ukrainian soprano Yelena Dyachek, who sang Marie Antoinette with delicate passion and superb English diction, Glimmerglass's Young Artist program staffed the cast. Jonathan Bryan's Beaumarchais and Peter Morgan's Louis XVI stood out for their gravitas.

Christian Sanders was marvelously nasty as the villain Bégearss. Wm. Clay Thompson did a fine job in the caricatured role of Suleiman Pasha. Joanna Lantini and Katherine Maysek stood out as Rosina and Cherubino. Maestro Joseph Colaneri gave a fine reading of Corigliano's sophisticated score.

Richard Wagner, *Lohengrin*
Bayreuth Festival, August 18, 2019

"The true pilgrim goes on his knees," a French guidebook to attending the Bayreuth Festival insisted in the 1890s. Going to Bayreuth, the festival Richard Wagner established in 1876 to perform his own works in a theater he designed for that purpose, still resembles a pilgrimage. Situated far from any major airport and only accessible by road or regional train and still run by the family, it draws a peculiar crowd of the faithful but seems to repel the tourist hordes that mob Salzburg, Verbier, Aix-en-Provence, and similar locales in the burgeoning summer opera season. Bayreuth audiences are quite happy to endure the lack of air conditioning, sparsely padded wood seats, hour-long intermissions, the absence of subtitles, and general remoteness to drink in the works of their favorite composer. Some of the legendary obstacles have been removed or lessened. Political pressure led to a reform of ticket distribution so that at least some seats are available to the general public rather than limited to those patient enough to brave decade-long waitlists or rich enough to gain expedited access through charitable sponsorship. Commercial ticket orders are now accepted online rather than through postal mail. But other eccentricities remain. Vehicular traffic around the *Festspielhaus* is rerouted to prevent even the faintest hum of someone's BMW from disturbing the atmosphere (rumor has it that air traffic over Bayreuth is also diverted during festival season). The doors are still closed exactly on time and covered with heavy curtains – even German Chancellor Angela Merkel was recently denied admission for being a few seconds late, – and the heat of every summer seems to yield a handful of victims, who must be carried out past grumbling patrons. The slightest disruption to the hall's famed silence is met with acute hisses of reprobation.

Yuval Sharon's *Lohengrin*, which opened the Bayreuth Festival last year and returns now, bears the distinction of being perhaps the first work of art self-consciously inspired by the election of Donald Trump, which preceded the director's commission by a few weeks. Ostensibly a response to the attendant #MeToo hysteria, it attempts a feminist reinterpretation of Wagner's fairy tale exploration of romance and the male rescue fantasy. In a post-apocalyptic world that has the look and color schemes of 1940s-vintage science fiction comics, Elsa's persecution by the men around her does not yield to her salvation by the purity of Wagner's knight-errant, but rather to her noxious confinement by him. She is led to the altar in the second act's famous ruined wedding with her hands bound by a blue ribbon, which the scheming Ortrud unties in what Sharon would like us to believe is a moment of enlightenment about the gender dynamics behind her predicament. By Act III, when Elsa wants to ask Lohengrin the forbidden questions of his identity and origin, he ties her up to stifle her curiosity.

The trouble with this approach is that as #MeToo recedes in potency, as all witch hunts eventually do given humanity's inability to sustain rage, its relevance to what is happening on stage falls by the wayside, a mute byproduct that would have been virtually undetectable to anyone who did not read the program. Indeed, since the production premiered in 2018, Brett Kavanaugh was confirmed to the Supreme Court, Joe Biden remains the Democratic frontrunner despite all the allegations of lascivious hugging, mostly successful Title IX lawsuits against universities are filed at a rate of one per week, and Plácido Domingo continues to receive rapturous ovations as accusations against him pile up.[20]

Another disappointment in this *Lohengrin* came in the cancellation of the superstar Russian soprano Anna Netrebko, whose career has moved in the direction of heavier roles, including Elsa, which she was scheduled to sing in two performances this summer, including the performance I attended. She cancelled on medical advice, however, and

---

[20] Domingo was virtually erased from North American stages in subsequent months, but his career in Europe has remained almost totally intact and shows no sign of faltering post-pandemic.

was replaced by Annette Dasch, who sang in the last production, which cast the opera as a scientific experiment in which characters were costumed as lab rats. Dasch's creamy, lustrous soprano has become shrill, however, and too often the high notes did not reach their loveliest extent. Piotr Beczała's Lohengrin fared rather better, though he has no claim to being a *Heldentenor* in the classic mold. More enjoyable were the evil duo of Elena Pankratova's Ortrud and Tomasz Konieczny's Telramund, both in excellent form. Pankratova appears to have lost whatever vocal inhibitions she may have suffered when I heard her two years ago and is now a Wagnerian villainess par excellence. Under the baton of Christian Thielemann, a conductor so dynamic that he is now the subject of a 300-page coffee table book featuring him in impassioned conducting poses, the score radiated the inimitable sound that draws people to Bayreuth notwithstanding all its inconveniences.

Richard Wagner, *Tannhäuser*
Bayreuth Festival, August 20, 2019

The signature event of most years in Bayreuth is the advent of a new production. This year it was *Tannhäuser*, the second of Wagner's mature operas, which has gone down in musical history for the titanic failure of its revised "Paris version," which was booed, whistled, and laughed off stage when it was presented in the French capital in 1861. Director Tobias Kratzer chose the earlier and rawer "Dresden version" for his debut production in Bayreuth. The major difference is that the Dresden version lacks the ballet that Wagner was compelled to write for Paris, but the music of the opera's overture is also rougher and more rebellious.

This is how Kratzer, who studied philosophy as well as theater, decided to explore the opera. In this he rises to a recent trend to make productions self-referential to Bayreuth itself – Stefan Herheim's ethereal production of *Parsifal* and Barrie Kosky's recent *Die Meistersinger von Nürnberg* situated those works in and around Wagner's local villa, which is preserved as a museum. Kratzer places *Tannhäuser* in the milieu of the *Festspielhaus* itself. The title character, sung by the brilliant American tenor Stephen Gould in the Wagner role best suited to his voice, is no medieval knight, but a Bayreuth soloist who has fallen away from his calling to serious art into the realm of Elena Zhidkova's enchanting Venus, here the leader of a countercultural band of street artists rounded out by a dwarf and a black drag queen. As the overture plays, they drive around rural Germany in a van, stopping to steal gas and fast food while distributing posters with a catch phrase borrowed from Wagner's young adult theoretical writings about the point of an artist's life: "Free in Will! Free in Deed! Free in Enjoyment!"

Caught while defrauding a Burger King, Venus stirs Tannhäuser's doubts by running over a security guard. His return to the grace of high art is his discovery by fellow artists behind a recreation of the *Festspielhaus*, where he is to perform the opera's title role. His old love Elisabeth, voiced with passion yet some room to grow by the young Norwegian soprano Lise Davidsen, is a fellow singer, who inhabits the character as she forgives him. The opera's Act II song contest unfolds during a highly traditional staged performance, which Venus and her confederates infiltrate in order to tempt Tannhäuser back into their deranged company. Ironically, the scene was the opera's least believable, since it asked us to accept that Bayreuth would actually stage a traditional production of a Wagner opera. Our hero succumbs, of course, but during the solemn music of Tannhäuser's decision to seek absolution in Rome he runs off with Venus. By Act III, Elisabeth awaits his return among the marginal down-and-out, giving a bout of pity sex to Tannhäuser's besotted friend Wolfram before ending her life in a bloody suicide. When our hero returns shriven nevertheless, there is little hint of redemption, only a video image of him driving off into the sunset with Elisabeth in a pale wallowing in what might have been.

One could easily dismiss the effort as "Eurotrash," but Kratzer balanced irony with philosophical insights that deserve respect. Notably, his production responds to the idea that the spiritual, or the realm of the soul generally, has become less about place than affect and experience. In an age of social media, "experience," as such, has become the main priority of the younger generation, over stability and settling down. It made perfect sense that Tannhäuser's suspension between the sacred and the profane should emerge from the company he keeps and the difference in his surroundings. Just to remind us, Kratzer engineered an intermission show with Venus and her band frolicking around a pond in the park in front of the theater. Its only tie-in with the performance was the drag queen's rendering of Elisabeth's ecstatic entrance aria "Dich, Teure Halle" transposed for bass voice. The frivolity at least lightened the mood during what can often be a somber intermission hour. The eminent Russian conductor Valery Gergiev made his Bayreuth debut with this production of one of only two of Wagner's operas he has never presented in his home theater, the Mariinsky Theater in St. Petersburg, and led a magnificently disciplined performance from Bayreuth's specially assembled orchestra.

Chapter Ten

2019-2020

Arnold Schoenberg, *Erwartung*/
Béla Bartók, *Bluebeard's Castle*
New York Philharmonic Orchestra, September 26, 2019

Opening week in New York rose to dizzying heights of excitement with the Metropolitan's Opera opening night new production of Gershwin's *Porgy and Bess* and the hysteria over the sexual harassment allegations against Plácido Domingo, who withstood them until the eve of his scheduled Met performance in Verdi's *Macbeth*, when he withdrew from the production and all future Met appearances. The mood for the New York Philharmonic's innovative staging of this double bill of explosive works of the expressionist genre, offered in collaboration with the Royal Stockholm Philharmonic Orchestra, gave the audience much to think about in the realm of gender relations, if that is all music now means.

Rarely for performances of Schoenberg's monodrama *Erwartung*, which the late soprano Jessye Norman memorably sang on the Met stage, Bengt Gomér's production was preceded by a performance of Schoenberg's song "Erwartung," one of a four-song cycle. Nina Stemme's strong interpretation, modulated through her cool Nordic tones, made one wish she were on all night, but alas it merely whetted our appetites for the second part of the concert, in which she took the role of the naïve Judith in Bartók's *Bluebeard's Castle*. Katarena Karnéus, however, did a superb job relating the wavering emotions of the nameless woman of *Erwartung* the opera, who searches for her unfaithful lover while cycling through feelings of anticipation, anxiety, and fear of abandonment before finally finding him dead. Gomér depicts her as a traveler, carrying around a suitcase. When she discovers the body, which is concealed under a white sheet on a hospital gurney, it turns out for no readily apparent reason to be a dead deer. The musical quality was there, but this odd production trick seemed like a satire or joke on her profound feelings, which I, at least, came to enjoy.

Bluebeard made rather more sense. Performed, as was *Erwartung*, on a platform over the orchestra, the opera's title character, voiced with ardent desperation by the talented baritone Johannes Martin Kränzle, forces his attentions on Judith while taking her on a tour of his castle. Its secret doors lead variously to his torture chamber, treasury, lands, and finally, his wives, but in the video projection the footage merely followed a tunnel in what looked like the depths of a mine. Stemme's powerful voice captured the part with smooth lucidity, bringing the anxiety of Judith's naïveté and the final horror of her imprisonment forward in a captivating performance.

The New York Philharmonic has taken a critical beating over the past decade or so, but under its relatively new maestro Jaap van Zweden it delivered a strong performance.

Gaetano Donizetti, *Don Pasquale*
London, Royal Opera, October 18, 2019

Amid Brexit chaos, constant protests, and a rising new generation of other royal woes, comic relief is hard to come by in the British capital. A tense audience at the Royal Opera left it all aside to take in a new look at Donizetti's funniest opera, *Don Pasquale*. Designed by Europe's arguably most innovative director Damiano Michieletto and shared with the Paris Opera and Palermo's Teatro Massimo, this cheerful romp on family politics sees the hilarious victimization of its title character, a fading and indolent landowner whose friend Doctor Malatesta ("headache") contrives a marriage for him with the coquettish Norina. Norina, however, is in love with Don Pasquale's besotted nephew Ernesto, who stands to be disinherited upon his uncle's unexpected new marriage. The object of the scheme is to get control of the old bachelor's fortune. For it to work, Norina must prove to be so unbearable a wife that Pasquale will stop at nothing to get rid of her. In the end her tempers and caprices have the desired effect, and the happy young couple are united, with Pasquale's blessing and with Ernesto safely remembered in the will and a handsome allowance, too. If only marriage were so simple.

Michieletto has updated the opera from its mid nineteenth-century setting to a rough present. It may be hard to imagine fading landowners as we approach the third decade of the twenty-first century, but they are around and about, and supplemented by a superordinate *rentier* class that can imitate its slide toward decadence. In a perfect clash with the ugliness of our modern world, Norina's scenes, in which Malatesta grooms her for the rouse, are a series of poses and moues in the style of that most nebulous of postmodern careers, the "influencer." As Malatesta coaches her attitudes and affectations, she poses against a vast green background that allows her to be filmed and projected onto a large screen that dominates the background. Intercepted notes and letters are text messages snooped off of lost mobile phones. Norina's expensive makeover of Pasquale's dilapidated digs includes swapping his rusting Fiat for a sleek Maserati. Michieletto's unique insight extends even to the normally insipid. Ernesto, sung by the sunny Romanian tenor Ioan Hotea, pours out his determination to escape his plight in the saccharine yet principled aria "Cercherò lontana terra," but here he complicates his naïve intentions by vandalizing the old Fiat and stealing his snoozing uncle's wallet.

Our Don Pasquale, played as a larger-than-life lout by the wonderful bass-baritone Sir Bryn Terfel, lounges in his bathrobe around a ramshackle old house with no walls and a roof suggested only in outline by fluorescent tubes. Malatesta looked like the type of urban quack who might have issued medical marijuana licenses before that branch of natural medicine became respectable in the last few years. Markus Werba hit the comedic high notes but his more lyric baritone proved too light in color to answer Terfel's stentorian broadsides. The characters' second act patter duet "Aspetta, aspetta, cara sposina," a run through of Pasquale's plan to rid himself of Norina, resounded as the evening's most engaging music, yet it was Terfel's blusterous majesty that carried it to its greatest heights. It would be unfair to point of out that Olga Peretyatko has succeeded superstar Anna Netrebko as a powerhouse Russian bel canto soprano, excelling in roles that her countrywoman has left behind as her voice embraces the challenges of heavier Verdi and Puccini parts. A more just assessment is that her spiraling candenzas and girlish exuberance are charismatic enough to resound in their own right as the gifts of an exceptionally talented stage performer.

Evelino Pidò will not go down as one of history's greatest conductors. The pacing of the orchestra was at times sloppy and at others rather jejune, and the playing of Donizetti's lighthearted score lacked drive and focus. William Spaulding's choral work, however, announced the townspeople's brief scene with aplomb.

Christoph Willibald Gluck, *Orfeo ed Euridice*
New York, Metropolitan Opera, October 24, 2019

"Antique" opera has enjoyed a vogue for the past twenty or thirty years, but sometimes the results leave audiences wondering why someone would bother to revive whichever obscure seventeenth or eighteenth-century opera they spent an evening yawning through on a leading stage. All too often, the genre escapes engaging presentation and can be reduced to concert performances in all but name. A short work like Gluck's, which in its original 1762 version clocks in at eighty-five minutes with no intermission, can raise questions about seriousness, even though it is thought to have "revolutionized" operatic convention. But with the creative impulses of director-choreographer Mark Morris, whose imaginative production premiered in 2007, the Met has revived an unexpected crowd pleaser that has flitted in and out of the repertoire since the company's earliest seasons. It premiered at the Met in 1885, and this was its 100th performance

Mr. Morris's concept truly makes this a successful production. For a work of paper-thin simplicity, he imaginatively cast much of the work with the chorus of underworld denizens styled as noted historical figures costumed by fashion designer Isaac Mizrahi. They include celebrated royals (Princess Diana, Queen Elizabeth I, Henry VIII, Queen Victoria, Louis XIV), noted African-Americans (Harriet Tubman, Frederick Douglass, Martin Luther King, Jr., Ella Fitzgerald), dictators (Stalin, Mussolini, Mao Zedong – no Hitler, though), celebrities (John Lennon, Jimi Hendrix, Will Rogers, Judy Garland), figures of the ancient world (Salome, Livia, Cleopatra), and even Abraham Lincoln in his iconic top hat. Arrayed in rows above the stage, they take maximum advantage of the Met's high proscenium to suggest the universality of the afterlife and eternality of the work's moral message of self-restraint. Hades is suggested by caverns, through which Orfeo must lead, lose, and regain Euridice. Amor descends a long way down from above the stage, singing all the way, but adds the production's only major eyesore with her contemporary casual pink outfit. The dance sequences are Mr. Morris's standard airy passages and have more than a hint of jazzercise about them.

Met music director James Levine, who just settled a lawsuit against the Met after his summary dismissal amid sexual harassment allegations, championed the work with the argument that a steady dramatic hand can absorb the audience. Mark Wigglesworth brought less gravitas to the score, but the reduced Met orchestra delivered it with elegance and precision, while the chorus lived up to its fine reputation. Excellent principals added considerably. The title role went to the rising mezzo Jamie Barton, whose dramatic presence and adept singing riveted the whole house and reminded us that she is now the Fricka and Eboli of choice. Veteran soprano Hei-Kyung Hong accompanied her in the smaller role of Euridice. Her lustrous soprano and superb acting convinced the audience of real matrimonial love. Hera Hyesang Park accomplished Amor's dexterous stunt entrance from above the proscenium arch artfully and sang with feeling.

Giuseppe Verdi, *Otello*
Washington National Opera, October 26, 2019

Opening an artistic season on the weekend before Halloween can invite certain pitfalls in the nation's capital. Among them, as one found at this opening night premiere of Verdi's penultimate and most cinematic opera, was the confusion of whether other audience members were wearing costumes or whether they were just bizarre. An elite Washington audience of patrons, socialites, arts leaders, and political celebrities – including Supreme Court Justice Ruth Bader Ginsburg, who received her customary standing ovation just for showing up – mixed and overlapped with people who seemed determined to advertise that their work weeks force them to dress up and celebrate five days before what used to be a children's holiday.

For an audience submerged in the hysteria surrounding Donald Trump's impeachment hearings and other traumatic political headlines, the intrigues did not stop at the proscenium arch for Giuseppe Verdi's operatic adaptation of *Othello*, Shakespeare's tale of murderous jealousy arising from a wretched case of workplace betrayal. I have never before – in perhaps twenty performances of the opera around the world – known an audience to laugh aloud at Iago's dissembling excuses, biting cynicism, and sheer malevolence, but Washington brims with backstabbers aspiring to match wits with him.

Director David Alden, who staged a subtly allegorical production of Verdi's *Don Carlo* here two seasons ago, offered a rather unimaginative update of this later opera to the turn of the twentieth century. The trope follows Kenneth Branagh's picturesque but heavy film of *Hamlet* and is now starting to feel overused for Shakespeare's plays and works derived from them. Bartlett Sher's recent Metropolitan Opera production of *Otello*, which attracted controversy over its prospective use of blackface for its title character, is set in the exact same era. Sher's effort was ameliorated by some clever stage tricks, but Alden relies on the same monochromatic set – a courtyard inside a worn-down medieval fortress – for all four acts. This does allow the characters and their relationships to emerge in greater relief than in busier productions, but, combined with John Morrell's frowzy costumes, one wondered if the opera's Cypriot setting might have been presented with more dazzling visual appeal. It also forced Otello to seduce, confront, and then murder Desdemona in what is effectively a public place, vitiating the evolving intimacy of each scene.

Under Daniele Callegari's skilled baton, the Washington National Opera's orchestra rendered some of its better playing in recent seasons. *Otello*'s brisk pace must be paired with a dynamic lead from the podium, and the pit brimmed with stormy energy. Washington's chorus, however, was small and sounded underpowered in the opera's ensemble moments, which are more symphonic in architecture than the standard Italian opera chorus.

The fine tenor Russell Thomas essayed the opera's title role at Deutsche Oper Berlin earlier this year with decidedly mixed results, but sounded much more comfortable here and faced fewer distractions from Alden's sparse staging. From the treacherous first notes of Otello's entrance, the resounding call to exult (*Esultate!*) at the Venetians' victory over the Turks (to the company's credit, his second line, which proclaims the pride of Muslim fleet to be buried in the sea, was not sanitized into something more politically correct in the supertitles), to the delicacy of his wounded pride, Thomas proved through and through a noble warrior brought down by the flaws of his passions. As Desdemona, he was delightfully paired with the exquisite soprano Leah Crocetto, who is establishing herself admirably in Verdi heroine roles. Her "Ave Maria," the late hour prayer soaked with presentiments of death, rivalled her duet singing with Thomas as the evening's highlight. The splendid Georgian baritone George Gagnidze drew on unmatched technique to deliver an Iago that emerged straight out of the Golden Age. The raw anger of the character's creed, a monologue that has no antecedent in Shakespeare (referring, as it does to theories of evolution and the atom), resounded with extraordinary spite. It was a performance of menace that would not have been out of place in the back corridors of Capitol Hill.

Giacomo Puccini, *Tosca*
Milan, La Scala, December 7, 2019

Every year La Scala celebrates its annual opening with a new production. This year it was Puccini's *Tosca* with superstar Anna Netrebko in the title role for an audience of the international great, good, and not-so-good willing to pay up to three thousand euros for the privilege of attending. Preening actresses, captains of industry, titans of fashion, royals and aristos, and the paparazzi who capture them for the glossy magazines crowd into Europe's most important annual cultural event, which always sells out and hums with energy. The favored few continue the party afterward at Milan's historic private club, the Società del Giardino, where they are deluged in champagne before a gala dinner with the performers and creative team. As an *"Omaggio a Cavaradossi,"* the opera's ill fated tenor lead who is bloodily tortured and finally shot by a firing squad, this year's menu sardonically featured a gorgonzola risotto drizzled with lines of red turnip.

At one point in second act, *Tosca's* villain, Rome's sadistic Old Regime police chief Baron Scarpia, mocks the title character, the singer Tosca, for her real-life dramatics over the fate of her politically suspect lover Cavaradossi (described, among other things, as a "Voltairean"), declaring that she has never acted better on stage. La Scala openings are rarely immune from the dramatic intrusions of Italy's turbulent political life, with an annual demonstration by anti-globalist leftists trying to challenge the sensibilities of their betters across the piazza. This year's demonstration was surprising muted given the raging protests that are rocking corrupt regimes from Beirut to Bolivia. Milan's local police and the paramilitary *carabinieri* easily outnumbered its few participants, while the well heeled crowd inside the theater showered Italy's centrist President Sergio Mattarella with more than five minutes of sustained applause for his deft handling of his country's divisive politics and attendant crises.

La Scala's music director Riccardo Chailly has indulged in what Italian critics have called "a personal Puccini Renaissance" revolving around an excavation of original versions of the composer's operatic scores, presented as they were before they were revised into the versions we know and love today. This curatorial approach begs the question of whether artistic mistakes recognized and corrected by a work's own creator truly deserve our attention. Chailly's earlier treatments of Puccini's *Madama Butterfly* and *Manon Lescaut* proved interesting and well cast, but were not exactly crowd pleasing favorites.

Tosca, an opera set in Rome that premiered in the Italian capital in 1900 and has never before opened a La Scala season, is not all that different in its original version, and the divergent material neither adds nor detracts much from the *Tosca* we know. The first act duet, for example, includes a couple of extra lines for Cavaradossi to assuage Tosca's jealousy, though they leave the impression that he attaches more importance to it than he really should. In the original score, Tosca's famous second act aria "Vissi d'arte," a meditation on the injustice of her pain and suffering, has an anti-climactic coda in which Scarpia crudely asks her whether she has yet made up her mind to yield to his lust to save the imprisoned Cavaradossi's life. After she deceptively assents and stabs the police chief, a minute or so of music suggests superfluous reflection on the deed before she finally muses that all Rome had trembled before him. The opera's original finale moves the loud and devastatingly ironic strains of the love motif that normally end the opera to the moment right after Cavaradossi's execution, which is followed by a slightly different orchestration of the rest of the scene, culminating in Tosca's suicidal leap from the walls of the Castel Sant'Angelo.

Anna Netrebko's move into Puccini's heavier soprano roles has not been universally well received, and her first Toscas were mixed successes. Here, however, she showed an uncanny command of the role's vocal demands with absolute control, a splendid middle range, and riveting high notes. "Vissi d'arte" stood out brilliantly. Netrebko also captured the role's almost hysterical jealousy, which other performers tend to submerge under the character's more attractive mixture of pathos and saccharine goodness. The sunny voiced tenor Francesco Meli sounded underpowered in the opera's first two acts, and some high notes were noticeably strained, but his lighter lyrical talents were well suited to Act III's intimacy, especially in Cavaradossi's bittersweet aria of memory and lost hope "E lucevan le stelle." The role of Scarpia demands moments of aristocratic charm to balance his psychopathic ruthlessness, but baritone Luca Salsi's coolly collected malevolence allowed for little refinement. Chailly's conducting ably navigated the score and its odd additions with aplomb in a performance that sometimes seemed a bit lost under the weight of the plot.

Director Davide Livermore staged Verdi's *Attila* here last season in a quasi-fascist production that meditated on Italy's complicated fate in World War II. His new *Tosca* has delivered Milan's audience from the late Luc Bondy's despised production of the opera, which La Scala had the misfortune of sharing with the Metropolitan Opera, where it was also swiftly replaced. The first act sets for Rome's church of Sant'Andrea della Valle slide around the stage to change perspective and highlight the religious service in preparation for the Te Deum finale. The effect might have been cinematic but it tended to draw attention away from the action. Scarpia's headquarters resembled the Farnese Palace in other traditional productions but curiously looked in on the action from the side rather than the front. The stage elevator raised the floor to allow a distracting visual of Cavaradossi's torture, which is typically left off stage to focus attention on Tosca and Scarpia's more compelling drama. In Act III, the set wrapped the Castel Sant'Angelo in the wings of the angel whose statue rests atop it, but the stage elevator came to the rescue and restored the dual set of Cavaradossi's jail, here a prison cell he shares with thieves and prostitutes, and the parapet where he is executed and from which Tosca jumps (and from which a flamboyant Washington acquaintance of mine once jumped). While Bondy's hapless production staged Tosca's suicide as the beginnings of a simple leap, Livermore suspended a stunt double illuminated by spotlights to create the illusion of Tosca's body falling through space. The music stops before the descending soprano hits bottom, but the fade out was probably more tasteful than a splat or splash.

Giacomo Puccini, *Turandot*
Palm Beach Opera, January 24, 2020

After some worrisome pitfalls, including the bankruptcy of the Florida Philharmonic earlier this century, cultural life in the Sunshine State is on an upswing, fueled by a rising population of permanent residents seeking to avoid less accommodating climes and tax environments. The Palm Beach Opera, founded in 1961 as the Civic Opera of the Palm Beaches, presents a modest season of four productions but also engages heavily with the local community and annually hosts a prominent gala fundraiser featuring a solo recital by a guest vocal artist. Since 1992, it has performed in West Palm Beach's Kravis Center for the Performing Arts, an attractive modern venue of vaulting glass walls that serves as the metropolitan area's major theater for the lively arts. Under the direction of Daniel Biaggi, who recently stepped down after fourteen years as general director but was seen in the audience at this premiere performance of Puccini's final opera, the company has grown in stature and quality. Biaggi has been ably succeeded by David Walker, who proudly announced that the production run has sold more tickets than any other Palm Beach Opera production in the past ten years. Pessimists who lament what they believe to be the decline of classical music should take note of this intrepid company, along with other regional theaters that regularly post comparatively better numbers than the famous one in New York, with its forests of empty seats.

Allen Charles Klein's production of this narcissistic tale of a Chinese ice princess who is conquered by the wits and charms of her suitor, aided by the unmourned sacrifice of the woman who truly loves him, has been around for nearly forty years. It is owned by the Lyric Opera of Chicago and has appeared here as well as in Miami, Houston, Dallas, and San Francisco. It has held up well and veers toward what might be described as stylized traditional. It did not anticipate the Met's famously representational production by Franco Zeffirelli, which seems fated to remain forever in place. Rather it magnifies tropes of ancient China to accompany the action without overwhelming it. The imperial palace that dominates Act II, for example, is suggested by a dragon sculpture and an enormous pearl, but the effect encourages a refined focus on the characters.

The evening's star was the rising soprano Leah Crocetto in her company debut, a casting decision that places Palm Beach Opera in the top ranks of American opera companies. She was not chosen for Turandot, which requires a heavier voice, but for the role of the sacrificial slave girl Liù. She tends Timur, the blinded father of the tenor hero Calàf, because Calàf, whom she adores, once smiled at her. In the end she kills herself rather than reveal his identity, which Turandot demands to escape betrothal to him. In shimmering slivery tones, Crocetto delivered the part with moving sympathy, placing an exquisite trill on the word "*sorriso*" ("smile") when she reveals her devotion. She was equaled by the revelatory Italian tenor Stefano La Colla, also in his company debut, who sang a bright and clarion Calàf. The role's greatest challenge, the famous aria "Nessun dorma," unfolded with an exciting charisma that I have not heard in the part since Pavarotti and Domingo. Russian bass Evgeny Stavinsky, another newcomer to Palm Beach, sang a stentorian Timur. The promising young baritone Zachary Nelson made a strong impression as the courtier Ping.

The opera's title role is one of the repertoire's most difficult. It allows no onstage warm up before the treacherous aria "In questa regia," Turandot's recounting of an ancestress whose brutal murder by a lover inspires her deathly riddles, which a suitor must answer correctly to win her. If he fails, he is executed. Soprano Alexandra Loutsion got off to a rough start, with strained high notes that seemed beyond her. She fared rather better with the part's piano lows before rising more resolutely to the challenge in the final scene, when she overcomes her fears and insecurities to surrender her love to Calàf.

The company's chief conductor David Stern, son of the celebrated violinist Isaac Stern, led a solid performance, though sometimes Puccini's exquisite first act – widely regarded as the best act in his entire oeuvre – dragged a bit. The chorus sang strongly under Gregory Ritchey's direction.

Peter Ilyich Tchaikovsky, *The Queen of Spades*
Lyric Opera of Chicago, February 15, 2020

Tchaikovsky's ultimate opera of fate is interwoven with fate at the Lyric Opera of Chicago itself. Absent from the company's repertoire for twenty years, it was the first opera that music director Sir Andrew Davis conducted here. Now, as Sir Andrew prepares to leave his post next season, he has returned to *The Queen of Spades*.

Musically, the effort could not have scored a greater success. Every aspect of Sir Andrew's conducting let the score reverberate in all its creepy magnificence, though at times he slowed the tempo in what seemed like an effort to create suspense when in fact suspense is already amply written in. Brandon Jovanovich's Gherman, the opera's oily, desperate hero, pursued Liza with effortlessly resounding high notes through an entire evening performing a role commonly called "the Russian Otello." As Liza, the object of his fatal attraction, Sondra Radvanovsky bloomed in smooth, round tones. Gone are the pitch issues and metallic sound that had generated some critical comment in years past. Radvanovsky is back, fully on point, and should look forward to a stunning and accomplished midcareer. Samuel Youn's purring baritone, known from his gripping Alberich in Lyric's unfolding *Ring* Cycle, delivered the meddling Count Tomsky with a devilish charm that Richard Jones's production made quite literal. Lucas Meacham sang well as Prince Yeletsky, showing off a superb legato in a role that, in losing Liza to a ne'er-do-well like Gherman, is fundamentally a bore. The fine character mezzo Jane Henschel made a long overdue Lyric debut as the Old Countess, a hag if ever there were one. The endearing Jill Grove was a touch of luxury casting as Liza's governess, in this production a chain-smoking vamp.

Jones, who staged Lyric's bleak but vocally impressive production of Handel's *Ariodante* last season, seems to have a penchant for making the operas he directs downcast and depressing. This *Queen of Spades* did not unfold in the glory of Imperial Russia, but in some kind of grim 1930s dystopia. The program describes the setting as "fascist," but the opera's inescapably Russian idiom more immediately suggested a post-revolutionary Soviet Union, in which the opera's aristocratic characters hold on in greatly reduced circumstances. Either way, it just did not work. Bland totalitarianism lends itself poorly to passionate romance and the stuff of obsession, but even if it did the production's highly abstract conceit, which argues that Tchaikovsky's music anticipated the expressionist music of the chronological era depicted, rests on a false premise. *The Queen of Spades*, which premiered in 1890, stands toward the end – and is in many ways the highest expression of – the swelling Late Romantic. The composer rejected the Wagnerian label, but he wrote an opera about a love that can find no earthly resolution, unavoidable fate guided by the morbid supernatural, and a hero who becomes suicidal – and then filled it with an impressive catalog of leitmotifs that twist and bend to reflect the opera's emotive associational vicissitudes.

The expressionist genre lay rather in the future and belonged to a later generation. All we are left with in its absence is a sea of gray sameness in John Macfarlane's nondescript sets and bedraggled costumes, punctuated with kitschy puppetry that replaces the Act II *pastorale* and then, with comic effect that was almost uncertainly unintended, animates the haunting scene, where the Old Countess appears to Gherman as a chalky skeleton that shares his bed while her lines are voiced offstage. The final scene, a lively gambling sequence in which Gherman loses everything, includes a bizarre drag show by a solo dancer, who prances about in a dubious illustration of Tomsky's bawdy ballad. Tomsky's final act is to crawl like a devil stalking the dying Gherman, unnecessarily magnifying the character's importance while diminishing the central tragedy.

The musical effort rated high, but Tchaikovsky's intoxicating opera deserves a better visual effort to explore its full effect.

Wolfgang Amadeus Mozart, *Don Giovanni*
Washington National Opera, February 29, 2020

Washington National Opera has opened the spring portion of its season with a production of this standard repertoire favorite by Wolfgang Amadeus Mozart featuring arrestingly abstract geometrical sets by Erhard Rom and alluring video projections by S. Katy Tucker.

In our present age, mixing sex, violence, and power is a powder keg just waiting to go off, and the company is plainly unafraid of controversy. Indeed, it chose *Don Giovanni* to launch a new public discussion series under the hackneyed title "Let's Go There," with its first installment, under the even more hackneyed title "Bad Romance," dedicated to an all-female panel consisting of director E. Loren Meeker, a popular culture contributor to National Public Radio, a woman described as a "former" classical music critic, and a writer with no apparent connection to any form of music.

Premiering only a few days before tarnished superstar singer Plácido Domingo's name was unceremoniously removed from the company's young artist program, which he founded in 2002, Meeker's bitter approach to *Don Giovanni* recasts the work as an accusatory probing of male culpability. Irresistibly, it seizes onto the wayward title character's condemnation to hell not as the traditional moral lesson for hormonal teens or existentialist challenge to the dull bourgeois mores to which they so often succumb, but as a dour social comment on "toxic masculinity." From the first strains of the opera's celebrated overture, our lusty anti-hero is shadowed (dare one say "stalked"?) by spectral female apparitions. That Don Giovanni never actually kills any of his conquests (or, as the company's program notes call them, "survivors") is beside the point. Even when consensual – Zerlina, whose seduction is the only complete one we see, voluntarily agrees to go off with him at her own wedding to the oafish Masetto, – his womanizing is so foul that he is beyond redemption and must be consigned to perdition's flames. And even if he did repent at the end, perhaps by offering one of those meaningless blanket apologies to anyone who may have been hurt by his alleged actions, would he have to "step back" from whatever else he does in life to "reflect" on his misdeeds?

Despite the national hysteria, the message eluded Washington's audience, which still presumed to chuckle at the enormous number of Don Giovanni's conquests "documented" in his servant Leporello's rollicking "Catalog Aria," giggle at lines suggesting the insatiability of his lust, and peal with sardonic laughter at the distress of the seduced and abandoned Donna Elvira, who, far from being an early avatar of #MeToo victimhood, was originally conceived by Mozart and his librettist Lorenzo da Ponte to be a funny character at whom people should rightly laugh. Intriguingly, the same audience greeted the arrival of Supreme Court Justice Ruth Bader Ginsburg in the hall that evening with its customary standing ovation, perhaps without even knowing that she has publicly advocated full due process rights for men accused of sexual harassment.

Even if Meeker's production concept proved, for lack of a better word, meek, the company registered a modest success. Its main draw was the rising baritone Ryan McKinny in the title role. His vocal performance was steady, but lacked the lower range that demands a singer more comfortable in the bass-baritone range. Dramatically, he lacked flair. A successful Don Giovanni needs seductive charm, roguish guile, and a devilish shamelessness, among other qualities that North American men are no longer supposed to exhibit. It may well have been professionally inadvisable for McKinny to have explored them in this tendentious production, but whatever the reason their noticeable absence rendered the character unconvincing. Kyle Ketelsen's Leporello was a stronger presence in both voice and character. In her Washington National debut, Vanessa Vasquez delivered an affecting Donna Anna, though one shorn of the hints of attraction the character often emits in Don Giovanni's direction. Vanessa Becerra's Zerlina scored another excellent debut, without letting the production concept get in the way of the character's seduction. Keri Alkema managed the same feat with Donna Elvira, but seemed to lose her way in the part's coloratura, here added into the score to reflect her amusing pain. Basses Norman Garrett, as Masetto, and Peter Volpe, as the Commendatore, rounded out the cast with promise. Only tenor Alek Shrader's weak and tortured Don Ottavio seemed out of place, although the character's benign wimpishness may be the standard of manhood to which we are now supposed to aspire. Evan Rogister, Washington's new music director, led a slow-paced performance of a work whose many scenes demand a more dynamic thread.

Richard Wagner, *Der Fliegende Holländer*
New York, Metropolitan Opera, March 2, 2020

Wagner's *Der Fliegende Holländer* (*The Flying Dutchman*) the composer's first mature work, has not had a fresh look at the Met since August Everding's spectral industrial-age production appeared in 1989. That effort aged poorly over its three decades. In a barometer of its decline, the snow storm that blasted through its finale withered over successive revivals from the original blinding blizzard to the light flurry we saw at its last outing in 2017. Strong casts, however, generally made it worthwhile.

Director François Girard made a (bloody) splash with a *Parsifal* that opened to general approval here in 2013. I never saw much in it. The Act II bloodbath looked gimmicky, and the rest said little of interest about the work. Girard's *Dutchman*, his second Met production, fared little better. The overture is one of Wagner's most evocative and can stand well on its own as a kind of short dramatic tone poem. Here it was cluttered with a showy and inconsequential lightshow projecting shapes that come to resemble a ship breaking up in the waves. As Mariusz Treliński did with his own misstep in the prelude of *Tristan und Isolde* in his new production of that opera in 2016, the busy nautical projections were a pointless distraction. Girard made it worse by adding a superfluous dancer whose weird undulations were bereft of any connection to the unfolding plot that follows.

John Macfarlane's uninspired sets were bland and basic. The cursed Dutchman does not even get a ship and is left to wander around awkwardly on foot. Daland's vessel, which has some visual merits, is heaved on and off stage as necessary, but its presence merely announces the absence of the Dutchman's ship. The Spinning Chorus, which gives rise to Senta's ballad, the opera's focal point, heaves on vertically suspended ropes that recall an adolescent's gym class. This could have poked fun at Senta's raging passions, but the effect did not seem intended to be humorous. Her portrait of the Dutchman appears only as a huge eye that looked like it was repurposed from a failed *Ring* Cycle. There was no hint of legend, mystery, or attraction – just an empty gesture toward obsession that made one think of later Wagnerian characters and wonder what they were doing here. *Dutchman's* finale has been tricky for the last generation or two of directors. The music movingly proclaims the doomed couple's redemption through love, but our alienated creative caste is too uncomfortable with both of those concepts to give them any credence. Girard has the traumatized townspeople look out over a crimson sunset in a moment that screams, "So what?"

This new production was intended to mark the magnificent Welsh bass-baritone Sir Bryn Terfel's return to the Met after an eight-year absence. A broken ankle, however, removed him from stage performance. He was capably replaced by the Russian baritone Evgeny Nikitin, whom I first encountered in the role under conductor Valery Gergiev's baton at St. Petersburg's Mariinsky Theater some twenty years ago. Nikitin gave alluringly brasher performances in those days, when he was still under thirty. Later, in 2012, he suffered a terrible career setback with *Dutchman* when he was summarily fired from a new Bayreuth Festival production after an old video surfaced of him sporting what looked like a swastika tattoo. Being "cancelled" *avant la lettre* may have tempered his engagement with Wagner, but his solid baritone, which has given the Met memorable Klingsors, Kurwenals, and Gunthers, has not really grown into the part. The lower range, which conveys the grave depths of the doomed mariner's devilish predicament, proved elusive.

Soprano Anja Kampe made a big, bright, and long overdue house debut as Senta. Having mastered heavier Wagner parts elsewhere – her Berlin Isolde last year was enthralling – she brought a powerful effort that in many ways saved this drab production. Like Nikitin, she sounded tired by the end of the evening, but Met audiences should look forward to hearing more from her. Nikitin's countryman Sergei Skorokhodov proved an ardent Erik, delivering a manlier effort than we usually see in this cloying tenor part. And mezzo Mihoko Fujimora, a Wagnerian stalwart who has enjoyed a long and accomplished European career, made a fine Met debut as Senta's watchful governess Mary.

Gergiev was back on the Met podium after an absence of five years. Rumors have long swirled that the Met orchestra chafes under his reportedly authoritarian manner, and he has appeared regularly enough at Carnegie Hall to suggest that he has not just been too busy or too disenchanted with Bill DeBlasio's decaying New York to have stayed away from the Met. He ran a tight performance, with a finely balanced touch that lingered over the sensitive moments while delivering a tenacious drive in the stormier scenes.

George Frideric Handel, *Agrippina*
New York, Metropolitan Opera, March 3, 2020

Despite the world's current woes, we at least live in a Handelian Renaissance. The Metropolitan Opera has been slow to catch up, long having left the composer's works aside. But more than a decade after the collapse of the neighboring New York City Opera, which indulged them to an admirable degree, and whose anemic rebirth has had little time for them, bolder Met repertoire choices are giving the eighteenth-century composer the New York platform he deserves.

Agrippina, one of the composer's first operas, premiered in Venice in 1709 when Handel was just twenty-four years old, and after only five weeks of intense work. It preceded the pathbreaking *Rinaldo* by less than a year. Handel's librettist Vincenzo Grimani was one of the grandest Roman cardinals, a fractious bunch who punctuated their lavish patronage of the arts with intrigues and power plays that recalled the excesses of Rome's Julio-Claudian dynasty, the first to rise to imperial prominence before squandering it all on inbreeding, petty bickering, and mental illness. It does little justice to call *Agrippina* a case of "bad people doing bad things badly." Its libretto, suffused with wry irony and arguably the best Handel ever set to music, could have served as worthy inspiration for the popular series *House of Cards* before it plunged into preposterous irrationality. Much public commentary argues that the opera is relevant to today's political world, where allegations of collusion and treachery for the sake of power simply abound.

New York has not been unaware of *Agrippina*. City Opera's production in its final proper season a dozen years ago gestured toward an update, placing the opera in a kind of decadent 1930s. Sir David McVicar's production, a Met premiere, departs from his normal gray hues to give us something like modern Manhattan, suggested by a film projection of New York City street traffic when Poppea, the object of three men's affections, runs out to hail a cab. The cunning title character prances about in the short black dress that has become a virtual uniform for female Manhattanites under fifty. Joyce DiDonato stunningly delivered the role's dramatic narcissism – with all its tempers and vices – while conquering its musical challenges with a precision that could easily make it her greatest role to date. The lithe Act II aria "Pensieri" suggested perfect pitch as its lines unrolled spools of finely woven coloratura. Her surroundings served her well, though McVicar probably went too far with a giant yellow staircase that leads to a seemingly unreachable throne.

DiDonato's triumph paled in no way by comparison with her colleagues, who formed one of the most dynamic ensembles seen on the Met stage in many years. As Agrippina's callow son Nerone – the future Emperor Nero – Kate Lindsey used androgyny to her advantage, delivering a splendidly sung performance while acting like a spoiled Manhattan teen who gives the middle finger, snorts cocaine (marvelously during an aria about clouds), and acts the young seducer whenever time and opportunity allow. Brenda Rae, who makes her long overdue Met debut in this production, sang a light and airy Poppea, too innocent to do real harm but too flighty to demand the type of seriousness that would spoil the plot, which ends with Emperor Claudio remaining on the throne with Nerone as his heir while the besotted military commander Ottone gives up his ambition in exchange for Poppea. Further developments in history were truly appalling, but countertenor Iestyn Davies scored a pronounced success in artfully delivering the part. Matthew Rose's Claudio was sturdy and plumbed attractive low notes. Duncan Rock's Pallante and Nicholas Tamagna's Narciso – dupes for Agrippina's scheming – were excellent foils.

Conductor Harry Bicket is best known for early music and has an extraordinary ability to make a modern orchestra sound like it is playing on period pieces. Handel's score, which attenuated the evening for nearly four hours, unrolled with an arresting dynamism that made one lose track of time.

The Met clearly has the resources, and, given the small number of empty seats, the audience to deliver excellent Handel and the work of other composers who preceded Mozart. It should certainly shift its repertory in that direction, even if it means cutting a few of those stale Puccini revivals.